Kowtow

Kowtow

GEORGIAN BRITAIN, IMPERIAL CHINA *and* THE IRISHMAN WHO INTRODUCED THEM

EOIN McDONNELL

FONTHILL

Fonthill Media Language Policy

Fonthill Media publishes in the international English language market. One language edition is published worldwide. As there are minor differences in spelling and presentation, especially with regard to American English and British English, a policy is necessary to define which form of English to use. The Fonthill Policy is to use the form of English native to the author. Eoin McDonnell was born in Ireland and educated in Ireland and the UK; therefore, British English has been adopted in this publication.

Fonthill Media Limited
Fonthill Media LLC
www.fonthillmedia.com
office@fonthillmedia.com

First published in the United Kingdom and the United States of America 2021

British Library Cataloguing in Publication Data:
A catalogue record for this book is available from the British Library

ISBN 978-1-78155-821-8

Typeset in 10.5pt on 13pt Sabon
Printed and bound in England

Preface: A Note on Chinese Names for Places and People

Given the vast differences between the writing systems used in China and Europe, transliterating Chinese names into the Roman alphabet can prove difficult. This challenge is compounded by the fact that a number of different solutions have been proposed over the years, none of which has proven entirely satisfactory. Thus, the city now known as Beijing to foreigners was once known as Peking in English (and indeed still is in French). Yet to the Chinese, the name has always been pronounced the same (although they, too, have changed how it is written, at least in mainland China).

Add to this the fact that Europeans have often misheard or misunderstood the names of Chinese people and places, and the picture becomes more confusing still. So, what Europeans once called the southern port of Canton, capital of the province of Canton, and home to speakers of the Cantonese language, has always been Guangzhou, capital of Guangdong, and home to those who speak guangdonghua to the Chinese themselves (or at least for those who speak Mandarin).

To summarize, trying to develop a uniform approach to Chinese names for use in this book has been taxing. As a compromise, Beijing has been used to refer to the modern city, while Peking refers to the imperial capital of Macartney's visit. Similarly, Guangzhou has been used for contemporary references to that city, Canton for historic. Generally, other Chinese cities' names have been rendered as they were in the source material. For the most part, personal names have been written using the modern pinyin romanisation system used in the People's Republic of China, except for a few individuals (most notably the brothers Fuchang'an and Fukang'an), where I have relied on names derived using earlier systems.

Acknowledgements

Given this book began life as a simple hobby to keep me in touch with Chinese history when my career took me in another direction, it has only reached the point of publication through the support, guidance, and expertise of a number of people to whom I am deeply grateful.

Alan Sutton, Jay Slater, and Jamie Hardwick from Fonthill Media have been vital in transforming what was a pastime into an actual book, and I am immensely appreciative for the professional polish they have provided and their continued support.

Thank you also to the former colleagues in the IIEA who gave welcome feedback that helped shape the final product. Needless to say, any remaining errors or mistakes are entirely my responsibility. Writing this book has been a personal undertaking and the views expressed in the book are entirely my own.

Many thanks also to the Ireland China Institute for the use of my profile picture, and to its chairman, Ken Duggan, for his advice over the years. Of course, the greatest support of all came from Deirdre, Niall, Oisín, and Siún, even if the book has been in existence longer than the last two. To them, always, all my love and thanks.

Contents

Introduction: Learning to Kowtow

If you ask the average person in Europe or North America to list the Chinese words they know, they will probably finish very quickly. Most will claim total ignorance of the Chinese language, while some might list popular Chinese dishes or name figures, such as Mao Zedong, who have achieved global renown. Tell someone in Britain or the United States that they know a term deriving from Chinese court etiquette formed over 2,000 years ago and they will surely express bafflement. Yet, ask most educated people in the English-speaking world what the word kowtow means, and they will immediately understand that you are referring to an act that is submissive, servile, and obsequious in manner. The word is synonymous with humiliation, prostration, and powerlessness.

It is a term still regularly deployed to describe one party's symbolic prostration before another. Indeed, deriving as it did from the *koutou*, the formal prostration of a subject before the emperor of China, the word often appears the ideal term for detractors to describe the attitude of anyone they see as too eager to please the modern rulers of that nation. Thus, Prime Minister David Cameron's very warm welcome to Chinese President Xi Jinping during the latter's visit to the UK in 2015 led some members of the press to claim he had 'all but kowtowed to [the] visiting Chinese leader'.[1]

Businesses, too, in their enthusiasm to access the Chinese market, see their efforts to win over China's regulators and market authorities described as kowtowing, particularly when it is claimed that such commercial interests lead them to act in ways that may not be in keeping with their stated corporate philosophy. In recent years, such charges have been levelled at Apple, Hollywood, and the NBA, all of whom have displayed a remarkable responsiveness to official or public opinion in China over issues that may seem very peripheral to their businesses. From banning apps in China that would never face censor in the West, to editing films to add in Chinese heroes or remove problematic villains, to disciplining team managers for tweeting their views on the political situation in Hong Kong, many international brands seem desperate not to offend Beijing.

Although perhaps describing this as kowtowing is merely Western bias? Could it be that the use of such an inflammatory term is merely the outward symptom of a growing unease felt by some at the slow shift of economic weight away from the US and Europe and towards China? Yet, the term is also deployed in the Chinese press, even in English. The *South China Morning Post* has printed articles explaining why 'China insists foreign organisations ... kowtow to its nationalistic red lines'.[2] The state-owned *Global Times* describes how the interference of external powers in the Middle East means that the 'the regional security situation is forced to kowtow' to the desires of outsiders, rather than reflect the needs of its inhabitants.[3] Even away from China, in stories with no other reference to Asian culture, kowtow finds itself deployed; to describe how 'HP wouldn't kowtow' to Xerox, how 'the NFL wants to kowtow to crybaby Kaepernick', or how US athletes 'are unlikely to kowtow to outdated regulations which purport to limit their marketing freedoms'.[4]

More than two centuries ago, the term kowtow also featured heavily in the headlines of the British press. The event that brought this obscure piece of Chinese court etiquette into the popular lexicon of the English-speaking world, where it has remained ever since, was the refusal of a foreigner to bow down before the Qianlong Emperor, ruler of China, fourth emperor of the Qing dynasty, in 1793. This man, George Macartney, was not the first European to refuse to bend to court ritual in China. However, as the ambassador of George III, Macartney's refusal has come to be seen by history not simply as a simple question of protocol, but rather as foreshadowing what the Chinese refer to as 'the Century of Humiliation', a period of shameful weakness where China was at the mercy of Western imperialism. Although neither side understood it at the time, that fateful break with tradition marked a fundamental clash of worldviews, a psychological collision that would result in China's downward spiral, leading to the Opium Wars, the cession of Hong Kong, the dismemberment of Chinese sovereignty, and the nation's prostration before rapacious foreign powers.

History need not have taken that direction. The Qing had ruled China since 1644 and had paradoxically strengthened the nation's position as a major global economy, while preventing its subjects from freely developing extensive contacts with the Western world. Despite this guarded approach, the dynasty presided over the largest economy on the planet. Such commercial opportunity drew interest from across the globe, including from Britain. Yet while the British Empire, through what was effectively its commercial arm in the East India Company, was dominating the trade between East and West, she lacked the regional base that Portugal had found in Macao, or the representation at court that the French enjoyed through their compatriots employed by Qianlong as advisers on astronomy and other sciences. Britain's only toehold in China was the 'Thirteen Factories', a complex of warehouses and commercial office on the banks of the Pearl River at Canton.

Macartney had travelled to China in an attempt to win greater trading access for Britain's goods, to ensure better rights for its subjects who visited the Qing Empire, and perhaps for his nation to be ceded a small island on which to establish a permanent trading presence. The embassy aimed to impress on the emperor the advanced nature of British technology as well as Britain's role as a key trading partner for China, opening up the possibility of further collaboration. In almost all these goals, the mission was unsuccessful. The tragedy of this failure was that it set the tone for the following century and a half of relations, with the result that what should have been resolved by diplomacy was instead settled by violence. Britain forced its way into the Chinese market through the smuggling of opium, won stronger rights (indeed, effective immunity from Chinese law) for its subjects at the point of a bayonet, and seized the island of Hong Kong as a war prize. The price for all this was paid not in diplomat's time or the ink of treaties, but in Chinese blood.

Thus, this first meeting between China and Britain was the root of much of the pain that followed. Could either party to this first unproductive engagement have changed the course that the subsequent relationship took? Why was the Qianlong Emperor so reluctant to engage with the British from the very start? Did Macartney's refusal to perform the kowtow really scupper any possibility of agreement? What would have become of China had the Qing Government opened up its territories to Western commerce more willingly? Such questions are key to understanding how China engages with the world today and how it plans to deal with its increasing global interests in the future.

The first meeting of Qianlong and Macartney also holds lessons for all incumbent powers on the dangers of clinging too tightly to accepted truths. Britain and China had competing, indeed contradictory, worldviews, and their disagreement over the kowtow perfectly embodies this. The assumptions that underpinned Macartney's approach to the

Qianlong Emperor were those of a strident, outgoing maritime power whose global reach was defined as much by trade as by naval and military force, and which expected to become the equal, if not the superior, of any other empire.

From Qianlong's seat on the Dragon Throne, the world appeared governed by a very different set of norms—rules that lay on a foundation of the assumed superiority of the Qing Empire as a political entity and as China's central role in the international order. After all, while Qianlong was not Han (i.e. ethnically Chinese; like all rulers of the Qing dynasty, he was Manchu), he shared something in common with all previous Chinese rulers, Han or not, and indeed with all the myriad rebels and barbarians who had unsuccessfully sought to rule the nation over so many centuries. This was a belief that Chinawas the locus of all global power; all other nations, no matter how vibrant their trade or imposing their military power, were by nature's design inferior to this realm. That was, to Qianlong and his court, an undeniable, immutable fact, and why the emperor of China deserved to be kowtowed to as a matter of course.

Thus, two very different, mutually exclusive, views formed the starting points for this first round of Anglo–Chinese engagement. One of the parties would be proven right in their assumptions of strength and power; the other would be disabused in a most painful, humiliating manner. At the outset, a neutral observer could have been forgiven for picking either side to gain the upper hand; indeed, as we will see, even after Qianlong had bade farewell to Macartney, it was not immediately obvious whether China or Britain would emerge as the ascendant party in the relationship.

Since that initial rebuttal, the first meeting of Britain and China in an official capacity has become the archetypal clash of cultures—a morality tale applied to many situations down the years. The standoff over etiquette has been used, depending on one's prejudice, to illustrate Chinese insularity, British arrogance, and the importance of viewing negotiations from the perspective of the person across the table. It has formed the introductory chapter to numerous books on the relationship between China and the West and has even inspired a school play designed to educate students on the importance of cultural sensitivity. From how the US manages the emergence of China as a peer competitor, to how Britain's national self-image has shaped its decision to break with the European Union, the modern world is still faced with many of the questions raised by the experience of the Macartney mission. Yet there is one place in the West where this story is not widely known, and that is in Ambassador Macartney's birthplace: Ireland.

For an Irishman to have played such a pivotal role in this key moment of diplomatic history, and to have fundamentally shaped the relationship between two great powers, means that this is a profoundly important chapter in Ireland's engagement with Asia. Born in Antrim, Lord George Macartney, 1st Earl Macartney, was a dedicated servant of the British Empire, but a man intensely aware of his origins and who surrounded himself with his countrymen throughout his career. He has a good claim to being the most influential Irishman that most of Ireland has never heard of. His experience offers key guidance to his homeland as it, too, attempts to navigate the currents of a global economy going through profound change. Yet because Macartney worked under a flag with which most modern Irish people do not identify, he has been largely forgotten in the land of his birth.

No matter where you are from, no matter what your background, the tale of when Britain and China first met reveals much about human nature. It speaks to us about the illusory comfort of assumed superiority, the dangers of ignoring change and of how money, force and knowledge can change a nation's political and economic landscape in an historical blink of the eye, in ways no one can foresee. Most of all, it warns us that the world may not always be as it seems, and that the most fundamental of political, economic, or social structures can come crashing down when subjected to the stress of brutal reality. Tradition, that things were ever thus, is no guard against that.

1

'It Must Not be Difficult to Impress the Chinese'

Thankfully, words such as 'rape' rarely feature in debates on foreign policy. In an election that was full of sensationalist scandal and spluttering rhetoric, however, the term was used by one of the candidates running for the position of forty-fifth president of the United States, to describe America's treatment at the hands of China on trade matters. The eventually successful Donald J. Trump was particularly exercised by what he saw as unfair Chinese practices, claiming that Beijing weakened its currency artificially for an unfair advantage in exports, engaged in sharp practices that would fatally undercut the US economy, and had even concocted global warming as a scam to harm American industry. Of course, all these claims were wrong—in 2016, China was trying to strengthen, not weaken the renminbi; trade between China and the US is broadly mutually beneficial; and China suffers, and will suffer, greatly from the effects of climate change.

If nothing else, the venom of these exaggerations highlights just how emotive the give and take of trade relations can be when your commercial partner is a country of 1.4 billion people, and you feel your nation is unable to affect the balance of that relationship. Given the scale of China, the vastness of its territories, and the sheer volume of its economic activity, governments globally often feel they can do little to shift the course of this trade juggernaut. Most recognise that they start from a weak position. Their economy will likely be smaller than China's and will probably grow more slowly; they have fewer people and a smaller market. So how can you affect change when you feel the relationship is uneven?

These are not new concerns; they have existed throughout history during those periods when China has been open to global trade.

Such feelings were particularly keen in Britain at the end of the eighteenth century, when popular and political opinion felt that the nation was hard done by in its trade relations with China. At the time, high society and the burgeoning middle class were buying so much porcelain, tea, lacquerware, and silk that a huge balance of payments gap with China had developed. As a result, Britain was suffering from the buyer's remorse familiar to those who decry their nations' ballooning trade deficits with modern China.

At the highpoint of porcelain imports to Britain, in 1721, over 7 million pieces were shipped from China. These imports arrived in lots of thousands, after journeys of over a year and a half, in commercial ventures of colossal complexity. So common was the presence of such china and lacquerware in middle-class homes that it became something of a cliché bourgeois marker; as early as 1708, Daniel Defoe was poking fun at the trend. The French writer Louis-Sebastien Mercier noted the inherent foolhardiness of wasting vast sums on porcelain, so that 'with a touch of its paw, a cat can do more damage than the plunder of twenty acres of land'.[1]

Enterprising Chinese porcelain makers, realising that the greatest demand was for antique pieces, simply increased the supply of such goods, or at least a close substitute—newly produced vases dipped in a patina to give them the vintage look so sought after by Western buyers. Naïve consumers with excess income were eager to buy; Chinese producers and Western merchants were certainly more than willing to sell, usually at a massive mark-up.

Quite apart from questions of taste and common sense, this hunger for Chinese products had serious economic consequences. In the 1760s, the cost of British tea imports from China alone outstripped exports in exchange by 200 per cent, and as a result, silver had to be shipped directly to Asia make up the payments shortfall. Between 1760 and 1770, silver shipments from Britain to China had more than doubled, then doubled again in the following decade.[2] Moreover, this deficit showed no signs of decreasing. By the 1780s, Britain's trade with China exceeded all the rest of the trade of the East India Company (EIC, or simply, the Company) combined, consisting almost entirely of imports.[3]

Political pressures conspired to encourage this trend. In 1784, Prime Minister William Pitt slashed the import duty on tea from 119 per cent to a mere 12.5 per cent in an effort to strangle tea-smuggling. Instantly, tax revenues increased by £2 million, and sales of tea (which was officially still a monopoly of the East India Company) shot through the roof. While this certainly cut down on criminal enterprise, imports from China inevitably galloped to ever-higher levels. This inbound flow of goods did help stimulate domestic British industry in some sectors, such as ceramics, by encouraging the development of similar consumer products that could appeal to lower price points than the authentic Chinese wares. Yet there was little stimulating the movement of goods in the opposite direction, with the output from the mills of Lancashire and the metalworkers of Birmingham finding sparse interest in the Chinese market.

Only one export commodity offered potential cause for optimism, and whatever economic opportunities it brought with it, the moral costs were immense. Opium, grown in India and shipped by the EIC to China, was in great demand. From 200 chests in 1729, shipments of the drug to China increased to 1,000 chests in 1770, and over 4,000 in 1790, equivalent to more than 500 tonnes.

The British Government was not ignorant of the potential human toll of this product, and even at the time, the debate surrounding the trade was politically sensitive. One MP termed the poppy 'the most noxious weed that grew' in all of India, and while preparing for his voyage east, George Macartney himself expressed a wish that 'we could substitute ... any other better production in its place,' and so expunge the stain on the nation's character.[4] Such a controversial product did not offer a firm foundation for developing trade with China to mutual benefit, and the levels of opium sales were still far from some sufficient to offset the trade deficit. Something had to be done to broaden Britain's export opportunities, and a voice was needed to press for Britain's trade interests at the highest level of Chinese government. An ambassador had to make Britain's case in person at the court of the Qianlong Emperor.

Both the government and the EIC had been eager to establish influence in the Qing capital for some time. Indeed, there were even those who lobbied for an attempt to exert direct control over China, in the same manner as the British had done in India. As early as 1741, a retired British admiral had argued in his memoirs that where economics had failed, cannon should be used to open up the Chinese market. Following his stunning victories against the Mughal Empire, Robert Clive was, by 1763, suggesting that attention should now focus on a military campaign against China.

Thankfully, Pitt recognised the impossibility of conquering outright such a unified, populous nation. Given disparities in size, the distances involved, and the sheer lack of knowledge about China (never mind any moral considerations), diplomacy remained the best route to furthering Britain's interests with the Qing. From the late 1780s, an ideal opportunity for such an expedition seemed to be emerging, with Britain finding herself in a position where entanglement in European conflicts appeared unlikely. There was now the mental space to consider wider strategic issues, such as how to develop deeper ties with the world's largest economy.

This led to the first attempt by London to dispatch an envoy to Peking. In December 1787, Lieutenant-Colonel Charles Cathcart, MP, departed aboard the frigate HMS *Vestal*, bound for China with a comparatively narrow set of demands. He was to end the circumstances under which 'Great Britain ... has long been obliged to pursue this Trade under Circumstances the most discouraging (and) hazardous to its Agents'. Indeed, in the city of Canton (modern Guangzhou) 'the only Place where His Majesty's Subjects have the Privilege' of buying and selling 'the fair competition of the Market is destroyed by associations of the Chinese'. In essence, the full effects of free-market economics in China were hampered by the limited access the Qing were willing to give to foreigners, allowing contact through one port only, and even there under very strict controls.

Cathcart was tasked with widening this constricted window for commercial activity, and the goals of his embassy were closely linked to the specific desires of the East India Company itself. He was instructed to convince the emperor to grant British traders 'a place of Security as a Depot for our Goods' and to assure him of 'mutual benefits to be derived from a Trade between the Two nations'.[5] Sadly, Cathcart never got the chance to make the case for the benefits of Chinese engagement with Britain; he died of consumption off the island of Java on 10 June 1788, before reaching China. The now ambassador-less embassy returned home.

By the time a fresh delegation could be organised, further consideration had been given as to the impression Britain should aim to make on the Chinese emperor. Until this point, it had been assumed that the driving force behind establishing official contact would be purely economic, with the end goal of merely ensuring that British goods could reach Chinese consumers. The problem with this approach is that it placed the East India Company front and centre of any diplomatic effort, which represented not only a dilution of the British Government's own control over any proposed embassy, but, more crucially, would also weaken the position of the embassy itself when it finally came before the Qianlong Emperor. Why should the Celestial Emperor, a man believed by himself and his subjects to reign over the literal centre of the earth, deign to treat with the representatives of a grubby foreign commercial body?

Coupled with this was a sense within the British Government that the Company was not doing enough to further the national interest in Asia. Understandably jealous of their controlling role in Anglo–Chinese trade, the directors of the EIC were loath to allow anything that might put their tenuous foothold in Canton at risk. In their own words, any embassy should aim 'first and foremost neither to impair nor injure' the Company's existing trade in China, nor its relations with the Chinese state.[6]

Other than the commercial intelligence that any mission to the court in Peking was likely to acquire, particularly on the production of silk, tea, cloisonné, and other in-demand items, there was little immediate benefit to the Company's shareholders from such an expedition. While the EIC had proved eager to open the Chinese market for goods produced in India, it had shown less interest in forging a path for the products of England's booming factories, which would be the focus for the putative embassy.

Often, the choices made by great powers reflect internal bureaucratic tussles as much as grand external strategy, and so it proved in this case. There were growing concerns about the British state's control, or lack thereof, over the East India Company. While the Company's political functions had been brought under the sway of the government with the 1784 East India Company Act, Home Secretary Henry Dundas was determined to tighten this grip and to consistently and rigorously ensure that the Company recognised that the needs of the state were paramount.

Following recent scandals in India, the primacy of political direction over the EIC was strengthened, and it was no longer the independent bailiwick of its directors that it had once been. What is more, the EIC had always depended for its success on the coercive power of state-backed violence. True, it had its own army, ships, and bureaucracy, but these elements could be easily taken away by the sovereign state if it was felt that the EIC was becoming a little too independent. Lastly, there was grudging recognition that the long-term strategic interests of the Crown and the EIC coincided, whatever short-term disagreements might exist. This cut both ways; as Edmund Burke noted in parliament in 1783, 'To say that the East India Company is in a state of distress, was neither more nor less than saying the country was in a state of distress'.[7] Everything must be done to protect the EIC's commercial position in China, but equally, the Company had to recognise its responsibilities to the Crown. To ensure its ongoing profitability, the time had come for it to play the patriotic part. To this end, the directors even agreed to foot the entire bill for the embassy.

The tasks set for this new mission had also expanded since Cathcart's failed attempt. Commercial goals were still to the fore, but rather than greater profits for the Company's shareholders, now there was an additional emphasis on reducing the trade deficit between Britain and China. There were also very clear political and diplomatic objectives. The request for a British trading hub in China was expanded from merely a location for securely storing goods, to a foundation on a par with Portugal's colony in Macao, coupled with greater access to the Chinese interior. The mission was also charged with encouraging the emperor to allow Britain to establish a permanent embassy in Peking, and to seek immunity for British merchants in China from the local legal system.

First, however, Britain would need permission to dispatch an embassy. Standard petitions to the court in Peking from the EIC were transmitted through the *Cohong*, a trade guild that managed foreign commerce in

Canton on behalf of the imperial court. The letter announcing King George III's desire to send his representative to Qianlong would take a political channel, however. Members of the EIC's Secret and Superintending Committee arrived in Canton in September 1792, insisting on delivering a message directly to the local governor-general of Liangguang province, Guo Shixun, whose remit included the city of Canton.

'His Majesty,' it began, 'desirous of improving the connection, intercourse and good correspondence between the Courts of London and Peking, and of increasing the commerce between their respective subjects, resolved to send his well-beloved Cousin and Counsellor the Right Honourable George Macartney' as an emissary.[8] Macartney was not, of course, related to the king, but a slight flourish seemed justified in order to gain imperial attention. The letter from George also claimed that he wished for his ambassador to be with Qianlong to celebrate the emperor's birthday in September 1793. This was a clear attempt at portraying the visit as part of diplomatic protocol, while at the same time downplaying, for now, the commercial goals of the mission. From the outset, the British aimed to distance the embassy from Chinese officialdom's former engagements with the EIC, hoping to mark a new phase in the relationship.

That the delivery system belonged to the Company while the message was sovereign to sovereign proved unclear to the Chinese, however. Subsequent communications between Guo and Peking show that he struggled to process the concept that representatives of a commercial firm could deliver a message announcing an embassy sent by a sovereign. What was merely an administrative channel for the British, alerting Peking to Macartney's arrival, was of much greater significance to the Qing. For them, every step in an embassy's journey, from the opening invitation to court onwards, was a carefully choreographed diplomatic action. All the embassies that regularly called to Peking from states throughout Asia understood this. Yet even at this early stage, it was obvious that what was arriving from what they termed the 'Western Ocean' was an envoy the likes of which the Chinese had never before faced. The British claimed that they were sending an ambassador to mark Qianlong's eightieth birthday, yet they announced they would be bringing a large body of scientists and artists as well. How then should the court in Peking interpret the purpose of the proposed embassy? Was it some lowly commercial enterprise, or a genuine, high-level engagement?

To be fair to the hosts, the mission's ultimate aims were also open to debate among the British themselves. Such a diversity of impulses, across a wide range of questions on issues of foreign, trade, and legal policy, meant that maintaining a unified message proved to be a challenge. Planning for the expedition was bedevilled by this question of purpose; after all, if the goals were not readily clear, what would constitute success or failure? No one doubted that the economic imbalance between the two markets needed to be corrected, but how this could be achieved depended on whom you asked. Macartney, the East India Company, and the British Government would have all provided very different responses, and the tension between these competing views was to feature throughout the mission.

The ambassador himself saw his visit as a clear attempt to impress on the Qianlong Emperor that Britain was a leading global power in trade, science, and statecraft. Given the lack of contact between the two nations, there were few reliable guides that Macartney could turn to for advice in making this case. The European obsession with chinoiserie went beyond consumer culture to include a mania for China's philosophical and intellectual output; this often led to an excessively rosy view of the country among those writing on the topic.

In the eighteenth century, many of Europe's thinkers felt that China set an example that the rest of the world should follow. From Oliver Goldsmith's *Chinese Letters*, to the belief that China, ruled by reason, was 'a green paradise of free thought', the Qing Empire was romantically portrayed as an ideal, held up as the paragon of an enlightened state.[9] This was largely down to the fact that much of the information then available to outsiders was derived from accounts of Jesuit missionaries, who had been active in China since the 1580s. Understandably, they saw much to admire in a society structured around the hierarchical, rules-based Confucian values, and were also keen to emphasise to their sponsors in Europe than China was sophisticated and advanced, and thus worthy of attention.

This positive take on imperial China seeped into subsequent commentary on the nation from a host of sources. Voltaire himself had said of the Chinese 'that what places [them] above all the earth's peoples, is that in four thousand years neither their laws, nor their morals, nor the language spoken by their men of letters has changed'.[10] Even those critical of some aspects of Chinese society operated under a presumption of the nation's superiority. Adam Smith, while recognising that China was in dire need of economic reform and international trade, still felt it was 'long one of the richest ... most fertile, best cultivated, most industrious and most populous countries in the world'.[11]

This rosy view needed filtering by Macartney as he prepared for the embassy's departure. Much of the writing available to the British reflected how philosophers and intellectuals wanted China to appear, or even used the nation as a utopic allegory for how the author felt states in Europe should be run. There was little hard research on what China and its people were actually like, what their society lacked in terms of commercial goods, or, crucially, how they viewed matters such as foreign policy and engagement with other states.

The files of the East India Company could at least bring Macartney up to date on the story of Anglo–Chinese relations so far, and the twenty-one volumes that the Company had provided him offered considerable background. For wider questions on Chinese culture and society, he turned to the writings of the French missionaries. These stressed the importance to the Chinese of the study of astronomy and mathematics, which is unsurprising given that so many French Jesuits found employment with the emperor as consultants in these areas. Macartney thus formed the opinion that the way to open up the imperial court was to appeal to its deep-rooted respect for these sciences. This could be done through displaying the advanced state of British technology, particularly in the fields of telescopes and timekeeping, underlining his nation's potential as a supplier of such items to the Celestial Empire.

Previous European missions to the imperial court had relied on what the British mockingly derided as 'toys and sing-songs' to win over their audience, automated gadgets that were entertaining, but useless.[12] Instead, Macartney's team would display items 'whose merit lay in their utility', aiming not simply to entertain the emperor, but to overawe him with tools that would help pick apart the mysteries of the heavens and the earth.[13]

Such a lofty aim required skills beyond the experience of diplomats, bureaucrats, and statesmen. As a result, the embassy included ninety-five scientists, artisans, and technicians, each a high-calibre practitioner in their chosen field and handpicked by the ambassador. Two scientists were seen as being particularly important—the Scottish natural philosopher James Dinwiddie and the Swiss horologist Charles Petitpierre—and were tasked with bringing together the collection of scientific instruments. These formed the core not so much of an exhibition, but of a technological performance, with the planned display including a demonstration of electricity and a hot-air balloon.

Dr Hugh Gillen and Dr William Scott would lecture the Chinese court on the latest advances in European mathematics and physics. Two painters, William Alexander and Thomas Hickey, were also included in the team, tasked with recording, for a curious British public, scenes from the other side of the world. Five German musicians would play the works of Handel and Haydn, while a mathematician, a metallurgist, a botanist, and hosts of artisans and craftsmen rounded out the itinerant academy of sciences that would travel to China. Perhaps worrying that the generosity of the EIC in footing the bill might be exhausted, the home secretary grumpily reminded Macartney that he was not 'leading a delegation of the Royal Society', but the envoy appointee was convinced that this was the right approach.[14] To Macartney, it was clear that his team should include those 'who, by being versed in such sciences or arts as are admired in China, might then increase the respect for the country of which such men are native'.[15]

The only problem with such sentiments was that, in an effort to impress the Chinese, Macartney was perhaps diluting the 'Britishness' of the message being conveyed—a potentially dangerous approach given that the Chinese understandably found it difficult to discern one group of European barbarians from another. The embassy's display of wonders centred on a specially commissioned, German-made planetarium (costing more than £1,500, at a time when the average annual salary in Britain was just under £21). Telescopes, a celestial globe, and a globe representing the earth would also be presented to the emperor, as would a wide range of weaponry, many of which had no connection to Britain beyond the fact that they could be purchased there.

Indeed, some of the items later displayed in Peking were not even brought out from Europe by the mission. Macartney's team went so far as to acquire Western-made telescopes and toy automata from Western sources in Macao and Canton after they arrived in China, having lost confidence in the ability of their gifts to grab the attention of their hosts. Despite the cobbled-together nature of the mission's collection of technological wonders, Macartney was confident of success; after all, he reasoned with supreme over-confidence, 'it must not be difficult to impress the Chinese'.[16]

In adopting this focus on the most cutting-edge knowledge the West had to offer, Macartney also eschewed the opportunity to maximise the benefits for less glamorous British industries. Despite communicating with leading tradesmen and craft workers from Birmingham, he passed up the opportunity to bring any of their number with him to China. For the envoy, this was not an attempt to simply win orders; rather, it was a chance to create an impression, accurate or otherwise, of overwhelming technical prowess. The humble workers of Britain's steelworks and factories had no place in the image he wished to project.

Such was Macartney's view. For the East India Company, however, the success of the mission would be coldly measured in the increased opportunities for profit. Whether they were achieved via exports to, or imports from, China mattered little. The creation in the minds of the Chinese elite of a vague association between advanced knowledge and British industry was also of no concern to the Company's shareholders, unless it had concrete commercial benefits. The main objective that Macartney had to achieve from their perspective was the lifting of restrictions on British trade in China; all else was secondary. The emperor must open up ports further to the north along the Chinese coast, which would be nearer the production zones of those goods that British consumers most desired, such as tea and silk. More competitive prices for such goods should also be sought, as would the abolition of duties charged on imports, with British trade to be placed on at least an equal footing with that of Portugal.

To a lesser extent, it was hoped that the Chinese internal market might also be opened to consumer goods produced in British factories. Nevertheless, lingering in the dark recesses of the minds of the Company's directors was a terrible fear; what if the Chinese did not want anything that the British could offer? 'I cannot recollect any new article that is likely to answer. Almost everything has been tried,' to entice demand among Qianlong's subjects, wrote an exasperated EIC director in 1791.[17] Maybe the Chinese really had all that a society could want, and there was nothing worthwhile the British could provide. For the board of the EIC, the pursuit of export opportunities for British goods in China should under no circumstances threaten the Company's access to the unique luxury goods the Chinese produced. In the opinion of the Company's board, if Britain had to suffer an ongoing trade deficit, so be it.

In many ways, such thinking was the commercial equivalent of the idealisation of China engaged in by many European philosophers. Both beliefs rested on supposed Chinese exceptionalism. Europeans had long recognised the technical prowess of the Chinese, as their voracious consumption of products such as silks and porcelain since the early seventeenth century shows. Many had reached the conclusion that the Chinese were simply so far ahead in the production of consumer goods that the West could never hope to catch up. When the Macartney mission was preparing to set out, however, scepticism over China's inherent superiority had begun to develop. Joseph Banks, an adviser to the ambassador, was convinced that by this point China was merely 'the ruins of a state of civilisation', and that Britain could match it in any area of science or industry. Even in those areas where the Chinese might have an edge, the British would soon catch up, he felt. Contact between the two empires would lead Britain to 'in a few years acquire a mass of information for which if placed in the industrious and active hands of English manufacturers the whole revenue of the Chinese empire would not be thought sufficient equivalent'.[18]

Surely, then, this fear that Qianlong would turn up his nose at Britain's wares must be unfounded. No market in the world had yet resisted the temptations offered by England's merchants. Her factories could produce wonders that would be highly sought after in any marketplace, and her merchant fleet was capable of supplying demand across the globe. If only the entrepreneurial British could get unfettered access to the Chinese market, and really get an opportunity to sell to the consumer, their buccaneering can-do spirit would win over even the most doubting of foreign customers. That was how the government imagined the Macartney embassy could bring real value—sales in China not of the latest European gadgets, or German telescopes, or of the Indian-produced goods favoured by the EIC, but of the basic household products, blades, steel, and ironwork of Birmingham and Liverpool.

Despite the fact that the British had experienced little appetite for their wares in Canton, this optimism about the Chinese consumer's enthusiasm to purchase masses of British 'broad cloths and camblets, of lead, tin, and ... articles of manufacture' remained unfettered. Indeed, an assumption grew that this lack of interest in southern China was a regional phenomenon. Some in Britain wondered that if a 'market could be opened on the northern part of the coast of that extensive empire, a new and increased demand for these articles, and others not wanted in the southern provinces' might result.[19] As soon as the population in northern China had access to what Britain had to offer, the thinking went, the trade imbalance would begin to level out.

True, there was some logic behind the idea. For cloth or steel imported into Canton to reach the north, it would have to pass through many hands, each adding a margin. By the time an import arrived in the stocks of merchants in Peking or Tianjin, price inflation had taken its toll. The lack of a system of trade credit within China exacerbated the situation, as transactions were by barter or with bullion, making long-distance commerce inefficient. Yet, setting these wider economic issues aside, there was no tangible indication that British goods would be in any greater demand elsewhere in China than they were in Canton. With optimism undimmed nevertheless, the mission brought with it a wide selection of 'modern kilns, tapestries, carpets, saddles, two yellow carriages, muskets, pistols, swords, cannon, cloth and woollens, and lustres'.[20]

The British Government was also determined that the most be made of Macartney's mission from a political and diplomatic perspective. Given that the expedition would cost roughly £80,000 (steep, but nothing compared to the rumours circulating London that the real price tag was £500,000) and that the EIC was thankfully picking up the bill, the opportunity was seized to cram as much state business into the official itinerary as possible. Thus, Macartney was not only accredited as an envoy to the Qing court, but also to the rulers of Japan, Annam (modern Vietnam), Korea, Manila, and the Moluccas.

For his engagement in China, the ambassador was also tasked with discovering why British trade faced such stringent controls. Was this a deliberate policy of the imperial government in Peking, perhaps motivated by 'jealousy of our national influence'?[21] Were the British suffering at the hands of over-empowered local bureaucrats who were using the powers vested in them by the emperor to make a quick profit through corrupt practices? All Europeans suffered from what seemed to be arbitrary decision-making by mandarins in Canton, but British merchants were in a far weaker position than their competitors from Portugal, the Netherlands, or France, as all the other European states had achieved some form of formal contact with Qianlong. Along with the embassies dispatched by many of the European states, France and Portugal were also able to take advantage of the presence of their nationals among the ranks of Jesuit missionaries in Peking.

The British, however, had no such voice in the emperor's ear, despite the fact that their vessels carried 80 per cent of the foreign traffic through Canton. Their merchants operated alone, without any seal of governmental approval. Viewed as commercial freebooters by the Chinese authorities, and dismissed as *hong mao* (red-haired barbarians) by the average Chinese person, not only did they lack the same level of influence as their European competitors, the British feared they were seen as a separate species, even less worthy of respect than the other foreigners. This needed to change; otherwise, Britain might find herself frozen out of the opportunities secured in China by imperial rivals, with potentially drastic consequences for the balance of power in Europe.

At the same time, the ambassador's political masters were also keen to stress that he was not to seek commercial advantages at any political cost. Although the exact nature of China's relations with foreign nations was imperfectly understood before Macartney's departure, the British would have been aware that the Chinese viewed their own position as unique. Perhaps the best example of the Sinocentric thinking that has often dominated China's attitude to other states lies in the Chinese word for their own country, *zhōngguó* (literally the 'Middle Kingdom', or the 'central country', although this originally referred only to the central plains of China).

Even more obvious in its underlining tone of superiority is one of the terms the Chinese imperial court used for the empire, *tianxia*, or 'everything under heaven'. In essence, Qianlong's domains were not simply those areas that had formally agreed to his overlordship; the Chinese believed he could claim rule over all creation. So strong was this belief of their nation's centrality to world order that it could even undermine the usually great Chinese appreciation for the sciences. When Matteo Ricci, the sixteenth-century Italian Jesuit missionary, first tried to win favour at the imperial court in Peking by displaying a contemporary European globe, he came up against a surprising criticism. The globe must be disastrously inaccurate he was told, for China was far too small.

Macartney could thus expect major challenges in attempting to present George III as an equal to an emperor who believed that, whoever you were, you were his subject. This mindset would have to be addressed from the embassy's first moments in China, and Macartney had been given strict instructions when it came to handling the rituals of the imperial court. He should 'engage with all ceremonials of that Court which may not commit the honour of your Sovereign or lessen your own dignity, so as to endanger the success of your negotiation'. Yet at the same time, the departing ambassador was also given considerable leeway to follow his own judgement; his government masters were 'satisfied you will be too prudent and considerate to let any trifling punctilio stand in the way of the important benefits which may be obtained by engaging the favourable disposition of the Emperor and his ministers'.[22] For Macartney, as for so many ambassadors since, the message was clear—achieve the goals set at all costs, but do not do anything to cause controversy for the government. Failure would be all his own, despite the constraints put on him.

If he were hoping to find encouragement in the records of other diplomatic missions to Peking, Macartney would have been very disappointed. Since 1521, fifteen missions had visited China's imperial court, with the Netherlands, Russia, France, and Portugal all trying to make inroads into this promising market. Results were mixed, but certainly none of the previous visitors had achieved the recognition of their nation as an equal party to the Chinese emperor. This time, the British hoped, things would be different.

Despite the long odds of success, the upper echelons of the British government had great faith in Macartney. From a career spent in Russia, India, and the Caribbean, he had the right blend of diplomatic, commercial, and administrative experience. They believed he would be up to the challenge of working with an alien culture and navigating a byzantine bureaucracy while mollifying the ever-louder protests of the outraged traders of the EIC. In fact, the latter organisation (due in part to Macartney's service in India) was pleased by his selection:

> The propriety of fixing this Embassy on a person thus dignified (as yourself) is enforced by the decided opinion of those who have been most experienced in the Company's concerns in Canton, and who have been witness of the vexations under which they labour.[23]

In January 1792, Macartney's complete list of objectives was delivered in a letter from Henry Dundas, 1st Viscount Melville, the home secretary. No doubt, the levels of British optimism revealed by the document seemed reasonable and realistic at the time. Today, it is hard not to scoff that anyone could believe it would be possible to wrest such concessions, in a first engagement, from the longest-established state on earth. Macartney's orders were to achieve the following:

> Open new ports to the British, beyond the existing entry point at Canton;
>
> Achieve agreement with the Qianlong Emperor to address the concerns of the British traders in Canton, and to win redress for abuses suffered;
>
> Open up the Chinese market for new goods, and expand the existing export opportunities for British products in China;
>
> Establish a permanent Embassy in Peking;
>
> Win the cession of a small territory, possibly an island, to Britain for use as a permanent trading base. Ideally, this would be near the centres of tea and silk production;
>
> Have a successful round of diplomatic engagements with other kingdoms and territories in East Asia;
>
> In addition, of course, gather intelligence on 'every circumstance likely to throw a light upon the present strength, policy and government' of the Qing empire.[23]

Had the British openly admitted to these motivations, it was unlikely that they would have even received permission to send such an embassy. Never mind whether the emperor's closest advisers would have entertained such a notion, the prospect of the request making its way successfully and uncorrupted from Canton, north through a complex web of Chinese bureaucrats to the imperial court was highly doubtful. Hence, to ensure that Macartney would at least have the opportunity to press the British case in person, the fiction was created that the embassy was visiting Qianlong to offer him congratulations on his eightieth birthday. To avoid meddling from self-interested regional mandarins, the embassy would refuse to follow the usual Chinese requirement of landing at Canton. Instead, they would aim to land at Tianjin, the northern port closest to Peking. While it was almost certain that this would raise protests from Qing officials, these could easily be quelled by pointing out the logistical benefits of reducing, by as much as possible, the land transit facing the many cumbersome and delicate presents for the emperor.

Such were the drivers behind British officialdom's decision to send their envoy to China. Yet, there were also more personal motivations at work on this mission as well. Nearly 100 officials, artists, musicians, experts, and physicians journeyed east with Macartney, and when one counts the sailors, soldiers, and attendants who travelled with them, the total number of those who visited China under the ambit of the embassy reaches nearly 700. Some of these, notably the soldiers and sailors, were travelling under orders. The rest, however, chose to go. What led those ordinary men to risk their lives in this venture?

It is easy today to dismiss the motivations of such people as naked colonialism; surely, like all imperialists, they were merely concerned with the base exploitation of foreign races, and they had little concern for the people among whom they travelled? Yet the fact is that many of those who signed up for the Macartney mission were driven by desires closer to those of a gap-year student than an empire-builder. Sir George Staunton, Macartney's right-hand man, who was intended to remain on as resident ambassador in Beijing, described his travelling companions in quite wistful terms:

> They had just quitted their former stations, oldest habits, and most close connections, to engage in a hazardous, but interesting, enterprise. They were not Argonauts, indeed, actuated by the hope of obtaining a golden fleece; but, impelled by the strong incentive of curiosity, and eager to indulge the spirit of inquiry, they already contemplated China at a distance, while objects and topics, occupying the attention, and agitating the minds, of those about them, and formerly their own, seemed to lose the interest they had hitherto excited; and a more captivating, though distant prospect, appeared rising from the horizon to take possession of their thoughts.[25]

Simple curiosity, rather than greed, drove many of Macartney's colleagues, motivated as they were by a desire to learn that was stronger than a base hunger for a new source of wealth or to gain fame.

Of course, not all the volunteers were motivated by such wide-eyed idealism. On the return from China, and despite Macartney's best efforts to corral all the mission members into contributing to a single, edited, and unified published account of the embassy, many of his colleagues, particularly the junior members, subsequently released their own unauthorised descriptions. While certainly revealing a profit motive, these unofficial books also give us an insight into how the average British clerk or soldier accompanying Macartney viewed his Chinese hosts—often with less superiority than one might expect and regularly with a good deal of respect. This obviously does not excuse the exploitation that followed in Macartney's wake in the decades after the embassy, but it does perhaps underline that for many of its members, the decision to join the embassy's team sprung from a very simple desire indeed—to see China.

Also, what of the ambassador himself? What drove him, at the age of fifty-five, to risk travelling to the other side of the globe to argue Britain's case at the court of the Qianlong Emperor? His motivations were decidedly more complex than those of most of his colleagues, and considerably less idealistic.

2

'Who in the World is this Young Man, Who Knows So Much About So Many Things?'

If you are in need of a good wedding venue, Lissanoure Castle is certainly worth a look. Located just outside the little village of Loughguile, set among the green fields of Antrim, the castle has an almost fairy-tale setting. With a dining room that can take 120 people, a church on site, and within easy driving distance of the picturesque north coast of Ireland (for breath-taking photos of the newlyweds), it would surely satisfy the fussiest of wedding planners.

Indeed, the estate is so picture-perfect that even George Macartney himself, a man with very high standards and expectations, might be pleased with the fabulous condition of his former home. Whether this would help him get over the shock of learning that the castle is now open to hire by the public is hard to say, although he might be mollified by the knowledge that the castle's website at least details his impressive globetrotting CV, noting his time in Russia, the Caribbean, India, South Africa, Italy, and, of course, China.

No doubt, after a lifetime of service to the British state, Macartney might have felt that he deserves a little more recognition. Yet, both the island of his birth and the nation that he represented so faithfully have largely forgotten him. Despite seeing himself, most decidedly, as Irish, history has overtaken this identity. Modern, nationalist Ireland's heroes rarely include British diplomats (Roger Casement being the exception). Neither is his story widely known in Britain. For those who are aware of his mission to China, it is usually synonymous with a collapse in cross-cultural understanding, diplomatic failure, and as the introduction to more than a century of Chinese suffering at the hands of Western powers.

It is hard to know which reaction would have upset him more—the Irish apathy to his achievements or the British tendency to attach his name to disappointment.

Ambition guided Macartney in all areas of his life. Be it personal, professional, or political, every decision he made was done with the aim of furthering his advancement in society. From his earliest days, he was fascinated by heraldry, history, and genealogy—the markers of power and success in Georgian Britain—and he would later claim that these 'events, dates, and other facts gleaned up when a boy were [*sic.*] of great service' later in his professional life.[1]

Born in 1737 in Lissanoure, George was the only surviving son in his family. The Macartneys had come to Ireland in 1649 from Scotland, settling in a land that had only recently witnessed a bloody uprising by the native Gaelic Catholics against the newly arrived English and Scottish settlers who professed various Protestant faiths. His great-grandfather, also called George, had led troops into Belfast in 1688 to support the claim of King William and Queen Mary to the throne, which resulted in him then hastily fleeing to England to avoid Jacobite retaliation. Steeped in the traditions and beliefs of a frontier society, the Macartney family would come to combine a deep-rooted loyalty to the Protestant British state with a lingering sense of insecurity. Members of the Irish aristocracy were never at ease among the predominantly Catholic peasant population of Ireland, but so too were they on the margins of court and high society in England.

While in Ireland they represented the elite, once transplanted from home to the more competitive leagues of the Empire's ruling class, Irishmen had to be constantly striving to progress, unable to rely on the natural ascension enjoyed by their English counterparts. George Macartney was the archetypal example of this drive. His bookish childhood was a focused preparation for adult life. Entering Trinity College, Dublin, at the age of thirteen (admitted so young only though lying about his age), after a leisurely course of study, he graduated in 1759 as a master of arts. Initially, he sought to launch his career in medicine, although this path was later discarded as not offering sufficient power. Instead, he took up the study of law at the Middle Temple in London, despite having no intention of being called to the bar. Rather, he considered this the best introduction to the world of politics, where he felt true authority lay.

Following his legal studies, he embarked on several tours of the continent, but even this light-hearted diversion became a productive exercise in résumé-building. Using his travels to gather as much information as possible on the countries he visited, Macartney hoped that with this knowledge, he could portray himself as something of a foreign policy expert and hence launch himself into the House of Commons. Even social activity during this tour served a strategic purpose; rather than simply seeing the sights, he cultivated a relationship with Rousseau in Neuchatel and Voltaire in Geneva, impressing the latter to such an extent that he wondered, 'Who in the world is this young man, who knows so much about so many things at such a young age!'[2]

The most productive ties he would forge on the continent would be with the Englishman Stephen Fox, an inveterate gambler who was heavily in debt. Macartney helped his friend out in a delicate, somewhat mysterious, matter, which was fortuitous as Fox was the son of Lord Holland, leader of the House of Commons. His favour to Fox thus provided the entrée to the political life he so longed for. These vital ties to the Holland family were kept up throughout his life, with his correspondence over the years peppered with queries on his sponsors' health. In 1764, Lord Holland introduced him to Lord Sandwich, secretary of state for the Northern Department, and the two power brokers decided that Macartney would be well-suited to parliament. Happily, the seat for Midhurst was due for election soon, with all the election rights for this rotten borough held by Viscount Montague. This guaranteed Macartney a seat in the House of Commons.

Yet before he could take his seat, the aspiring MP was distracted by the promise of a fresh possibility—envoy to Russia. The opportunities presented by this position were not lost on Macartney; he could already see that through becoming involved in Britain's relations with the wider world, he would achieve a prominence that might be slow in coming on the domestic scene.

He also understood the potential offered by what today we would term an emerging market. Russia, he noted, 'is no longer to be gazed at as a distant glimmering star, but as a great planet that has obtruded itself into our system, whose place is yet undetermined, but whose motions must powerfully affect those of every other orb'.[3] To be Britain's man at the court of Catherine the Great would allow his influence at home to grow with that of his host nation. Russia was seen as being a power of the future; indeed, only ten years after Macartney was ambassador, the acquisition by Catherine of the art collection left by the late British Prime Minister, Sir Robert Walpole, would be held up by some in England as proof that Russia was in the ascendant, while Britain was in decline. Macartney hoped to share in this upswing in the country's fortune.

He may have been encouraged by other, more particular, factors as well. Lord Holland, on writing to his protégé to induce him to take up the post in St Petersburg, notes 'that the Empress is about the age you like, not a slim woman, and, I add, growing older every day, and when she passes the turn of perfection you will be coming away.'[4]

Almost immediately, his sense of promise seemed to be justified. The new role brought with it a knighthood, in order to give the freshly minted ambassador some additional gravity. Given he was only twenty-seven years of age upon taking up the post, no doubt Sir George welcomed any help he could get in strengthening his position at the Tsarina's court. His new environment proved tricky to navigate, and the challenges Macartney faced in unravelling Russian politics would prove good training for his later mission to China.

On arrival in St Petersburg, he was made immediately aware of the lack of progress achieved by his predecessor, Lord Buckingham, who had not only failed to conclude a commercial agreement with Catherine to replace that initially signed by Britain and Russia in 1743, but had also proved unable to address Russian demands in the geopolitical sphere. With Russo-Turkish relations tense, the Tsarina demanded that any treaty between Britain and Russia include a clause that would bind London to pay a subsidy to St Petersburg in the event of the latter going to war with the Ottoman Empire. From a Russian perspective, such a promise would underline the trust necessary for closer economic ties. Yet the entanglement the clause would create ensured that Lord Buckingham avoided providing a concrete response to the Russian proposals, a situation his hosts understandably found deeply frustrating.

Given this history of disappointment with Britain, Macartney was encouraged to bring the full force of his charm to bear on the Tsarina in order to make up lost ground. On his first audience with her, in January 1765, he informed Catherine how grateful he was to be posted to St Petersburg. At her court, he declared, he would 'have the happiness of more nearly contemplating those extraordinary accomplishments, and those heroic virtues, which make you the delight of that half of the globe over which you reign, and which render you the admiration of the other'.[5] This neat piece of flattery not only impressed the Tsarina, but also won Macartney plaudits when it was repeated back in England.

However, silver-tongued diplomacy would not alone prove sufficient to overcome the obstacles towards reaching an agreement. In St Petersburg, the environment was generally inhospitable to British diplomatic overtures, but thankfully, Macartney had a willing ally in Count Nikita Ivanovich Panin, Catherine's *de facto* minister of foreign affairs. In return, Panin saw the young envoy as an ideal channel to convince Britain to join his proposed Northern Accord, which aimed to counter the Bourbon and Hapsburg influence in northern Europe through an alliance of Russia, Denmark, Sweden, and Prussia.

Macartney's superiors in London were open to the idea of actively opposing French influence. By carefully emphasising the potential for an alliance, and by accepting less favourable conditions for British traders, the young ambassador was finally able to achieve agreement on the text for a treaty with Panin, minus a clause relating to war with Turkey. However, his characteristic impetuosity was now to cause Macartney serious grief. From his on-the-ground perspective, it seemed that the pact struck with Russia was the best deal possible, and Macartney promptly signed off on the document.

When the agreement was transmitted back to London in full, the Duke of Grafton, secretary of state for the Northern Department, initially wrote in reply to state the ministry's satisfaction. Yet there then followed a series of disputes over the actual impact on British interests, with Macartney being told this new treaty would clash with the existing Navigation Act of 1651. The ambassador's response was that he knew that the treaty caused no issues under the act because he had memorised the entire piece of legislation and could recite any section of it at will. No doubt, such exacting command of detail, combined with absolute confidence in his own judgement, made Macartney much beloved by many of his colleagues and superiors.

Of greater concern to Britain's leaders, however, was the question of whether Count Panin was authorised to sign on behalf of Catherine's court. Needless to say, the Russian took a very dim view of this when such quibbles were communicated back to him. Macartney found himself in an impossible position; he had arrived in Russia determined to apply great energy and effort to the challenges facing British diplomacy there, and he had made great efforts to win over his hosts. Yet wrapped up in his efforts in St Petersburg, he had failed to recognise that he must also persuade the audience at home if his efforts were to truly bear fruit. Evidently, the somewhat confused management of the treaty ratification was noticed in London as much as in St Petersburg. When Macartney finally received notice, in August 1766, that his superiors were happy with the treaty, he was also informed that he was to be replaced as ambassador.

In his letters to friends and colleagues, Macartney's disappointment and frustration are evident. Noting that 'the nomination of [a replacement] did not at all surprise me', he expresses wonder that his political masters 'did not turn me out without further ceremony'. His sense of abandonment is palpable, given he had 'happily accomplished a very laborious and a very difficult negotiation, and brought to a conclusion a treaty of commerce which, but for my zeal, industry, and activity, I will venture to say would have been lost to us for ever'.[6]

When one balances his treatment against what he had secured for British merchants in the treaty, it is easy to see how bitter a blow this was for a still young man. Every corner of Catherine's domains was now open to British commerce. Where once British merchants had been subject to punitive taxation, they were now charged at the same rate as their Russian counterparts. In return, the man who had negotiated all this was to be summoned home under something of a cloud as soon as his replacement arrived.

As he waited, Macartney's humiliation was compounded when the Russian court relocated from St Petersburg to Moscow in the autumn of 1766; without official orders from London, Macartney was forced to stay put. Awaiting his successor, Macartney peevishly noted:

> If he were my enemy I could not wish him a greater punishment than his present commission. Were he my friend, I could not wish him a greater happiness than to be relieved from negotiating with this Court. Had he been informed of the real situation of things here, I am persuaded he would have declined so disagreeable an employment.[7]

Given the personal financial loss suffered by Macartney in Russia (as he had to finance large portions of the embassy's budget himself), his disillusionment is understandable. Nonetheless, he had received a valuable lesson on the importance of effectively navigating bureaucratic channels and the dangers of leaving oneself exposed. What is more, we can imagine that he must have been wryly amused to hear, shortly after arriving back in London in 1767, that his successor had in fact turned down the role of envoy to Russia. The cabinet was now eager to reappoint Macartney, who, understandably, also refused this offer.

Not that his reluctance to return to Russia needed strengthening, but his marriage to Lady Jane Stuart in 1768 ensured that Macartney was even firmer in his rejection of the post than he might otherwise have been. Even in his choice of a wife, Macartney was ever on the lookout for opportunities to advance, and his match with Jane, the daughter of former Prime Minister Lord Bute, brought considerable social elevation. Arranged by his ever-supportive patrons in the Holland family, Macartney was alive to the possibilities that such a marriage might offer, and it mattered little that he did not find Lady Jane particularly attractive.

To modern readers, it might seem depressing that an eighteenth-century gentleman on the ascent would marry for advancement and not love; solace can at least be found in the fact that Macartney was always consistent in his approach to matters of the heart. Many of his romantic attachments were driven by cold logic rather than true emotion. Writing of an earlier lover in Russia, he noted:

> Madame Keyshoff was of a great family, but neither young, handsome, nor clever. She had neither beauty nor wit to engage, to captivate, or to

> retain. Her only merit in my eyes was a passion which she either had, or affected to have, for me.[8]

His marriage was similarly utilitarian. While there may have been a large degree of respect and fondness, nothing approaching genuine love seems to have developed. Her family believed that Lady Jane's marriage was an unhappy one, but then this was the lot of many of her female contemporaries. Her husband seems to have made a conscious decision to elevate his career over affection in his life, coldly affirming:

> Now I ... instead of glowing with desire and love, must be in future a British person with a Roman soul, and an admiration of what I wish myself to be ... When we let ourselves be carried away by some particular affection, the pursuit of it makes us incapable of anything else.[9]

For their part, Jane's family felt that she had married beneath her station, and that Macartney's careerism was vulgar in the extreme.

In April 1768, Macartney was again tempted with the offer of a seat in parliament, but despite his election as MP for Cockermouth, he quickly resigned from his constituency. Instead, he stood for and won the seat of Armagh in the Irish Parliament in June; this was followed by his appointment as chief secretary of Ireland in January 1769. Once more, he had chosen to forego the temptations of an easy life as a secure backbench MP in Westminster, preferring to take the advancement offered by tougher jobs away from London.

While he resisted actually moving back to Ireland for as long as possible (to the increasing despair of his superior, Lord Townshend, lord lieutenant of Ireland), by the following autumn, Macartney was on his way to Dublin, dragging Jane with him. Lord Townshend had quickly recognised that his new chief secretary's understanding of the land of his birth might help bring a sense of tact and subtlety to an administration that had been somewhat tone-deaf up to this point. He was thus eager to ensure that Macartney should begin work as soon as possible, so he sent a series of flattering letters, underlining how valuable his skills and experience would be, and perhaps more persuasively, how beneficial to his career the post in Ireland might prove.

The delay in Macartney's arrival in Ireland and swearing-in was down in part to his hope that he might yet be appointed ambassador to Spain. As always, other pastures appeared greener to the ever-driving Macartney. In the end, he had little choice but to accept the position, as the role of envoy to Spain was not offered to him (no doubt leading to him regretting making public his belief that he would soon be on his way to Madrid).

Despite the disappointment that no doubt accompanied him across the Irish Sea, he applied himself to his duties with relish, and he brought with him an intimate knowledge of key local figures and political tensions. In the face of initial suspicions from the leading personalities of the Irish Parliament, some of whom apparently suspected that he had become a 'papist' during his time abroad, Macartney had an effective, if personally unprofitable, three years in Ireland. His mind, however, was still on matters international; indeed, in 1773, he was allegedly the first to refer to Britain's imperial possessions as 'this vast empire on which the sun never sets'.[10]

Apart from seeking broader horizons, he also hoped for more lucrative employment, retiring from his position in Dublin to weigh up his options. He was then elected again to the British House of Commons in October 1774, this time for the constituency of Ayr; this was followed shortly after by the decision to make him governor of Grenada in December of that year, a role that might offer considerable financial benefits. An elevation to the Irish peerage also accompanied the new position, whence the new governor became Lord Macartney. Deciding against a new title for what we might today refer to as brand awareness reasons, he retained his surname, 'as I had passed through several employments, and was pretty well known everywhere as Macartney, I thought it better not to alter it, at this time of day'.[11]

Given that he had sustained serious losses during his time in Russia and Ireland, Lord Macartney now hoped that his time in the Caribbean would help restore his wealth. Of course, such profit would be charged against the misery of the slaves working the cotton, sugar, and tobacco plantations on the island, over 100,000 of whom would be brought to the colony between Britain taking control of Grenada in 1762 and the final abolition of slavery in 1834. Yet such considerations seemed to provide little discomfort to Macartney.

As things turned out, his posting to the region certainly brought him some benefit, albeit decidedly not of the material kind. It was here that Macartney was introduced to Sir George Staunton, who would become a lifelong friend and accompany him to India and China. Like Macartney, Staunton was an Irishman, born in Galway, and educated as a doctor in France by the Jesuits. He, too, had come to the Caribbean to make his fortune and had found sufficient success to purchase a sugar plantation and the necessary slaves to work it. Having risen to the top of colonial society, Staunton acted as the right-hand man of the new governor, a role in which he would effectively continue for the next twenty-five years in a global career that travelled in tandem with Macartney's.

While the governorship of Grenada might have brought a close friendship, it proved financially disastrous. The Caribbean had just become a front line in the naval theatre of what we now know as the American War of Independence. Not only did this mean that Macartney spent his journey out to Grenada in 1776 dodging US privateers, but he also had to worry about an invasion of Britain's island possessions by America's ally, France. While the new governor applied considerable energy to trying to shore up the defence of Grenada, through organising a local militia, establishing an artillery battery, and even laying the groundwork for a new shipyard, these efforts were all to come to nought.

When a fleet under Jean Baptiste Charles Henri Hector, *comte* d'Estaing, arrived off Grenada on 2 July 1779, Macartney's enthusiastic but amateur efforts at soldiering dissolved before the might of a professional army. Despite initially offering an attempt at resistance by abandoning the town of Saint George and holing up in a fort overlooking the coast, it quickly became apparent that any opposition was futile. Macartney departed for captivity in France, in the process losing not only what wealth he had accrued while in Grenada, but also all his clothing and personal papers.

His colleague Staunton was quick to place the blame on the British commanders in the Caribbean, Admiral Byron and General Grant, who never arrived with expected reinforcements. One suspects that this was the line the politically astute Macartney was peddling, hoping to shape what would become the accepted truth about the loss. Whatever he may have lacked in prowess on the battlefield, in the bureaucratic skirmishes around dodging of blame and claiming credit, Macartney was a capable strategist.

Thankfully, a relatively short imprisonment in France followed. His freedom came in 1780, thanks in large part through the skilful negotiation of Staunton, who convinced the French court to let his patron go. Returning to England, Macartney began anew in making his fortune. Through Staunton's efforts, he was not even subject to limits of parole by the French, and this proved vital to his quick resumption of an effective career. Had the French imposed such conditions, Macartney would have been honour-bound to avoid positions where he could come into conflict with his erstwhile captors. As these did not apply, he was free to seek promising roles across the whole of the British Empire.

Yet again, he was elected as an MP (this time for Beeralstone in Devonshire) in September 1780, but as per usual, he seemed to have little interest in actually taking up the seat. Instead, the following December, he was appointed governor-general of the colony of Madras, a position that gave him the opportunity to make his name in one of Britain's most important overseas possessions and which would see him once more in competition with the nation's chief imperial adversaries.

His opponents would not all be foreign, however. One of the reasons Macartney had been chosen by the Company's directors was that he represented a new broom that could sweep away the corruption that mired the East India Company's efforts in India. At this time, Britain had effectively outsourced her imperial activities in the sub-continent to the private sector, with the EIC representing the monopoly contract holder. To this end, it was able to call on a professional army separate from Britain's own forces; additionally, the Company also had a major hand in developing policy for Britain's interests in the region, but usually with commercial rather than political interests to the forefront. As a result, there was an unholy mixture of profit-motive and coercive power at play in the administration of Britain's Indian possessions and in the empire's relationship with local rulers.

Unsurprisingly, this offered well-placed EIC employees the opportunity to make vast personal fortunes, and both of Macartney's opponents for the position in Madras had become stunningly wealthy during their time in India. His victory had rested on Macartney's ability to portray himself as the untainted candidate, with no prior baggage to hamper his effective running of the colony. Speaking in his favour at a meeting of the EIC's Court of Proprietors, Edmund Burke had said that if there was already an honest candidate available from within the Company, they should elect them; if not, they should choose Macartney.[12] Yet even upon taking up his post, there was still considerable internal opposition to his selection. At the forefront of the new governor's mind must have been the experience of a predecessor, Lord Pigot, who died under house arrest after he fell afoul of the internal political wrangling within the EIC.

On arrival in India in June 1781, Macartney immediately began to stamp his authority where he could, all the while mindful not to alienate powerful factions within the colonial administration. In his efforts to shore up his position, he was perhaps fortunate that Britain was engulfed in a war with Haidar Ali, sultan of Mysore. With an external enemy to focus on, the new governor's internal opponents were at least distracted, and he could initially focus on prosecuting the war.

To do this, he first had to rectify basic failings in the defence of the territory. Refugees—both Europeans and those Indians identified as sympathising with the British—were streaming towards Madras, in flight from the victorious sultan. The army units available to Macartney had not received pay for some time, and he had to convince the resident military commander, Sir Eyre Coote, not to dissolve the forces available and simply start recruiting from scratch again. In addition to all this, the precarious state of Britain's interests in India had led both the French and the Dutch to start undermining its position further.

In response, and wanting to win over as much support from within the Madras administration as quickly as possible, the new governor decided to focus on a relatively easy early victory, dispatching his forces against the Dutch colonies along the coast. This would not only reduce the pressure from one European opponent, but it would also leave Haidar Ali with no access to ports on India's eastern seaboard. While he may have failed militarily in Grenada at a tactical level, on the strategic theatre level of operations in India, Macartney proved more successful. Quick results against the Dutch at Sandras and Pulicat boosted Macartney's position, providing him with the funds to pay all his troops in full. This success was soon followed by Coote's victory over Haidar Ali at the Battle of Porto Novo in July 1781, which seemed to offer the chance of a negotiated peace. The sultan, however, remained defiant.

The victory did give Macartney the space needed to remove the Dutch from the theatre completely, by assaulting their colony in Negapatam. However, Coote—highly successful, brave but cantankerous—opposed the plan in what was to prove the first of many clashes between civil and military authorities in Madras. The governor won out, Negapatam was besieged and captured in October 1781, and the positions of the EIC in India—and of Macartney within the Madras leadership—were strengthened considerably.

He next clashed with the governor-general, Warren Hastings, in Bengal, who was the head of the EIC's civilian administration in India. Hastings pressed Macartney to take punitive action against the nawab of Arcot, Muhammad Ali Khan Wallajah, whom he felt had been less than supportive of Britain's efforts against Haidar Ali. No doubt wishing to reduce, rather than increase, the number of enemies he faced, Macartney negotiated a diplomatic settlement with the nawab that saw him contribute financially to the British war effort.

Ironically, this was not the first time that Macartney had found himself at the intersection of colonial politics, the nawab's vast personal wealth, and Britain's wider interests. Shortly after arriving in India, Macartney had earned the ire of several of his compatriots for refusing to accept a 'gift' equivalent to £20,000 from the nawab, but this principled stance did see him praised for his honesty in the House of Commons. Declining this offer put him in stark contrast to a number of other leading figures in the administration, who had willingly accepted the nawab's generosity. Now, Macartney was tapping that same wealth for the good of British interests in India.

In 1782, Coote left Madras for Bengal, complaining both of ill health and of Macartney's interference in military affairs. While they may have disagreed bitterly as to the best way to conduct the campaign against Mysore, at least the two men held each other in high esteem as individuals. The same cannot be said of Macartney's relationship with Coote's replacement, Major-General James Stuart. As the man who personally arrested Lord Pigot in 1776, it is not hard to see why the new governor viewed Stuart with suspicion. An even greater failing—Stuart's indecisiveness—compounded this original sin in Macartney's eyes.

In December 1782, Haidar Ali died, leaving his son, Tipu Sultan, scrambling to assert his authority. To Macartney, this seemed the ideal time to strike, but Stuart prevaricated, not believing Haidar Ali was actually dead. Enraged by what he saw as a lack of backbone, Macartney replaced Stuart in the field, calling him back to the Company's headquarters in Madras, Fort St George. This was a bitter humiliation for Stuart, who had 'at the age of fifty, cheerfully dropt a bloody limb' in battle for the Company, while administrators like Macartney 'at their ease are only dropping ink on their paper in black characters'.[13]

In recognition that Macartney and Coote made a better team, the latter was dispatched from Calcutta to once more take control of military affairs in Madras, but died *en route*. The governor then turned to Sir James Burgoyne, offering him the leadership of forces in the region, but he was too close to Stuart and refused the position. Certain now that he had to strike first before he suffered Pigot's fate, Macartney sent the ever-faithful Staunton with a party of *sepoys* to arrest Stuart. With swords drawn and bayonets fixed, they confronted the general in his office, and in the face of superior numbers, he came quietly. Bundled on to the first ship bound for England, he returned home to lick his wounds and wait for revenge on Macartney.

France and Britain were now on the cusp of agreeing peace terms, and it was hoped that Tipu Sultan might prove similarly open to talking. Despite initial reluctance, he agreed to meet with representatives from the British side in autumn 1783, and Staunton was duly dispatched to Seringapatam (modern-day Sriringapatna) with a number of other senior figures from the Madras administration.

Macartney needed accord to be found quickly for a number of reasons. The Treaty of Paris in 1783 ended open conflict between Britain and France, but it also freed up the resources of the latter to stir up trouble against the former's possessions in India. Madras needed to end the threat from Mysore to deal with any new challenges the French might engineer among other Indian leaders. Added to this was the plight of the British prisoners of war held by Tipu, who were reportedly suffering greatly at the hands of their captors.

Granted, any strong Indian leader was going to find his name blackened by the British, and with Tipu, this tendency was no doubt strengthened by a subsequent later need to justify the British invasion of Mysore in 1799. Even given the likelihood of bias from British sources, however, it does seem that Tipu took a particular relish in the maltreatment of those enemies who fell into his hands. After all, his hatred of the foreign foe had led him to commission an automaton of a Bengal tiger savaging a British soldier for his court. If nothing else, life as one of Tipu's prisoners must have been precarious.

To bring negotiations to a quick close, the British offered a straightforward peace proposal; all territories captured by either side east of the Western Ghats would be restored to their original owners and the British prisoners immediately released. For Tipu, this offer had a major drawback; Mangalore, a city originally ruled by Hyder Ali until captured by the British in 1767, would remain in foreign hands. This proved unacceptable, and without the handover of Mangalore, Tipu would agree to no peace deal.

Some members of the British negotiating team wanted to give in to this demand, but Staunton stood firm in his refusal, backed fully by Macartney. They were both suffering from excessive confidence in the British position. In January 1784, Tipu attacked and captured Mangalore, forcing Staunton back to the negotiation table with a considerably weakened hand. In March of that year, the British signed a peace treaty with Tipu, who pointedly demanded it signed in his newly captured prize city.

The deal was immediately criticised for having given Mysore too much, and Macartney's stock with his superiors in India plummeted. His relationship with Hastings, which had always been cold, turned hostile. Aware that he may have fatally wounded Staunton's career, he wrote to Charles Fox, then leader of the opposition, to try to secure some significant role for his acolyte in India. While Macartney's fortunes might seem to be finished, he did not wish to see his friend destroyed as well. This rare display of selflessness suggests just how important Staunton was to Macartney.

Packing his bags and prepared for home, Macartney took particular care to lodge two documents in the Madras government files. The first was an affidavit swearing he had never accepted bribes or inappropriate gifts, nor had he misused the Company's allowances or assets. The second was an open and transparent overview of his own private fortune and expenditure. Satisfied he was now safe from accusations of malpractice by his opponents, he travelled to Bengal to give a frank account of his term in Madras to the East India Company's Council in Bengal.

Ultimately, success as a colonial administrator in India depended as much on perceptions in London as on realities in country. As Hastings pushed to have Macartney removed, he in turn found himself exposed, as the public became concerned at what they saw as mismanagement of the national interest. In particular, attacks on Hastings in Westminster by Macartney's old protector, Charles James Fox, scuppered any possibility that the Irishman would take full responsibility for the failings at Mangalore. On arriving in Bengal, Macartney found Hastings already recalled, and that the pendulum of fortune had swung so far that the consensus now was that he was the candidate best placed to take over as governor-general. In an echo of his earlier experiences in Russia, however, Macartney seems to have had enough of the petty politicking, deciding to keep his options open. He went home, despite considerable pressure to accept the promotion immediately.

On returning to London in January 1786, Macartney tried to turn this demand for his services to his advantage. In talks with the chairman and deputy chairman of the board of the EIC, he stressed that if he was to accept the position, he expected their full support, and that the military authorities in India would answer to him. Even with their agreement in hand, he was still less than enthusiastic about returning to the intrigue he had experienced in India. His health had suffered during his first tour in the country, and it was only ambition that led him to consider a second term of service there. When he received acclamation not only from Fox, but also from the prime minister, William Pitt, on the opening of parliament, he thought he might perhaps be able to exact a reward sufficiently generous to justify a return to Bengal. Macartney duly requested an elevation to the English peerage from Pitt, noting that such authority was required if he was truly to put his stamp on the position of governor-general. Pitt refused, and Lord Cornwallis was subsequently installed as Britain's top official in India.

Macartney was not too disappointed; on hearing the news at a ball, he passed his wife a note stating, 'I am the happiest man in England at this hour. Lord Cornwallis, I hear, is Governor-General of India'.[14] He had reason to be satisfied, too, with his severance package; the East India Company awarded him an annuity of £1,500, and silver plate with a value of £1,600. From a few years of hard service in India, Macartney had undone much of the financial damage suffered at the hands of the French in the Caribbean.

Not all of his former colleagues from India were prepared to part from him on good terms, however. A day after arriving back in London, Macartney learned that his erstwhile opponent, James Stuart, had petitioned the King, claiming that Macartney's account of their differences in India was a falsehood. Macartney informed Stuart that he was unconcerned by the petition, and that he would always call out incompetence where he saw it. Somewhat rashly, he also advised Stuart that he would only communicate with him in future through the offices of an appropriate gentleman appointed by the general—i.e. a second. In effect, Macartney was courageously suggesting that if Stuart had grievances towards him, they should resolve the matter in a duel.

The fact that this was not the first time Macartney had faced single combat only heightens the bravery and/or recklessness of his approach. In Madras, he had fallen out with James Sadleir, one of the officials who had favoured handing Mangalore to Tipu Sultan without waiting for the release of British prisoners. Despite Macartney's harsh criticism at the time, the enmity between the two men did not break out into open confrontation until after the unsuccessful diplomatic mission, when Sadleir blocked the bestowal of a special allowance on a colleague. Incensed by this obtuse attitude, Macartney exploded in anger, leading to Sadleir calling him out. Whatever his attributes as an administrator and diplomat, Macartney clearly was not an accomplished duellist. Thankfully, after wounding him on his left side, Sadleir felt that honour had been satisfied.

Inevitably, given the belligerent nature of Stuart, Macartney found himself facing a violent death once more. At 4.30 one morning in June 1786, the two parties to the dispute met near Kensington, along with their seconds and a physician. Armed with pistols, the combatants stood twelve paces apart in the dim pre-dawn light, leading Stuart, in an attempt at psychological intimidation, to query whether Macartney could see him, given his poor eyesight. Macartney gamely replied that he could see perfectly well. Both men then opened fire, and the Irishman fell with a wound to his right shoulder.

The seconds suggested that this should suffice, and that honour was served; however, Stuart was not about to develop generosity of spirit now. He demanded that the duel proceed, and Macartney, perhaps still allowing his ego to outweigh his judgement, proclaimed himself ready to continue. However, the seconds insisted that there was no justification for more violence and called for the physician, fearing the casualty would collapse for lack of blood. Macartney was lucky; despite the limitations of eighteenth-century medicine, he survived his wound and did not require amputation. His luck redoubled when the king, upon hearing of the dispute from Lord Townshend, intervened and demanded that they lay the matter to rest. No further duels were fought between the two men.

A long period of convalescence was required, as well as some time also, perhaps, for reflection. Recovering first in London, by the summer of 1790, Macartney had returned to Lissanoure, Ireland. Here, he seemed to retreat from the global and concentrate on the local, delighting himself through improving his estate. Local bogs were drained, the village of Dervock was rebuilt, and he became involved in the administration of County Antrim and in the local linen industry. Drawing on direct experience in Grenada and India, he raised a local militia dragoon company. His engagement with the wider affairs of state and questions of politics seems to have been reduced to reading the essays penned by his friend Edmund Burke, which were reprinted in the local newspaper. Perhaps there his résumé might have ended, had the British Government not decided that the need to dispatch an embassy to China could no longer be ignored.

Such was the career of the man who would meet Qianlong. What of his character? As an individual, Macartney reflected the beliefs and prejudices of his time. To modern eyes, it can be jarring. Generally, he was intrigued and interested in the wider world, open-minded and curious. Yet his observations easily slipped into bigoted generalisations. Russians he dismissed as 'barbarous, the clergy ignorant, and the nobility is but half civilized'.[15] In the Caribbean, he characterised the people of Grenada as 'a strange discordant mass of heterogeneous animals ... easily irritated to do mischief, and but seldom to be roused to do good'.[16] The inhabitants of Barbados had 'degenerated a good deal', and he noted 'that the inhabitants of the other West Indian islands did not scruple to say that in half a century more the Barbadians would be ranked in the monkey class by naturalists'.[17]

Europeans were not spared this prejudice. Clearly, Macartney thought little of the Spanish and the Portuguese; when visiting the Canaries, he was surprised at the standard of civilisation enjoyed on the islands. In Cape Verde, he could not help but be surprised at how positions among the colonial administration and military officer corps were opened up to people of all races. The common people of Brazil were 'thievish and imposing'.[18]

Coupled with this was Macartney's personal involvement in slavery, which began long before his time in Grenada. While in Russia, he was pressured into 'christening my negro ... so to save my character and avoid scandal I had him received into the bosom of the Church and the congregation of the faithful'.[19] That Macartney felt there may have been a moral lapse in not having a slave baptised, but none in slavery itself, speaks of the racist assumptions that acted as the bedrock for his worldview.

One might be tempted to dismiss all this as typical of any Georgian British gentleman, but his companions on the embassy to China proved more measured. Staunton regularly commented on the advanced nature of Chinese society in his diary. James Barrow, an embassy clerk who would go on to produce his own commentary on the mission, remembered Macartney's disgust at the perceived moral failings of the citizens of Rio de Janeiro. Such an opinion, formed as it were from a few days in Brazil, could hardly be objective, Barrow felt, 'It is scarcely fair to decide on the moral character of a whole nation from the occasional occurrences and observations of a few hours in the day during a week's residence'.[20] Clearly, Macartney was, even by the standards of the age, quick to entertain low opinions of other races and nationalities.

It can also be hard to discern where his racism ended and his snobbery began. In both Russia and China, he was willing to admit that, at least among the higher ranks of society, there were the trappings of civilisation. As for the peasants in these countries, 'the common Chinese, like the common Russian, is only half civilized'.[21] Nevertheless, we should not simply dismiss him as an unthinking bigot. In the Caribbean, he noted:

> It is curious to observe what a number of people are brought together here by various accidents who, one would imagine, were never intended to see each other's faces ... In short, the mixture is so great, and the inhabitants so chequered in respect to birth, breeding, colour, and consideration, that the contemplation of them is to me a highly philosophical entertainment.[22]

While not exactly extolling the benefits of a multicultural society, these words do at least suggest that Macartney was open to deeper considerations of how societies were formed and what happened when many and disparate cultures were brought together. This presents a more complex worldview than one might have found among many of Macartney's slave-owning, foreigner-dismissing contemporaries.

Similarly, his prejudices do not seem to have hampered his political antenna. One would assume that, given his belief in European superiority, he could not countenance a colony slipping the bonds of empire successfully. Yet he had some sympathies with the cause of the American revolutionaries and could see how a colony might surpass its supposed master. Speaking of Brazil, he noted:

> The Crown of Portugal must either soon transport its seat of Empire to Brazil or leave Brazil to take its own chance by itself. For, in spite of all political or commercial regulations and restrictions, it [Brazil] must soon burst the bud and unfold and exert its native powers, uninfluenced by the weight and unrepressed by the terror of a distant sceptre.[23]

Macartney's relationship with the land of his birth was also complicated, again pointing to some of the internal tensions he dealt with over the course of his career. Landed aristocracy he might have been, but he was Anglo-Irish and was consequently something of the poorer relation to his English peers. His Irish identity was, therefore, both a badge of pride and a source of insecurity. When serving as chief secretary in Ireland, he addressed the Irish House of Commons in a manner that makes his national origins clear, even if he stressed the point for political gain:

> If I have merited the approbation of my countrymen ... I shall rejoice not only as a servant of the Government ... but as an Irishman, as a man who thinks it an honour to have been born among you, ... and who has a heart that feels warmly for the interests and liberties of his country.[24]

In London, he mixed with Edmund Burke and other young Irishmen seeking to rise to prominence. Burke would remain a lifelong friend, featuring in his correspondence throughout his career. While his bond with Staunton was forged by a lifetime of shared hardships and victories, strengthened by a mutual loyalty and respect, it is hard to believe that their common national identity was not, at least partly, the germ of their friendship. The diary of his voyage to China contains numerous mentions of the various Irish people he met while travelling the globe. From the wife of the French consul in Tenerife, to wine merchants, to the wife of one of the soldiers in the Cape Verde garrison, Macartney always seemed to notice those members of the far-flung Irish diaspora wherever he met them.

His Irishness also provoked some anxiety. Notably, it would seem that tension sometimes developed between Macartney and Lady Jane when the former's Irish roots collided with his development as an English gentleman. She was clearly unhappy living in Ireland, particularly during the period of Macartney's convalescence following his duel with General Stuart in 1786. Earlier in their marriage, her relatives lamented that she was 'so tormented with those horrid Irish people', who were clearly a little too familiar, as it was 'the Irish way to make no difference between friends and strangers'.[25]

There can also be no question that Macartney's Irish identity was of a very specific kind—that of the Anglo-Irish aristocracy, an Irishness that folded neatly into a wider British national identity. There was no conception for Macartney of an Ireland separate from Britain; he was from Ireland in the same way that a colleague might be from Devon or Yorkshire. The Ulster Protestant root of this Irishness also shows through in his deep suspicion of Catholicism. As the embassy travelled out to China, whenever it stopped in territory governed by the Catholic monarchies of Spain or Portugal, Macartney's diary contains references to the tendency of the local population to hold 'religious prejudices'—that is, Catholicism.

In the Canaries, Madeira, Cape Verde, and Brazil, he makes careful note of how prominent and powerful the Catholic Church was. In each of these locations, Macartney genuinely expected the inquisition, although one can sense the disappointment in his diary as he recounts how powerless this once fearsome institution seems to have become. Yet his wariness of papal influence actually never quite slips into outright bigotry. Throughout his time in Spanish and Portuguese territories, he appreciated the craftsmanship and skill evident in the decorations of the churches he sees. Most noticeably, as we shall see, he proved himself more than willing to work with Catholic clergy in his search for Chinese translators and in matching the machinations of the other European powers at Qianlong's court.

Such was Macartney's achievements, his failings, his great strengths and his terrible flaws. It was this man, ambitious and arrogant, honest but prejudiced, interested in, but ignorant of, China and its culture, who in October 1791 opened a letter from Henry Dundas, 1st Viscount Melville, the home secretary. Inside, he found a request for him to lead a diplomatic mission to the other side of the earth, the first from the ruler of Great Britain to the emperor of China.

3

'Affable and Affectionate to His Subjects, Vindictive and Relentless to His Enemies'

In November 2016, a rare and very beautiful firearm came up for auction at Sotheby's of London. Coming in at nearly 6 feet, with a barrel finely inlaid in gold, silver, and copper, the *Tedeng Di Yi* or Supreme Number One, would certainly be a wonderful addition to any gun-lover's collection, or indeed as a standalone piece all by itself. Sadly, all but the most well-heeled fine weaponry aficionados would have been put off by the piece's guide price of £1.5 million, and most of those who could stomach this initial estimate would have fallen away well before the eventual sales price of £1.985 million was reached.

How could any weapon, no matter how richly decorated and lovingly handcrafted, command such a sum? Even taking into account that the piece comes complete with a *zitan* tripod, the price seems somewhat excessive. By buying the Supreme Number One, however, the lucky winning bidder was getting more than a simple antique musket. They were also gaining possession of a direct physical connection to its original owner, the Qianlong Emperor, one of China's greatest rulers.

It was this link that the somewhat vaguely described 'Asian private collector' who won the auction was actually bidding for, and this association with one of Chinese history's great figures was the centrepiece of Sotheby's marketing efforts. In their brochure for the sale, Sotheby's stressed Qianlong's great love of hunting, and the value he placed on muskets as the noble hunter's weapon of choice. Their description of the lot mentions the numerous poems written by the emperor, including 'Account of the Tiger Divine Gun', while their leaflets featured numerous paintings of Qianlong holding a piece not unlike the one that was up for auction. So the real question is not why this musket, but rather why this emperor? Why did this anonymous Asian (and we can safely assume Chinese) bidder part with the price of a luxury house for a two-centuries-old firearm, simply because of whose hands once held it?

Although known to history as Qianlong, the gun's original owner was actually born Aisin Gioro Hongli, the fourth son of the Yongzheng Emperor. Qianlong, or Lasting Eminence, was the era name he adopted on ascending the throne; this title was then used by his subjects to date each year of his reign (so 1736, the year he succeeded, was the first year of Qianlong. Thus, although often called the Emperor Qianlong in English, the Qianlong Emperor is more technically correct). Given the longevity of his influence at the apex of Chinese political power, until 1799, his era name proved remarkably prophetic.

Qianlong also had the good fortune to reign during a period when a number of economic and agricultural trends led to an explosion in China's population. Over the course of the seventeenth century, China's inhabitants had been decimated by famine and strife; in the 1670s, China's population had dropped to 100 million, down from 150 million in the middle of the fifteenth century, a level that was regained only in the 1720s, at the end of the Kangxi Emperor's reign.

By the end of his grandson Qianlong's reign, in contrast, China had 300 million people. A number of factors contributed to this, not least the fact that so much arable land was left available following the earlier drop in peasant numbers. Furthermore, these vacant fields could now be planted with new, energy-rich crops imported from the Americas, with maize, potato, and peanuts all improving the diet available in rural China. As well as being relatively high in calories, these plants were also hardy, which meant previously fallow hillsides and rocky stretches were now productive. Of course, this expansion in population brought challenges at the end of Qianlong's reign, but for most of the eighteenth century, China's economy expanded in step with its populace.[1]

Remarkably, this paragon of a Chinese ruler was, unlike the vast majority of his subjects, not ethnically Han Chinese. As with all of the rulers of the Qing dynasty, Qianlong was ethnically Manchu (an originally nomadic people from northeast Asia, referred to as 'Tartars' in most of the contemporary European accounts). The Qing had seized power in 1644 when they swept south from the wilds of Manchuria, unseating the ailing Ming dynasty, making the leap almost overnight from semi-nomadic warriors to imperial rulers. The China that Macartney visited would have thus shared one characteristic of the India he had experienced during his time in Madras—both had populations of many millions ruled over by a tiny foreign colonial elite. Even before he held formal power, there were hints that Qianlong possessed remarkable political intelligence, a vital trait if he were to maintain the Qing's precarious position at the apex of this power pyramid. In a dynasty riven by jealousy and intrigue, he achieved the distinction of not only becoming his father Yongzheng's favourite son, but also the preferred grandson of the illustrious Kangxi Emperor. When Yongzheng passed away in 1736, he left a locked box within which was a scroll inscribed with the name of his successor; there could have been few at court who would have been surprised that this parchment bore the name Qianlong.

The decades that followed brought the rapid expansion of the empire, as Qianlong doubled the size of China over the course of ten military campaigns, which required massive investment of both blood and treasure. By the 1770s, he had pacified China's border with Central Asia, securing a province that became known as Xinjiang ('The New Frontier'), while in 1790–1, he cemented his dominion over Tibet by repulsing a Gurkha invasion. Mongols, Tibetans, Zungars, and Uighurs were all brought into the fold of an increasing multi-ethnic state as Qianlong extended his control over their homelands, as well as Taiwan, Yunnan, parts of modern Vietnam, and Burma.[2]

While violence may have subjugated these peoples, it would prove far too expensive and risky to use force alone to maintain Qing control; greater tact was called for. Cleverly, Qianlong co-opted the elites of these new subject nations, fostering loyalty through solid promises of reward and veiled threats of punishment. When the Muslim peoples of Altishahr came under Qing domination, their leading figures were forcibly relocated to luxurious accommodation in Peking, where they would live in great comfort and under close surveillance.

The emperor also selected the daughter of one of these leaders to be his consort, and far from expecting her to adopt Chinese customs, he showed great respect for her Muslim faith. She was allowed to eat a diet consistent with her religious practices, and when she died, Qianlong ensured that her casket was inscribed with a Koranic phrase in the original Arabic.[3]

Similarly, the civil authorities in the territories incorporated into Xinjiang were granted titles and allowances that tied them to the Qing state. Following this approach to pacification, commerce expanded with, and through, the new regions, with copper, precious stones, woollen products, saltpetre, and slaves flowing along the empire's trade arteries.

Marriage alliances were also key to securing the acquiescence of the Lamaist Buddhist Mongols on China's northern frontiers, with one of Qianlong's own daughters marrying a Mongol prince. Some of the measures deployed to strengthen these ties were remarkably delicate. Knowing how devoutly these Mongols followed Tibetan Buddhist practices, Qianlong built a number of buildings in the Tibetan style at his summer retreat in Rehe, including a replica of the Dalai Lama's palace in Lhasa, the Potala. This instinct towards inclusivity also went beyond the grandly symbolic. Qianlong ensured that his realm reflected the diversity of its inhabitants in very practical matters as well. Coins, inscriptions, and official texts from the period have been found in Manchu, Chinese, Arabic, Mongolian, and Tibetan.

This willingness to embrace the foreign for the betterment of the state extended beyond the empire's own subjects; Westerners, too, could be useful, bringing as they did opportunities and skills that were not readily available within the realm. The tradition of welcoming Jesuit astronomers, mathematicians, and artists to the imperial court survived the fall of the Ming, with the Qing being enthusiastic consumers of the knowledge and cultural products they provided. Indeed, in the grounds of Peking's *Yuángming Yuán*, or Summer Palace, Qianlong commissioned the Jesuits to build a European-style palace, with features reminiscent of Versailles. European painters, most notably the Italian Jesuit Giuseppe Castiglione, were employed to provide Qianlong with a range of portraits and landscapes painted in a style that combined Western and Chinese techniques.

Of course, the most numerous of Qianlong's subjects, more than 90 per cent of the total population, were the Han Chinese. Accommodating the cultures that had more recently come under his sway would count for little if the emperor lost control of the Han themselves. Thus, keen to portray himself as a defender of the Confucian ideals that underpinned traditional Chinese society, Qianlong regularly referenced those texts that he had learned by heart during his long tutelage by Han scholars. The Confucian examination system for selecting the bureaucrats to run the empire endured, remaining one of the best routes to positions of power for members of the Han majority, who were employed in the top ranks of officialdom in numbers equal to Manchus.

Qianlong was also responsible for ordering, over the course of a decade, the assembly of the largest ever collection of Chinese literature on philosophy, history, and literature, an incredible body of work called *The Four Treasuries*. This anthology brought together 3,450 pieces of literature, as well as 6,750 commentaries on other works, the result spread across 36,000 manuscripts.[4] Of course, bringing these pieces together also allowed Qing censors to weed out those works that might be seen as undermining Manchu rule, an approach that led to over 2,000 different pieces being lost to history. Yet for the majority of Chinese scholars, and for the wider populace, the collation of *The Four Treasuries* seemed to suggest that Qianlong was an enlightened ruler, with a deep appreciation for the culture of his subjects. To this, he added an expansion in the imperial collection of paintings and calligraphy, although Qianlong caused controversy by adding additions and couplets in his own unremarkable script to many of the pieces.

Despite this embrace of the fruits of settled life, Qianlong never forgot his nomadic roots. He maintained the usage of the original Manchu language at court, took part in the traditional shamanic religious practices of his people, and encouraged their continued proficiency in mounted archery. The Manchu hairstyle—a long-plaited ponytail from the top of the head, called the queue or *biànzi*—remained standard for all men in China under Qianlong, an ongoing reminder of Han submission to the Manchu. Such reverence for Manchu tradition was a wise attitude, given that that the bulk of the 'Eight Banners' forces, the core Qing military organisation, was still comprised of ethnic Manchu. These garrisoned the major cities of the north and down along the east coast, forming the backbone of state coercion that ultimately guaranteed Qianlong's rule. This ruling caste needed to remain aloof from the Han Chinese, so that there would be no question of where their ultimate loyalty lay. It was therefore vital that they saw Qianlong as the ultimate upholder of Manchu identity.

The British knew little of these subtle details about the emperor when they set out. Western observations of Qianlong tended to confirm the clichéd European view of an oriental despot, semi-mythical and distorted by rumour and supposition. Only when they arrived in China were Macartney and his colleagues able to collect accurate information about the manner and personality of the man to whom Macartney would be envoy. Even then, what they did learn was interpreted as confirming the stereotype of a ruler who was capricious, cunning, and suspicious. When they discovered that the 'Emperor has had twenty-two sons, four only of which now remain alive', the foreigners decided that this poor princely survival rate was down to the fact that Qianlong had 'so jealous a nature' and must be murdering his sons (the majority of whom died from childhood disease). Such paranoia, they reasoned, must also explain why 'no person as yet knows with certainty which of (the surviving sons) he intends for his successor'. Those princes who were still breathing could not 'interfere in his government,' which Qianlong instead handles 'in a great measure alone, reading all the dispatches himself, and often entering into the minutest detail of affairs'.[5]

It does appear the father toyed with his potential heirs, claiming he was prepared to retire and setting out empty plans for a future handover date that never arrived. In 1778, he was forced to openly state he had made provision for a successor, when a scholar publicly questioned him on the matter (if nothing else, the incident reveals the deep respect held for the educated in China, even by the emperor). In a written response, Qianlong said that an heir had already been chosen, but that his identity was a closely guarded secret to prevent factionalism in the court.[6] At the time of the arrival of the Macartney mission in 1793, Qianlong still, at the grand old age of eighty-two, had his hand firmly on the tiller of the ship of state.

As their time in China passed, the British witnessed at first hand some of the qualities and policies that would lead Qianlong to be the second longest-reigning ruler of China, and still today one of the most celebrated. His reign had seen a reorganisation of government, necessary to ensure the efficient management of such a massive empire. His 'Grand Council' became a centralised management body, the power of its six or seven members transcending that of all six of the Qing Empire's ministries. With a dedicated secretariat of around 250, the new body provided effective control of administration, while also streamlining the development of new policies. The Council merged the talents of China's most experienced statesmen with new ministers capable of fresh thought.

Qianlong's first appointments were two of his father Yongzheng's closest confidants, Oertai and Zhang Tingyu, but they were joined by Qianlong's grand councillor, Heshen, a man who Macartney notes was 'a Tartar of obscure origin but considerable talents, whom he has raised by degrees from an inferior post in his guards to his present elevation'.[7] In Qing China, to a far greater extent than Georgian Britain, ability could see one rise to the very pinnacle of society. The competitive system of examination and promotion within the civil service ensured that a broadly meritocratic bureaucracy governed the country. However, Heshen's ascension took a less orthodox route. From 1775, he became a permanent and important fixture at the imperial court. At the time aged only twenty-five, he was still able to win over the then sixty-five-year-old ruler, rapidly progressing through the ranks. A senior position in the military was quickly followed with promotion to the imperial household, and then onwards via the taxation ministry to the heights of the Grand Council.

Whether Heshen's rise was solely down to ability was doubted even at the time, as the mandarin proved susceptible to graft and occasional incompetence. Perhaps inevitably, with such a career trajectory, tongues began to wag, claiming that the emperor's favour rested on Heshen for romantic rather than professional reasons. Qianlong believed, so the story went, that Heshen was the reincarnation of a much-loved concubine who had died earlier in his reign.

Regardless of how the young official had cultivated his position, he ruthlessly exploited the power available to him. Sent on numerous sensitive missions, with a direct reporting line to the emperor, Heshen was tasked with rooting out corruption in Yunnan province and quelling a Muslim rebellion in Gansu.[8] The reports the emperor received from him on these tasks were often tweaked to paint Heshen in a favourable light.

He also used his station as imperial favourite to line his own pockets. Inventories and supply stocks were misreported, allowing him to siphon off extravagant sums, all the while undermining the state's efforts in fighting insurrection and building effective social structures. Yet so complete was the spell weaved by Heshen over his master that Qianlong even offered him one of his daughters in marriage.

Despite his many gifts as a leader, Qianlong seemed easily influenced by those nearest him, unsurprising given the distance, both physical and institutional, between himself and the many provinces of the empire. Yet, any lack of awareness was not apparent to his foreign guests. The British ambassador described him as follows:

> A man of great parts, learning, and application, religious and charitable; affable and affectionate to his subjects, vindictive and relentless to his enemies; much elated with his greatness and prosperity, and impatient of the slightest reverse or mischance; jealous of his power, suspicious of his Ministers, and when angry not easily to be appeased.[9]

This impression of a ruler who was shrewd, cunning, and personally dynamic (in marked contrast to the bureaucracy that reported to him) tallies with what the British knew of his daily schedule, an agenda that reflected both his political and religious duties. Beginning at 3 a.m., the emperor went to worship at a private temple, before spending several hours reading and responding to dispatches from throughout his domains. These he annotated with his personal comments and instructions, recorded in the margins in brilliant vermillion ink. For the most part, the comments were terse and perfunctory (e.g. 'Noted', 'Read'), although considerably more description was provided when Qianlong was criticising the efforts of his civil servants.[10]

He finally paused to eat at 7 a.m., before, as Macartney euphemistically put it, he 'amuses himself about his palace and gardens with his women and eunuchs'.[11] Qianlong's female companions numbered more than 100 over his lifetime, with three empresses (all dead by the time of Macartney's visit), nineteen imperial consorts, and numerous concubines vying for his attention. Unsurprisingly, such an embarrassment of female companionship led to Qianlong producing twenty-seven children.

His morning recreation over, Qianlong would sit down with Heshen for a private meeting, before summoning his entire cabinet and other senior officials to account for their activities. Dining at 3 p.m., he would round out his day with theatre and then reading, before retiring at 7 p.m.

Through his maintenance of Manchu domination over the vastly more numerous Han Chinese, and given his ability to dominate both those peoples who had recently been subsumed by the empire while simultaneously keeping his own court and heirs on their toes, there can be little doubt that Qianlong was a capable political operator. Yet throughout his reign, on a number of occasions, poor judgement led him to commit unforced errors in the maintenance of his realm. In wars against Burma in the 1760s, and against a number of dynasties in modern Vietnam between 1788 and 1790, ineffective campaigning forced him to pragmatically accept defeats that were then spun as acceptable compromises. Stretched by so many wars of expansion, the Qing state found itself vulnerable to domestic opposition, and a number of rebellions erupted over the course of the 1770s and '80s, many inspired by religious fanaticism and ethnic hatred of the Manchus.

The faltering of state power also manifested in less violent ways. Emergency granaries, an important part of China's social infrastructure, were regularly empty, while the dredging of the Grand Canal, China's great inland waterway, lapsed. Corruption increased, while the excesses of soldiers and those in positions of power began to go unchecked.

Faced by such challenges, Qianlong felt it necessary to limit European access to the Chinese market as much as possible. Contrary to British perceptions that such rigidity in relation to foreign engagements was down to 'jealousy' or 'exclusionism' on the part of the Qing, the confinement of Westerners to only a few ports (and by the time of Macartney's visit, solely Canton) was a considered policy that addressed real concerns. After all, the last thing China needed in the latter half of the eighteenth century was the unchecked entry of potentially destabilising foreigners into the country. Instead, by funnelling foreign trade through only a few set channels, it became far easier for the imperial court to tap this commerce for tax revenues, while simultaneously managing this contact with the outside world. True, much could still be lost through corruption, but by focusing the flow of goods through key points with high-levels of government control, it provided Qianlong with an income stream that bypassed the usual taxation channels.[12]

As well as strengthening the Qing regime by ensuring it benefitted from the wealth created by this trade, limiting contact with the foreigners also helped prevent aid or support being channelled from abroad to those who would rebel against the emperor in Peking. It was feared that communities of ethnic Chinese overseas and meddling foreign powers might seek to foment unrest by supplying China's discontented subjects with financing or arms. Given the Qing would face six major rebellions in the century following the Macartney embassy, this anxiety over insurrection was well-founded. Using this approach, the central authorities were also able to vet and inspect any foreign military technologies that arrived in China. By preventing regional lords from acquiring European ordnance, there was no need for the emperor to worry that he might find himself outgunned by a vassal.[13]

Notwithstanding this desire to control foreign contact, Qianlong was nonetheless eager to bring these strange peoples from across the oceans into his political orbit. When the letter outlining Macartney's proposed mission finally arrived in Peking from Canton, Qianlong's councillors turned to the Catholic missionaries serving his court for advice. They confirmed that no British embassy had ever visited China before and that, significantly, the British differed considerably from the French and Italians who the Chinese were used to dealing with (the missionaries, unsurprisingly, highlighting the confessional differences). The court also learned that the British wished to land at Tianjin, the port closest to the capital, in order to facilitate the transportation of the large and delicate gifts it would be bringing the emperor.

Qianlong's response to the visit was unequivocally positive. Given that the embassy was travelling such a great distance, he felt that it would be right and proper, in keeping with his position as supreme global benefactor, to extend it the fullest welcome possible. Officials up and down the coast of China were alerted to its impending arrival, and they were to do everything in their power to support the British when they made landfall. On arrival in Tianjin, the embassy would be provided with smaller boats to help ferry its personnel and material upriver towards Peking, and the local salt commissioner, an official named Zhengrui, was ordered to procure these. He was also assigned as the primary liaison for the foreigners during their time in China and would come to have considerable impact on Macartney's fortunes.

It may seem odd that, given how reluctant the Qing had proven to be in hearing the complaints of the Canton traders, the court would be so eager to welcome an official embassy from the West. The fact is that the constrictions placed on contact with the West and the limited numbers of bureaucrats who were authorised to deal with these foreigners contributed to a confused picture about the nature and relative powers of these guests from afar. Qianlong hoped that direct engagement with the British might change this, but there was a long way to go. A major Qing-era work on foreigners, the *Huang Qing Zhigong Tu* (or *The August Qing's Illustrated Account of Tribute-Bearing Domains*), offers a remarkably muddied picture of the states of Europe, listing England as one of the Qing's tributary states, but then claiming that this kingdom also went by the names of Sweden and the Netherlands.[14]

Part of the challenge for Qianlong's bureaucrats was that the concept of freebooting, buccaneering merchants, operating overseas with only minimal oversight from their government proved profoundly alien. In China, there was little large-scale organised activity outside the remit of the state, and it was difficult for the Qing to grasp the idea of a private corporation like the East India Company. Previously, the engagement between Chinese officials and foreign peoples was defined by efforts to shoehorn each overseas visitor into a tributary relationship with the emperor. This was usually effective when dealing with other nations in East and Southeast Asia, but even in engagements with European powers, this approach could produce results. With the Portuguese, for example, their willingness to support the Ming dynasty in tackling piracy along the Chinese seaboard, and in apprehending mutineers fleeing the imperial army, had shown a willingness to recognise the emperor's superiority. For this, they were rewarded with the opportunity to establish a trading base in Macao.[15] The Dutch, similarly, were granted trading concessions by the Qing from the 1670s, but these were later withdrawn when the naval support on which they were contingent failed to arrive.[16]

A number of European nations that sent embassies to China over the seventeenth and eighteenth centuries also benefitted from having fellow-countrymen serving as missionaries in Peking. These priests were usually serving at court and consequently helped their compatriots approach the Qing on terms the Chinese understood. Indeed, according to Barrow, many acted as impromptu translators, and when asked about the gifts brought by the visiting delegations, they told the Chinese officials that this was indeed tribute in recognition of the emperor's suzerainty.[17] These other European nations were conforming, at least in part, to the pre-conceived idea the Chinese had about how their court should engage with foreigners.

Yet when a foreign trader arrived in China with purely commercial intentions, not formally representing his government (as was the case with most British merchants), the response from the Qing Government was to hand management of the relationship over to the *gonghang*, known to the Europeans as the *Cohong*. This body was a guild of Cantonese merchants, typically thirteen, who had a monopoly on trade with the foreigners. The only direct involvement the state wanted with the traders was to receive the customs duties levelled on the goods flowing through Canton. While the *Cohong* system allowed the Chinese Government to wash its hands of managing the day-to-day relationship with the Westerners, it also meant that the political effects, both domestic and foreign, of China's increasing exports were ignored.

Unlike with the Portuguese and the Dutch, there was no mechanism in place for guiding the development of engagement with the British, given that the traditional Chinese approach required a tributary relationship between the emperor and a foreign ruler as a starting point for ties to develop. The British had been of no use to the emperor; they had fought no pirates and had never promised any fleets. They only wanted to trade. As Barrow describes it, 'other nations of Europe were known to the Chinese by their services, and had received rewards for those services; the English were known only by their broad cloths and their bravery'.[18] Even this is likely a generous description of the Chinese view of the British. As far as Qianlong was concerned, they barely existed, except possibly as an irritant.

Increasingly, however, the British began to make up an ever-growing share of the traders putting in to Canton. With more trade came a greater number of what might be delicately termed 'incidents', the type that always happen when sailors land in foreign ports after many months at sea. As early as 1686, the Qing had placed restrictions on local contact with foreigners, but it was clear that this was not developing into the sort of control that Chinese officials expected. In 1741, a British vessel under the command of George Anson, which had been raiding Spanish merchantmen in the seas of the Philippines, was driven by storm damage to seek refuge in Canton. Expecting the typical courtesies extended to neutral vessels under the international laws governing maritime affairs, Anson instead found the local officials unhelpful and rude. Forced to depart with his ship only partially restored, his experience was later widely publicised in Europe.

If Anson suffered from the inexperience of the Qing state in dealing with Westerners, his hardships pale in comparison to those of James Flint. A Chinese speaker, Flint was specifically tasked in 1759 to present the complaints of the EIC to the Qing court. Bribing and cajoling his way via Ningbo, he was able to make it as far north as Tianjin, from whence his petition was brought to Peking. However, while he made his way back southwards, Flint suffered from a change in the imperial mood and was flung into prison. There he would remain for three years, guilty of the crimes of having visited a number of Chinese ports, having attempted to communicate with the court, and (most egregious of all) having had the temerity to learn Chinese.

More tragic was the 1784 case of the *Lady Hughes*, a merchant vessel plying between India and Canton. On arrival in the Chinese port, the vessel fired a salute from its cannons, accidentally killing two people ashore. The ship's captain attempted to protect his sailors by saying he could not possibly uncover which of the many gunners had fired the fatal shot. The response from the Chinese was to arrest the commercial manager aboard the ship, combined with a threat to cancel all trade with the West.

An unfortunate sailor was chosen as the most likely culprit and handed over to the authorities, who had him strangled in 1785.

All these incidents point to the haphazard handling of relations between China and the West, and Qianlong was aware that a more appropriate form of engagement was necessary. The decision to accept the Macartney embassy was motivated by the hope that the strange English traders in Canton might finally be tied into a relationship with a government that could act as a tributary of the Qing. Perhaps the British might be encouraged to develop the same level of respect for the emperor, and for existing Chinese practice, that the Dutch and Portuguese had displayed, however patchily. This would then allow relations between China and Britain to develop along the traditional lines that defined Qing foreign policy. Sadly, in hoping for such an outcome, Qianlong and his advisors were being tragically optimistic.

4

'The Severest Sufferings Both in Body and Mind'

In the spring of 2002, the Irish naval vessel *LÉ Niamh* set out from Cork, bound for the unfamiliar waters of the Pudong River, which flows through the centre of Shanghai. One of only eight vessels in the Irish fleet, the *Niamh* and her crew were making history; at over 9,000 km from home, this would be the furthest afield the Irish Navy had ever sailed. However, unlike most Western naval vessels that had sailed in Chinese waters over the centuries, the *Niamh* had commercial, not military, objectives. She had been dispatched by the Irish Government to act as a platform for a trade mission and would not only take in Shanghai, but would also call to Tokyo, as well as Penang in Malaysia.

While in Asia, the *Niamh* would welcome 2,000 guests aboard, providing a showcase for Irish food (in particular, and fittingly, seafood) and helping to launch a number of Irish cultural events. Although more pacific than most naval missions in China, nevertheless, the *Niamh* was not the first vessel to set out for the country carrying Irishmen and hoping to make a good impression. In fact, the vessel was following an almost identical mission to that pursued by HMS *Lion* in 1792, when she was tasked by the British Government to transport George Macartney, his embassy, and their assorted collection of scientific wonders to Asia.

The *Lion* was Macartney's personal choice, and the pick of the available transport was only one of the advantages that the ambassador had swung from his new appointment. His pay for his time overseas would be the staggering sum of £15,000 for every year spent away from Britain. He would also secure the much sought-after elevation to the English peerage, denied on his return from India. Departing as Viscount Macartney of

Dervock, he would arrive back in Britain to become Earl Macartney. Most crucially of all, he had also been allowed to select his own team for the mission.

This was vital given that of all the troubles that can befall expeditions such as this, Barrow wrote, 'none of any kind happen more frequently or are more pernicious than those which arise from disunion among the persons engaged in such undertakings'.[1] Inevitably, the ubiquitous George Staunton would be the second-in-command of the embassy; should things go to plan, Staunton would be staying on as permanent representative to Qianlong's court. Accompanying his father would be twelve-year-old George Thomas Staunton, known as Thomas, who would go on to become one of the great early British experts on China. His father recognised the opportunity that such a journey might provide to his son and resolved that Thomas would serve Macartney as his page. Thus, Thomas's childhood continued in a well-established precocious vein; fluent in Latin by four, the boy was taught to view toys and games as a waste of time. On the journey out, he devoted his time (willingly or not, it is hard to say) to the study of Mandarin, and he would be one of the few members of the embassy to make significant progress in the language. His Chinese skills joined an already well-developed conversational repertoire, which also extended to Greek and French.

The obvious language difference between the British diplomats and their hosts proved to be a difficult obstacle to overcome, efforts by the young Thomas notwithstanding. Daunting though the various dialects of Chinese might seem to modern visitors to the country, the mechanics of engaging in meaningful conversation with the emperor must have seemed particularly intimidating to Macartney as he planned the mission. In today's world, sourcing an interpreter would prove relatively easy. For eighteenth-century travellers, such services were not so readily available. Indeed, it seems clear that there was no one in the entire British Empire suitable for fulfilling the role of mission interpreter. While the East India Company had a number of 'supercargoes' operating in Canton who had picked up some Chinese, it was likely that what they had learnt was Cantonese, not the Mandarin dialect of the imperial court. Perhaps of greater concern would be the colloquial and idiomatic vocabulary that they would have absorbed from the salty company they kept in the port city.

This dearth of talent forced Macartney to search the European continent for the required linguistic skills, dispatching Staunton on his first task for the embassy. Only one organisation had the experience of Asia and the resources required to train large numbers of Chinese speakers—the Catholic Church. Travelling first to Paris, Staunton was told by the *Société des missions étrangères* that they had no Chinese speakers available, but that if he was to find the help he needed anywhere, it would be in Naples. There, he received aid from the unlikely pairing of Cardinal Antonelli of the Congregation for the Propagation of the Faith, and the resident British minister, Sir William Hamilton, husband of the soon to be infamous Lady Emma Hamilton. These directed Staunton to the *Collegium Sinicum*, the 'Chinese College', established to train missionaries in the Chinese language, and which survives today as *Università degli Studi di Napoli 'L'Orientale'*, the oldest school of Chinese studies in Europe. There he was able to recruit two Chinese converts to Catholicism who were training for the priesthood. Even so, Fathers Li and Zhou were only limited to translation between Chinese and Latin or Italian. The British would have to handle the translations between Latin and English themselves. Two further Chinese priests, Fathers An and Wang, would join the mission as far as Macao, at least offering additional tutors for anyone willing to learn the language for themselves.

All four of these priests also proved invaluable in advising Macartney on what gifts to present to the emperor, providing a level of cultural insight that had been sorely lacking. They also stand as testament to the extensive activities of the Catholic missionary orders, in particular the Jesuits, in China, where they were busy trying to win converts, using the order's typical methodology of appealing to the local elites. While the Chinese authorities might have found little of spiritual interest in what the representatives of the Society of Jesus could offer, the priests' skills as mathematicians, and indeed astronomers, were highly valued, for reasons we will examine in detail below.

However, the Jesuits' success as scientists was not matched in their missionary efforts. According to Staunton (who was not wholly unsympathetic to the missionaries), despite their efforts to convince the great and the good of Qing society, most of their converts were won from among children abandoned at birth by parents who could not afford another mouth to feed.[2]

Thus linguistically armed, on 26 September 1792, the mission set sail. Joining the *Lion* were two other vessels; the East India Company provided one of their own ships, the three-masted *Hindoostan*, while the brig, HMS *Jackall*, rounded off the fleet. Things began inauspiciously when the *Jackall* became separated from the other ships in a storm, shortly after departing Portsmouth. Leaving her to catch up, the *Lion* and the *Hindoostan* pressed on, their route taking them via Madeira, the Canaries and Cape Verde, then across the Atlantic to Rio de Janeiro. Along the way, Macartney was feted by a succession of Spanish and Portuguese colonial governors, some of whom were unimpressive (the governor of Rio was 'civil, but slow'), while others surprised him with their refinement (the governor of Tenerife 'spoke French intelligently, and ... was communicative in conversation').[3]

The voyage itself was to be an opportunity to increase the sum of British political, economic, and natural knowledge of the world—a lofty goal that was met with mixed, and indeed at times amateurish, results. Upon leaving Rio de Janeiro to re-cross the Atlantic to the Cape of Good Hope, the fleet attempted to survey the island of Tristan da Cunha. However, gales drove the ships away from the island before any serious exploration took place, and the sole result of the detour was some light butchery of the local fauna. A naval officer in command of a landing party claimed to have shot a huge sea lion, which was so big his crew could not haul it back to the ship. Mysteriously, the size of the creature seemed to decrease as the marksman was forced to recount the tale over and over again. The same hunter did, however, manage to wing and capture an albatross whose wingspan stretched to 10 feet. This small success was somewhat undermined when some of the crew claimed that this was a very small specimen, and that they had personally seen examples of the species with spans of 18 feet. The scientific credibility of this little excursion was ultimately erased by the final fate of this unlucky bird. Dr Gillen had intended to mend its wing, hoping to keep it alive for as long as possible to allow further examination. However, a member of the crew decided that the albatross could be put to better use as a dish than as a scientific exhibit, and one night, he roasted the animal on a spit. That this nautical gourmand was then laid-low with food poisoning seemed a fitting ending to the farce.

The mission skirted the Cape of Good Hope, making for New Amsterdam, an island in the middle of the Indian Ocean. There, they found a lonely team of five seal-hunters, a mixture of French and Americans, who were collecting pelts for sale in Canton. Nothing perhaps better encapsulates the global economic importance of China, or indeed the pressing need of the Macartney embassy, than the fact even this lonely, desolate part of the world was buffeted by the economic currents flowing from the Qing Empire.

New Amsterdam might have represented a neat example of global trade trends, but it also provided further proof that while the Macartney embassy might feature seasoned diplomats and administrators, rugged explorers were not among its complement. For a start, the skilled hunter from Tristan D'Acunha struck again, this time capturing a one-legged penguin that became something of a ship's mascot aboard HMS *Lion*. Several members of the embassy were then badly injured after sitting down beside a thermal spring, not realising that the heat from the ground was burning through their breeches until it was painfully too late. Macartney himself, in a somewhat bizarre aside in his diaries, wondered if New

Amsterdam might have the makings of health resort to rival Nice, Bath, or Montpellier, despite the notable handicap of being 3,000 km away from the nearest continent. While he may have been making the suggestion somewhat tongue-in-cheek, he did seem to think that the development of the hot-air balloon in the 1780s might make the trip a relatively easy commute.

Even this little community of seal-hunters seemed to end up worse off for its contact with the embassy. While the Frenchman in charge of the skinning operation showed Macartney and several senior members of his team around the island, one of the *Lion*'s crew bribed the remaining seal-hunters with some rum and managed to sneak the vast majority of their skins onto the *Lion*. This scam was only discovered when the *Lion* had put to sea again, and so Erasmus Gower, the captain of the ship, had no choice but to continue, intending to leave the recovered skins in Canton with the French agent who was officially authorised to sell them into the Chinese market. As we shall see, the Macartney embassy later managed to inflict even more suffering on these unfortunate seal hunters after its arrival in China.

This farcical stretch of the voyage between Brazil and Java, for all its comic asides, shows that in the eighteenth century, lack of experience was no barrier for the Georgian gentleman pursuing any goals that took his fancy. Macartney and his colleagues had achieved success in the fields of diplomacy, law, government, and medicine; why, they wondered, should they not be explorers, botanists, geologists, and zoologists as well? Yet from the numerous mishaps and downright failures, it is clear that they had no idea what they were doing. What is more, the acquisitive nature of their curiosity—where animals or plants were not merely studied *in situ*, but had to be captured and removed to be truly understood—speaks volumes about the essentially exploitative mindset of European society at the time. The Macartney mission arrived in Tristan da Cunha or New Amsterdam with the same basic mindset as it would display in Peking—aiming only to acquire material benefit, with little regard for the interests of the locals.

Any lingering feelings of embarrassment from their escapades among the lonely islands of the South Atlantic and the Indian Ocean were not in evidence when the British finally reached Java. Despite the outbreak of a number of cases of scurvy among the crew, they remained in a mood of perfect poise. Approached by a Dutch ship whose captain asked for details of the vessels, their complement, and destination (an effort by the Dutch governor of Batavia to exert his nation's primacy over the maritime approaches to the South China Sea), they responded in a manner befitting agents of the world's premier naval power. Other vessels flying the Union flag, such as the East Indiamen that regularly traversed these waters, might have complied to ensure an easy passage, but the captain of the *Lion* was not about to entertain any question about the primacy of the Royal Navy. The Dutch request was tartly met with the remark that the lead vessel was the HMS *Lion*, and given that it was easily observed to be a sixty-four-gun man-of-war, any other questions were irrelevant.

Despite this frisson of imperial rivalry, the British were warmly welcomed to Batavia (modern Jakarta) by Governor Willem Arnold Alting. Their encounter with the Dutch colonial establishment provides an interesting juxtaposition of the different approaches to imperial endeavours taken by the various European states. At first glance, the similarities between life in Britain's colonies and Batavia seemed remarkable. In both locations, the political elite enjoyed the same social rounds of sumptuous dinners, courtly dancing, and rapidly acquired, flamboyantly displayed wealth.

Macartney's diaries described in exacting detail the enormous and varied dishes served to the British as they dined at the governor's mansion, or at the house of his host, a Mr Wiegerman. The guests were treated to breath-taking fireworks displays, attended parties where the governor's daughter wore jewels rumoured to total £4,000 in value, and devoured luncheons that were so rich that everyone had to retire to bed for a few hours to prepare themselves for an even more extravagant meal at dinner. Of course, just as in Britain's possessions, this was all built on the exploitation and suffering of the local population, and of the slaves imported to Batavia from throughout South and Southeast Asia (at those delightful soirées, the wives of Batavia's rulers were attended by slave women whose only role was to hold highly polished spittoons).

However, it soon became clear that the Dutch had a far looser grip on their colonies than the British enjoyed in their own empire. Macartney notes that the countryside around Batavia had descended into lawlessness, with people not daring to travel any distance without being armed with at least a *criss*, the native dagger. The Dutch clearly had little interest in providing security for the local populace outside their own settlements. Large tracts of what was once farms was now reverting to jungle, pointing to a recent decline in population. Certainly, the embassy itself had good reason to view the northern coast of Java as anarchic. One of the *Lion*'s crew went ashore to wash some linens in a stream and was promptly killed by the locals. If the murder itself suggests how negatively native Javans viewed Europeans, the fact that nothing was done in response reveals the tenuousness of the Dutch position in the region.

As tended to be the case in Britain's own colonial possessions in India, Batavia itself was something of a melting pot. There were the native Javanese, who were all free and protected from slavery through agreements signed by the Dutch with the main local rulers. Nonetheless, it was clear to Macartney that violence kept the Javanese in line. Slaves were numerous, hailing from throughout the Indian subcontinent and Southeast Asia, although predominantly from the Malay Islands. Notably, female slaves vastly outnumbered the males. Freed slaves rented plots of land from the colonial authorities, cultivating crops for the marketplace. The Chinese community was the merchant lifeblood of the city, using their network of contacts throughout their far-flung diaspora to smoothly trade across Southeast Asia. The most successful Dutch merchants had a trusted Chinese partner who carried out commerce on their behalf, a system not unfamiliar to the British, who had similar Indian partners in Madras and Calcutta.

Above all these groups, but below the strata of the Dutch colonial rulers, was a class descended from Portuguese-speaking inhabitants of the city. Macartney took these to be the original settlers, who had been supplanted by the Dutch, but it seems more likely that these were actually the descendants of captives, primarily Asian, seized by the Dutch in their battles against the Portuguese in Asia. Known as *Mardijkers*, they had been pressed into service by their captors, before being freed and becoming an integral part of Batavian society, where their language was common until well into the nineteenth century.[4] Although initially clinging to their Catholic faith, by the time of Macartney's visit they had switched to the reformed churches, so that in Batavia, one could hear the teachings of Calvin being proclaimed in Portuguese. A result, Macartney imagined with relish, which would have been particularly appalling to Pope Leo X, who had been so pleased with Portuguese missionary activity in this region in the sixteenth century.

Evidently, the Dutch offered their guests much in the way of comfort and entertainment because they spent nearly two months there. Three weeks after their arrival, Macartney made the decision to purchase another vessel to replace the *Jackall*, which had been by now given up as lost. Parting with five thousand Spanish dollars, he acquired the French vessel *Nereide*, which he renamed the *Clarence*. Inevitably, shortly after the deal closed, the *Jackall* sailed into Batavia's harbour.

Despite the apparent reluctance among the fleet to move on towards China, a pressing motivation finally led them to weigh anchor: disease. Having had no fatalities before arriving off Java, Macartney's team now began to suffer seriously from illness. Dysentery carried off a number of the crew, and Batavia was seen as a breeding ground for the illness. Macartney himself put this down to the many canals that the Dutch had built through the city, tree-lined and full of stagnant water. The standard of medicine in the settlement was also abysmally low, and most of the doctors were nothing but adventurers with some basic knowledge of physiology. So deficient was the local medical community that the nephew of the surgeon on board the *Lion*, 'an ignorant young boy', was able to jump ship and find employment in the local hospital.[5]

Leaving Batavia on 21 April, by mid-May, they were off the coast of Vietnam, having lost men to disease all along the way. They anchored off the island of Côn Sơn, known to the English as Pulo Condore, a territory of the Tây Sơn dynasty, who were ruling large sections of what is now Vietnam from their capital in the modern city of Huế. The four ships were giving an apparently warm welcome by the islanders, who promised to provide all the supplies requested. Communication was through notes written by Father Wang, one of the Chinese translators; although he could not understand the words spoken by the Vietnamese, the two nationalities still shared a writing system at this point.

The next morning, the British awoke to find the village abandoned, with no sign of the locals or the promised supplies. A letter left behind for Father An explained that the villagers were terrified of the visitors, assuming that they would ransack the community and take all their belongings. The British departed, leaving a note explaining who they were, and that in the future, the people of Côn Sơn should not fear any ships flying the Union Jack. Macartney believed, or at least claimed to believe, that the island must at some point have suffered at the hands of an American ship's crew, who may have been mistaken as British. Given the volumes of trade heading to Britain, and the fact that the island lay on the route west and not east towards the United States, one might safely suspect that the local populace might have justly feared the British from prior experience.

Shortly after departing Côn Sơn, the *Hindoostan* suffered a terrible accident when one of the cables that held the capstan, used to raise and lower the anchor, snapped. As this rope flailed around, it left the deck strewn with heavily wounded men, many with smashed limbs. Despite initial fears that some were bound to die, miraculously all survived, but the fleet was forced to put into the port now known as Da Nang. The stop also allowed Macartney to pursue some diplomatic work as he was able to contact the governor of Da Nang, who relayed messages from the ambassador to Nguyen Quang Toan, the Tây Sơn Emperor. The British were now firmly operating in China's sphere of influence; the Tây Sơn dynasty were in the orbit of the Qing court and regularly sent shipments of ivory to Canton as tribute.

The governor of Da Nang hosted a dinner for the foreigners, where two lighted candles set in an alcove in the reception hall, representing the Tây Sơn Emperor, joined the diners. Entertained by a traditional opera—which was 'not very flattering to the ear, being strongly nasal' and reminded Macartney of the singing 'among the Presbyterians in the North of Ireland'—the British ate using Western cutlery borrowed from a visiting Portuguese ship. Determined that the Tây Sơn would have a positive view of the British, and to underline the extent of his gratitude, Macartney gave the governor a number of gifts to be passed on to the emperor. Whether the 'excellent plain gold watch ... a double-barrelled gun complete with pouch, powder-horn, etc., a pair of spring bayonet pistols, a fine steel-handled broadsword, [and] three pieces of fine camblet, red, purple, and yellow' would ever make it to the emperor was doubtful, the ambassador realised, but at least his appreciation was clear.[6]

Such diplomatic efforts were wise. Despite the outward hospitality, Macartney later learned that a force consisting of cavalry, infantry, and a half-dozen elephants was waiting out of sight, in case the governor received word from the imperial court that the British were to be treated as enemies. Given that the foreigners had already named a promontory overlooking Da Nang as 'New Gibraltar', perhaps even greater caution on the part of the locals would have been justified. As it was, behind the pleasantries and exchange of gifts, the Tây Sơn remained discreetly wary of the British throughout their period in Vietnam.

On 7 June, the cutter from the *Lion*, under the command of the ship's master, Jackson, had disappeared while surveying the local rivers. Viewed with suspicion by some local villagers, he and his men were seized and imprisoned. Not knowing what had happened to the cutter's crew, Macartney wrote to the governor of Da Nang, who promised to investigate. In truth, he already had the sailors in his custody and was merely waiting for instructions from the imperial court as to how to proceed. Happily, they were released, having 'undergone the severest sufferings both in body and mind, and no circumstance but their belonging to the British Embassy could have preserved them from being put to death'.[7] Before any further diplomatic challenges could arise, the British sailed for China on 15 June.

5

'The Greatest City on the Surface of the Globe'

When George Osborne, then-chancellor of the Exchequer, visited China in September 2015, his itinerary included cities that would have been unfamiliar to many Westerners. Of course, Osborne was first greeted in Beijing by Chinese Prime Minister Li Keqiang before he travelled onwards to Shanghai to visit the city's stock exchange. However, his itinerary also included Urumqi, in China's far western province of Xinjiang, where he toured the offices of a company that had improbably developed interests in both cement and mutton and was now looking to invest £60 million in housing developments in the north of England. This was then followed by a stop in Chengdu, capital of Sichuan province and a major centre for development in China's south-west.

That the man who, at the time, was widely expected to become Britain's next prime minister, and who was intent on ushering in a 'Golden Age' in relations between the UK and China, would visit these less widely known cities reveals an important truth about China. Understandably, for tourists, executives, and even visiting politicians, China can often mean just Beijing, Shanghai, and the cities of Guangdong province. After all, Beijing is where political power lies, where one can see the Forbidden City and take a day trip to the Great Wall. Shanghai has the waterfront of the Bund and is China's financial hub. The humming megacity that stretches along the Pearl River from Guangzhou to the border between Shenzhen and Hong Kong contains within it the many millions who, night and day, are turning out everything from iPhones to electric cars. These cities tend to draw Western eyes.

Yet China's true economic weight is most apparent when one goes beyond what the Chinese term their 'Tier 1' urban centres, when you travel through vast tracts of the countryside dotted by cities of over a million people each, of which China had 160 in 2012. Only then does the scale of the commercial activity in the country hit home. Every one of these cities, small by Chinese standards, but which would be considered major metropolises in any European state, is home to entrepreneurs, designers, financiers, and engineers who are constantly working to better themselves, consequently driving forward the national economy, and with it their country's role in the world. This reality is easily forgotten today, when one can, by aircraft or high-speed train, quickly zip between the main hubs, passing by the bulk of the urban areas that actually make up China.

In the eighteenth century, things were different. Macartney was forced, on both legs of his journey to and from the imperial court, to travel through towns and cities across China, all the time getting to understand the gargantuan nature of the empire. The sheer scale of the state with which he was to entreat was ever apparent.

His first glimpse of this massive country came on Wednesday, 19 June 1793, as the Chinese mainland appeared to the north-east, a great bulk that grew on the horizon throughout the afternoon. The following morning, at 6 a.m., the squadron came to anchor off the Ladrone Islands, within sight of Macao. A boat was dispatched to the Portuguese colony to seek out pilots for the journey north and to put ashore three of the Chinese missionaries who had been advising the expedition. Despite their initial enthusiasm, Fathers An, Wang, and Zhou, now that they were within sight once more of the Celestial Empire, had developed cold feet. The priests suddenly felt that accompanying a foreign embassy was too great a risk, particularly when compounded with their earlier sins of having left China without official permission.

Thankfully, there remained a fourth interpreter, Father Li, a heavy smoker with tobacco-stained teeth, whom Staunton described as being from Chinese Tartary, a term that blankets modern Tibet, Xinjiang, Qinghai, and Mongolia. As he was not a member of the majority Han community in China and was wearing an English military uniform, he felt more confident that he would not be found out as an errant imperial subject. The embassy was now also joined by two Italian missionaries who were travelling to Peking to enter the emperor's service as astronomers and mathematicians. Macartney's wariness of Catholicism did not blind him to the progress that that faith's missionaries had made in China, and he realised that by helping them, he might secure valuable allies to support his own efforts at the Qing imperial court.

Such support would no doubt have been particularly cherished once Macartney had studied the political currents that had been stirred up by the arrival of his embassy, both among the Chinese and the foreign community. Of course, the East India Company's own representatives in Macao were delighted that Macartney was in a position to make direct contact with the emperor, opening up the possibility that in future they might be able to communicate with Peking themselves, bypassing Canton, through which their petitions had to go at present. Up until this point, all their efforts at winning better trading terms and lighter regulation of their activities had come to nought, in part because they were easily dismissed as representatives of a merely commercial body. Now that they could use an envoy of the British Crown to make their case for them, they thought their position would improve considerably.

However, while the Dutch East Indies Company quickly promised Macartney the support of their resident in Peking, evidently having decided that any increase in the esteem afforded to the British would benefit all Westerners, the same was not true of Britain's traditional allies, the Portuguese, who proved a little less congenial. Macartney had hoped that they might be able to provide further translators for his team, but the Portuguese recognised that the embassy threatened to undermine the unique nature of their position in Macao as a gateway to the Chinese market. Anything that might increase the channels between China and Europe would harm their interests, and so they proved unenthusiastic. This explained an earlier instance in Da Nang, where a Portuguese captain who happened to be anchored in the harbour offered Macartney every obvious assistance in provisioning his ships. However, when the governor of the city viewed the British with some trepidation 'our good friends the Portuguese, notwithstanding their outward civility to us, did not, I believe, take any pains to remove those jealousies but rather confirmed them by an artful silence, or by expressive innuendoes'.[1]

The embassy also considered using French missionaries to flesh out the ranks of their interpreters, but they were discouraged as these priests had recently fallen under suspicion in China. In large part, this was down to the eruption of revolution in France. While the imperial government was only receiving snatches of reports from the West as to what was happening, they were understandably fearful of the spread of any ideology that might encourage peasants and the urban poor to rise up against an aristocracy. That the missionaries would have themselves generally been from among those sections of French society most threatened by the Revolution was a subtlety lost on their hosts.

On the other side of the Anglo-Chinese relationship, a range of impulses complicated the response of the local officials to the arrival of the embassy. Certainly, the word from Peking was that the Qianlong Emperor was eager to receive the delegation, assuming as he did that the British must be travelling in order to pay tribute to the Qing court. The provincial authorities in Canton were more tempered in their openness to the embassy, however, wary as to what direct impact the arrival of these foreigners might have on their own positions. After all, up to this point, they had regulated all foreign commercial activity in China; not surprisingly, the relationship between these greatly empowered regional officials and the striving, buccaneering merchants had not always been smooth. In particular, the provincial customs inspector, known to the foreigners as the Hoppo, feared that the emperor might soon be hearing from Macartney the tales of woe peddled by the traders regarding their treatment at his hands. Understandably, both the Hoppo and the governor of Canton were very eager to ascertain what exactly Macartney was planning to say when brought into the imperial presence.

The governor thus demanded that Macartney land in the city before making his way overland to Peking. Macartney easily dismissed this request on the grounds that transporting the vast collection of gifts for the emperor was only possible by sea. He had, of course, also realised that the surest route to success was to make directly for the imperial court, avoiding all the lower levels of Qing authority. To avoid entanglement with provincial bureaucrats, the mission set sail to the north on 23 June, without pilots and without additional translators beyond Father Li. These deficiencies forced Macartney to dispatch the *Clarence* under Staunton to the city of Zhoushan to seek at least local guides for the onward journey; this would be vital, as from this point forwards, Western knowledge of the waters began to peter out. The *Clarence* sailed west, leaving the rest of the ships at anchor in the muggy damp of a Chinese summer's rainstorm.

Zhoushan is spread across a number of islands off the coast of Zhejiang province and was subordinate to the nearby major port of Ningbo. Until 1760, it had been home to a number of Western merchants, when the Qing Government had decided to restrict all foreign trade to Canton. While the British assumed this was due to what they saw as an illogical Chinese aversion to unfettered commerce, the truth is of course a little more complex. According to one French missionary, the Westerners, when allowed relatively free rein to trade along the Chinese coast, abused this freedom through 'their extreme familiarity with the women, their haughtiness with the men, and repeated acts of insult and indiscretion … now they are only suffered to put in at Canton'.[2] Thus, the restriction of Western traders to Canton was less about China's alleged dislike of 'fair trade' and more about effectively controlling the potential destabilising social effects of the traders themselves.

While the squadron's visit was primarily to secure pilots, we also know that Macartney had greater plans in mind for the urban archipelago. As we have seen, one of the embassy's goals was to secure an island to act as a 'convenient depot … With the same privileges as were granted to the Portuguese at Macao'.[3] Macartney hoped that one of the islands near this city might prove ideal for this purpose, if Qianlong could be convinced to relinquish it. So the opportunity was seized to perform an unofficial survey of the sought-after territory.

As the British approached the city, a flotilla of sightseers and curious onlookers surrounded the *Clarence*. Having docked, Staunton sent some of his officers ashore to request pilots from the city governor, but the intricacies of Chinese bureaucracy were to complicate what they assumed would be a simple request. Stifled by the heat in their close-fitting Georgian clothes, surrounded in the audience chamber by delicately worked animal horn lamps and miniature *penjing* trees, the delegates were told that, alas, no pilots could be provided to the mission, as the governor was responsible to his immediate superior in Ningbo and could not make such a decision himself. His superiors had, regrettably, only authorised him to provide guides to take the British a little distance up the coast, where they would pick up their next pilots, and so on until they finally reached Tianjin. In such a manner, the bureaucrats of the empire hoped to keep the foreign fleet on a tight rein as it made its way north.

However, when arbitrary Chinese administrative requirements ran up against British stubbornness, there could be only one winner. Staunton stated that if the governor of Zhoushan would not provide them with the help they needed to get to Tianjin, then the *Clarence* would proceed directly to Ningbo and ask his superior for guides, but only after noting the unsatisfactory nature of the Zhoushan governor's offers of help. On hearing that the British might go over his head, exposing him as having failed in his duty as a host, in a panic, the governor combed the city for pilots, eager not to allow it be said that he had in any way undermined the empire's welcome for the foreign delegation.

Given the short notice with which the two pilots were rustled up, it should prove no surprise that they were less than expert. While both had been to Tianjin in the past, neither had been to sea in many years. Shortly after leaving Zhoushan, the *Clarence* was gripped by a whirlpool that dragged it to within touching distance of some jagged rocks. The pilots calmly told their charges not to worry as they promised the situation would resolve itself if the British sailors simply left the ship alone. Thankfully, things did turn out for the best, but as Staunton diplomatically noted, this relaxed approach to their duties, combined with their lack of English, would see the pilots 'sometimes pass for being ignorant of their business'.[4]

This near mishap notwithstanding, the *Clarence* returned to the rest of the ships without suffering any casualties, bar Barrow, who developed food poisoning from some poorly chosen fruit. The squadron passed north along the coast, every hour further outstripping existing European knowledge of the seas around them. By mid-July, they were passing along the northern coast of Shandong province, the scrubby, rocky hills of the peninsula not suggesting a warm welcome; the party cheered themselves up by presumptuously naming nearby features Cape Macartney, Cape Gower, and Staunton Island.

The pilots further distinguished themselves by having the squadron anchor in the wrong bay before the ships hove to in the right location, off the Miao Dao islands near Tenchoo (modern Penglai) to prepare for their landing at Tianjin. Macartney took this opportunity to have a notice he had prepared read out to the squadron, which drew everyone's attention to the fact that among the Chinese, the reputation of the British was not particularly high. All members of the mission, he declared, from the most junior up to himself, would have to do their upmost to win over their hosts. At all times, sensitivity and respect would be key. They would each be subject to Chinese law, and should they commit a crime, Macartney would not intervene on their behalf. The circular betrays the ambassador's recognition of his comparatively weak opening position. Despite the success of British force in securing economic advantage from India to the Caribbean, he recognised that polite persuasion was the only policy choice available this far from home. The Chinese would not brook any attempt at compulsion.

Once more, the advice of their pilots proved to be worthless as it rapidly became clear that the Miao Dao islands were not a suitable harbour for European ships. The squadron was forced to press on, delaying only to restock supplies, meet with the governor of Tenchoo, and to get much-needed competent guides. Having rendezvoused with HMS *Endeavour* (not, it should be noted, of Captain Cook fame), sent from Canton with dispatches for the ambassador and two more translators, they began their approach to Tianjin. HMS *Jackall*, the smallest of the British vessels, took the lead, and this precaution ensured that the squadron avoided a number of hazards along the route that could easily have snared the larger vessels, such as hidden sand bars and shoals. When they reached the mouth of the river Hai near Tianjin, officers from the *Jackall* went ashore to see if they could discover a suitable harbour for the *Lion* and the rest of the ships.

Then, as now, Tianjin was the largest port close to Peking, and a major population centre. The mandarins who governed the city at the end of the eighteenth century estimated the population at being roughly 700,000 people, and the British felt that this number chimed with their own observations. Today, the city is one of four Chinese municipalities treated as a province (putting it in the same league as Beijing, Shanghai, and Chongqing), and in Macartney's time, its officials were similarly empowered.

It was at Tianjin that the British mission acquired their two official minders for the rest of their time in China. The first of these was a civil administrator called Qiao Renjie:

> [A man] of grave, but not austere, manners. He was not forward in discourse; neither appearing to aim at anything brilliant in himself, nor to be dazzled by it in others. A faithful and benevolent discharge of his duty seemed to be the sole and simple object of his pursuit.[5]

In other words, he was the archetypical civil servant. A military official, Wang Wenxiong, accompanied Qiao. Wang cut a more dashing figure:

> Beside a red globe above his bonnet, he was honoured with another mark of favour for his services. This was literally a feather, and taken from a peacock's tail. It was given by the Emperor, with directions to wear it pendent from his bonnet. He had signalized himself in battle, and received several wounds.[6]

The juxtaposition of Qiao and Wang with their British equivalents provides an interesting contrast in different approaches to administration in these two great empires, European and Asian. In the former, promotion was very much based on patronage and depended less on ability than on either finding a powerful sponsor or on buying rank for oneself. Macartney had cultivated the support of Lord Holland to launch his diplomatic career, and it should not be forgotten that while being of the Anglo-Irish aristocracy was not the poshest of backgrounds, it did bring with it independent wealth and a healthy start for a political career. The English system favoured those who benefited from an accident of birth over those of humbler origins but greater ability.

Unlike their British counterparts, Chinese officials underwent a barrage of examinations to secure positions of power, while each subsequent promotion required braving another rigorous selection process. The knowledge tested under this approach was, perhaps, of questionable relevance to civil administration, with the works of Confucius featuring prominently. Military promotion was linked to more directly applicable skills, with elements such as archery tests and examinations on the works of Sun Tzu, a sixth-century-BCE strategic genius, standing between ambitious officers and higher ranks. The important fact is that in both cases, there was a relatively level playing field for all those hoping for a career with the government. While it still required substantial sums to be able to afford the study time and tuition necessary to have a decent chance of success, there was no implicit link between nobility and administrative rank.

The bureaucracy that managed China was, of course, massive, and the machine that fed it with new candidates was fittingly immense. On their journey home, the British saw in the town of Nanzhou one of the regional examination centres for aspiring civil servants. They failed to record exactly how large this test centre was, but it was big enough to provide shelter for seventy members of the mission overnight. This was just one exam hall in one comparatively small town; there were facilities like these throughout China—such was the gargantuan system that had selected and promoted Wang and Qiao.

One of the best illustrations of these different administrative cultures came when the mandarins began itemising the embassy's gifts for the emperor. Among the treasures listed was a large collection of paintings, many of which were portraits of leading figures in British life. To ensure that the emperor knew whose face he was gazing on, an official took notes on the subject of each painting. Among the portraits was a study of the young Duke of Bedford, described to the Chinese official as a *dachen*, or minister (i.e. a great man). That was impossible, the mandarin replied, laughing; the person in the painting was only a boy and at this point in his life could have done nothing worthy of such a title. While there were hereditary titles in China, greatness was still generally earned and not received at birth.

The arrival of these officials on board the *Lion* also afforded those members of the mission who had been attempting to learn Chinese an important opportunity to practice. An impromptu competition was held between two members of the crew, one a more experienced official who had studied daily, and the other young Thomas Staunton, who had apparently taken a more relaxed approach to learning. In an experience that many students of Chinese will readily identify with, the more diligent student found that his hours of tuition had come to nought as whatever language he was speaking was not understood by the two Qing officials. The younger student, meanwhile, seems to have had the somewhat unique experience of being able, on his first attempt, to converse quite happily with his hosts.

On 2 August, after so many months at sea and following so many tangles with Chinese bureaucrats, the embassy began to disembark. Over the course of the next three days, barges ferried the many gifts (590 in all) for the emperor and the mission's own supplies to shore; from there, they would be shipped along river and canal to Peking. At the request of Qiao and Wang, Macartney had already begun to prepare the requested 'catalogue of presents sent by His Britannic Majesty to the Emperor of China', which would best display 'the progress of science and the arts in Europe'.[7] No doubt, the ambassador felt that this was merely an administrative requirement, but in fact, Qiao and Wang had been ordered from the outset to solicit this list from the British. An inventory of the gifts offered by an embassy was a traditional requirement of the Qing court of all foreign dignitaries.

Already, the British were being drawn into the formalised Chinese manner of conducting diplomacy, but they remained unaware of the significance of the request. The importance of this seemingly innocuous manifest is best shown by its subsequent journey to Qianlong's hands. Despite being translated by the British translator from Latin into Chinese, the text was rendered once more into Chinese from the original Latin on arrival in Peking, this time by the missionaries in Qianlong's service. In so doing, the priests, possibly acting out of loyalty to their home nations, watered down the impact of the communication. In this second text, a reference to the common interests of the Chinese and British sovereigns was removed, as was the mention of a special golden carriage, which was seen as a gift that would be of particular interest to Qianlong. Any suggestion that George III was Qianlong's equal was carefully expunged and language more typical of documents sent to the Chinese court by vassal rulers in Asia was inserted instead. Macartney had given an opening to those who would do Britain's interests in China harm, but he was oblivious to this fact.

Unloading complete, the EIC ship *Hindoostan* was dispatched to Zhoushan, there to await its captain, Mackintosh, who would accompany the embassy to Peking and back. All the while, he would be taking stock of how the goods that interested the Company were manufactured and at what cost. It was hoped that the *Hindoostan* could load up on tea, porcelain, and other products prior to heading for home, subject to the agreement of the emperor. It was felt that HMS *Lion* and the rest of the squadron could not stay in a Chinese port awaiting the return of the embassy as there was a risk of their presence causing a diplomatic incident, either through the actions of one of the crew or of a curious Chinese observer.

Macartney decided it would be a better use of resources to dispatch the squadron to Edo in Japan once it had replenished and refitted, to see if the Japanese were as closed to foreign commerce as was thought. Despite a total lack of Japanese interpreters, he optimistically believed that the *Lion* would get by with the services of two Malay-speaking sailors and one of the mission's Chinese translators. Language difficulties notwithstanding, the squadron was to proceed from Japan to Manila and Mindanao in the Philippines, from there to Celebes in Indonesia, Borneo, and then back to Macao, where Macartney would meet it in May 1794. The squadron's orders were to take a survey of where in Southeast Asia would buy English goods and where Britain might establish colonies.

On 5 August 1793, Macartney and his colleagues, to the cheers of the assembled sailors, were rowed away from their ships, across a muddy bar, and into the mouth of the Hai River. Despite the military guard of honour provided by the local garrison on shore, Macartney preferred not to make land there, amid the swamps and boggy ground around the estuary. Instead, he pressed on to Taku, the location of fortifications that guarded the river mouth. There, his party boarded a yacht provided by the Qing Government. Lavishly appointed in the style of a mandarin's office suite, the small vessel had a bedchamber, a small sitting room, and a saloon, within which was a raised throne where Macartney would sit as he met guests who came aboard to pay their compliments. All in all, sixteen yachts of similar or larger size were needed to convey the personnel of the embassy upstream in luxury, the little boats being 'exceedingly convenient—more so, indeed, than any I have ever seen on our canals in England'. Nonetheless, comfortable though they might be, they lacked the convenience 'we Europeans regard as the most essential'.[8]

The emperor covered all the costs of hosting the mission, and the various mandarins and officials who accompanied Macartney and his team refused all attempts at payment. The warmness of the Chinese welcome was enforced with rigid discipline. When a delivery of supplies to the mission spoiled in the warm weather, the mandarins responsible were stripped of their rank, and the porters carrying the food were caned. At meals, only the finest dishes were served, with many of the delicacies, such as swallows' nests and shark fin, still mainstays of Chinese *haute cuisine* today. Less sumptuous were the attempts to mimic what the locals understood English cooking to be like, with Staunton charitably describing the resulting rough joints of beef and lamb as 'awkward'.[9] For those members of the mission longing for bread, the closest approximation they could find was cutting up Chinese *mianbao*, or buckwheat rolls, and then toasting the slices. Ironically, one of the biggest culinary challenges for the British officials seems to be finding an acceptable cup of tea; the Chinese leaves, they felt, were too fresh.

While the hospitality was generous, the foreigners were never let too far off the leash. Their government minders were keen to ensure that the guests had a very positive view of the empire and were determined to steer the British away from independent observation. When the diplomats, soldiers, artists, and clerks of the mission sought to go ashore by themselves 'to make little excursions from our boats into the towns, or into the country, to visit any object that struck us as we went along, our wishes were seldom gratified'.

There was never outright refusal, however. The mandarins, in a manner that will seem familiar to anyone dealing with Chinese officialdom today, gave the British 'immediate acquiescence in words with everything we seemed to propose, yet, in fact, some ingenious pretence or plausible objection was usually invented to disappoint us'. Very quickly, the visitors realised that laughter was really the only way to deal with this, with the 'refusal or evasion ... attended with so much profession, artifice, and compliment that we soon grew ... amused with it'.[10]

Wending their way along the Hai, the mission made its way into Tianjin proper, passing by masses of mud-built, thatched cottages that would not have looked out of place in eighteenth-century England. Along the banks on either side, onlookers gathered, so eager to see the foreign visitors that 'from a sense of mutual accommodation, none of the common Chinese, who usually wear straw hats, kept on theirs ... lest they should obstruct the view of the persons behind them'.[11] In the ports of the south, most notably Canton, the sight of a Westerner was not uncommon, but here in the north, such a spectacle was very rare indeed. The desire to catch a glimpse of the strangers was such that the curious even took to overloaded junks, one of which sank before the eyes of the British, drowning a number of people.

The extent of this fervour is hardly surprising given the imaginative, fantastic rumours circulating about the British. Macartney would later learn that the citizens of Tianjin believed that the embassy included:

> Several dwarfs or little men not twelve inches high, but in form and intellect as perfect as grenadiers; an elephant not larger than a cat, and a horse the size of a mouse; a singing-bird as big as a hen, that feeds upon charcoal, and devours usually fifty pounds per day; and, lastly, an enchanted pillow, on which whoever lays his head immediately falls asleep, and if he dreams of any distant place, such as Canton, Formosa, or Europe, is instantly transported thither without the fatigue of travelling.[12]

This sense of the ethereal attached itself even to the youngest member of the mission. A Chinese boy appointed as Thomas Staunton's servant refused at first to sleep in the same accommodation as the foreigner, convinced that as soon as he closed his eyes the barbarian would eat him.

Observing the crowds provided the mission members their first glimpse of women with bound feet, an agonising practice already synonymous with China in Western commentary. The majority of wealthy women, or those from families aspiring to wealth, had their feet wrapped tightly with ribbon from an early age. This forced the toes under the sole of the foot, which were then clothed in a silk slipper, to develop a dainty and petite appearance. The practice led Macartney to muse on the pressures that society places on the individual (most obviously, on women) to conform to the generally accepted standard of beauty. The tendency to be dissatisfied with one's looks crossed all national and cultural boundaries and 'seems to be felt by the whole human species, from the politest nations of Europe to the most barbarous islanders of the South Seas'. The universal refusal, common to both the Chinese and Europeans, to accept things as they naturally are led Macartney to the lyrical observation that 'we find beauty in defects, and we create defects where we do not find them'. It says something for his thoughtfulness that Macartney could see the innate cruelty of such customs, both in such practices at home and in the 'Chinese custom of squeezing their women's petitoes [*sic.*] into the shoes of an infant, which I think an infernal distortion'.[13]

Within the city they were greeted by Liang Kentang, the viceroy of the province of Zhili, an area that was composed of parts of modern-day Hebei, Henan, and Shandong, and also encompassed Peking and Tianjin. This elderly official was 'a very fine old man of seventy-eight years of age, of low stature, with small sparkling eyes, a benign aspect, and a long silver beard, the whole of his appearance calm, venerable, and dignified'.[14] Relaxed and calm, he was unperturbed by the fuss surrounding the guests; nearing the end of his career, he was probably past caring what impact the successful management of the occasion would have on his future prospects. His only concern seemed to have been that of a good host smoothing his guests' progress through China.

Accompanying the viceroy was Zhengrui, the ethnic Manchu assigned as official legate to accompany the mission on the remainder of its voyage. He was alert to the professional risks that engagement with foreigners could bring for a mandarin, and as a result, he clearly felt the need to stamp his authority on the situation and to ensure things were done in as risk-averse a manner as possible. Macartney quickly 'discovered a perverse and unfriendly disposition in the Legate toward all our concerns, and which struck me the more forcibly when contrasted with the urbanity and graciousness of his superior the Viceroy's'.[15]

Their hosts ushered Macartney and his officials towards a large tent, outside which a band played. Ducking through a triumphal arch, surrounded by green and red banners, bowmen, and musketeers, the British entered a private chamber, at the farthest end of which was a darkened sanctuary that represented Qianlong. In an echo of later difficulties surrounding proper court etiquette, Macartney and his entourage were expected to bow to this empty space—an acknowledgement of the power of the emperor, but also of the official who was greeting them.

The viceroy now informed Macartney of where and when he would be admitted into the imperial presence. Instead of meeting Qianlong in the Forbidden City in Peking, the British ambassador was in fact expected to travel far to the north, to Rehe (modern Chengde), where the emperor would greet him in his summer hunting grounds, on his birthday, 17 September.

On the positive side, this would give the mission the opportunity to see (and in their intelligence-gathering role, sketch) the Great Wall of China. Yet the change of plans also posed some significant problems. Most worryingly, the decision to host the British at his summer retreat suggested that Qianlong might, in fact, be eager for his guests to be on their way as quickly as protocol would allow. After all, if the British had come to establish a permanent legation, this could only be done in the capital, Peking. Moving the audience to Rehe put an immediate obstacle on the path to this goal. Macartney could only hope that the decision 'does not forebode his wishes for our speedy departure'.[16]

Additionally, the many delicate gifts that Macartney had brought for the emperor were safe enough while being transported by boat. The final stage of the journey to Rehe, however, was by road, across mountains and through forests, in the type of terrain that was unlikely to agree with the most advanced instruments of eighteenth-century science. Zhengrui, clearly reluctant to allow the embassy anywhere near Peking in the absence of his master, was adamant that there was no other option but to press on northwards to where the imperial court was waiting. The emperor, it was declared, would expect the foreigners to bring their offerings directly to him.

Macartney was accustomed to handling obtuse bureaucrats; whatever the cultural differences might be, administrators the world over have similar pressure points. Acknowledging that in China the will of the emperor was absolute, nonetheless, he explained that he could not, in all conscience, subject the gifts that had been bestowed to his safekeeping by his sovereign to the sort of mistreatment they would experience on the road north. If Zhengrui was willing to take responsibility for the presents from this point forwards, then by all means they could be taken directly to Rehe. Macartney would accept no responsibility for the condition that the more delicate items would arrive in, however.

This ploy, combined with the intercession of the more reasonable Liang, resulted in Macartney getting his way; the embassy could set up its more sensitive wares, such as the 'planetarium, the globes, the great lens, the lustres, the clocks, and some other articles' in a palace near Peking, before striking north for Rehe.[17] A few days later, word came from the emperor that two palaces would be set aside for use by the British, one located in Peking itself, and the other just outside the city walls, near the Yuanmingyuan, or Summer Palace (not to be confused with the summer hunting grounds in Rehe). Sadly, visitors to modern Beijing will find little of this once-beautiful building still standing. Burned to the ground in 1860 by British and French troops in the Second Opium War, the palace was never rebuilt, instead being supplanted by another palace originally completed in 1764.

Despite this early knockback, the legate remained determined to undermine the mission in any way he could. Certainly, the British felt it would have been better had Liang been given the role of liaison. So oblivious was Macartney and his colleagues to the internal dynamics of the Qing court, they failed to realise that with his first meeting with Liang and Zhengrui, the ambassador had scotched any possibility of this happening. One of Qianlong's great concerns was that the guest should be treated hospitably, but not offered such honours that they became arrogant. Ironically, the intervention of the missionary translators in Peking had actually helped Macartney appear humble, by toning down the Chinese descriptions of the gifts he was bringing the emperor. Yet when Liang and Zhengrui met with Macartney, he was ebullient in his declarations of how proud the British were of the technology they planned to display in Peking. In particular, the planetarium was described as being of immense importance and sophistication, taking as it would a month to be assembled by skilled artisans.

True though this may have been, to the Chinese it sounded like the crude bluster of an uncultured lout. When Liang reported this conversation to Qianlong, the emperor decided that the British needed taking down a peg or two. Rather than 'increase his boastfulness and arrogance' by offering Liang as key contact, Zhengrui would be assigned to accompany the British on their journey.[18] All these decisions were taken without Macartney even realising that such discussions were underway; he was playing a game while oblivious to the rules.

It was while he was at Tianjin, with communiques about his mission flying back and forth with the court, that Macartney himself received an odd, and somewhat troubling, letter from the capital. A young Chinese convert to Catholicism came aboard his yacht, demanding to see the ambassador. When finally admitted into Macartney's presence, he handed him a bundle of letters from a French missionary in Beijing, Father Joseph de Grammont, who held the British in the highest esteem due to their protection of evangelists and native Christians in India. The letters claimed that the Chinese Government had appointed a Portuguese missionary as official interpreter for Macartney's meeting with Qianlong and claimed (incorrectly) that this man had already made his way to

Rehe in preparation. The mysterious informant warned Macartney that under no circumstances could this priest be trusted as he was intending to do mischief to Britain's efforts to woo the emperor, most likely in order to protect Portugal's favoured position as trade broker between China and Europe.

With this warning playing on his mind, Macartney and his team left for Peking, sailing up the Hai. On either side, Tianjin extended along the riverbanks, blue- and brown-bricked houses continuing for many miles. Unusually for China at this time, there were significant numbers of two-storey houses, stemming from a desire among the inhabitants to be located as near to the waterfront as possible. Eventually, the houses thinned-out, giving way to fields of sorghum and sesame, living proof of the fertility of the land along the floodplain. This bounty, however, came at a price; the mission also observed granite-faced dykes and causeways, protection against the havoc that the river could create. Rich soil could also be encouraged by less deadly, if more odious, means. Many of the boats they passed carried a curious cargo of 'dry brown cakes' about the size of what 'we call crumpets'. These were actually sods of human waste, destined for the gardens of Peking, where gardeners 'dissolving them in urine, use them for manure'.[19]

Some 30 miles upstream, and freed from the grip of the estuary's tidal waters, the boats were driven mainly by wind when available. Along calm tracks of the river, crews were called on to propel their charges onwards, rhythmically paddling large multi-man oars in the stern of their vessels. Staunton notes they kept time using traditional songs, and on still moonlit nights, the riverbanks echoed with the sounds of hundreds of voices. When the current proved too strong, the fleet was pulled along by gangs of workers tramping along the towpaths; pointedly, the British commented on how human labour seemed to be more cost-effective here than the animal equivalent.

While the mission progressed through scenes of bucolic harmony, on board the yachts, there was mounting tensions between hosts and guests, instigated primarily by Zhengrui. At first, the members of the mission were able to jump ashore from their slow-moving craft, exploring along the riverbanks before re-joining their vessel further upstream; yet increasingly, the controls on them and the watchfulness of their accompanying escort made this more difficult. Throughout the journey inland, Zhengrui would meet daily with the embassy but would usually prove reluctant to answer even innocuous questions. He would regularly travel separately, overland, carried in a four-man sedan chair, with a great train of attendants and servants in his trail. In short, he seemed eager to keep the foreigners under close observation, while avoiding as much as realistically possible any situations where his guests might press him for information.

The British believed his surliness was down to a case of mistaken identity at the far end of the Qing Empire. Tibet had seen clashes between Chinese and Nepalese troops, who were backing rival lamas in the mountain territory. The Nepalese ruler had apparently claimed to have the support of the British and may indeed have had some fugitive *sepoys*, escaped from service in the East India Company's army, among his troops. To some factions in the Chinese court, this seemed to suggest the British were speaking out of both sides of their mouths and that their mission might simply be an elaborate ruse to cover espionage. While the emperor was still enthusiastic to receive the embassy, some of his courtiers were not, and the issue of engagement with the British was now becoming a focus for internal court rivalries. In particular, Staunton notes that the two Chinese officials, Qiao and Wang, ethnic Hans, seemed ready to believe the British protestations of innocence. Staunton suspected that Zhengrui, however, as what he refers to as a 'Tartar' or Manchu, was more willing to believe that their southern neighbours had goaded the Nepalese into action. The imperial legate was also suspected of being in sympathy with the faction around Heshen that was actively opposing the efforts of the embassy.

As they drew nearer to Tongzhou, the port where they would disembark for the overland route to Peking, the river became crowded with barges carrying loads of wheat grain. This was actually a portion of the imperial tax take, submitted in this form rather than in the more usual coin. Distributed around the country, and stored in warehouses, the grain was then on hand to provide emergency relief in the event of famine. There were budgetary benefits too; levying tax in this manner lessened the chance of corruption as it was harder for collectors to take a cut off the top. Additionally, given the amount of silver flowing into the Chinese economy at this point from the export markets of the West, monetary inflation was a major concern. By directly collecting grain, the Chinese state was certain it would have the quantities required, regardless of how the monetary value of the commodity rose or fell. Taxpayers, too, were safe from any fear that their tax bill would jump due to the falling price of silver. So extensive was the grain collection and transportation system along the Hai that Staunton estimated that 50,000 people lived and worked on these barges. Another embassy official, Aeneas Anderson, went further, claiming that on the 'most modest computation, we beheld at least half a million people'.[20]

The scale of this endeavour reflected more than just good planning and the forethought to fend off future disaster. Staunton also records that the emperor 'jealously' guarded his right as the sole source of charity for the common Chinese subject in need, which represented concrete proof of his semi-divine status as father of the nation. Thus, no attempt by other wealthy patrons to try to ease the suffering of the less fortunate could be brooked. While George III was, by the grace of God, king, he was a mortal appointed by heaven to rule over one empire. Qianlong was more than a servant of the divine; he was a direct embodiment of the will of heaven and therefore not simply without equal in China, but without any equivalent or peer anywhere. Only from him could all benevolence ultimately flow.

This need to tie in the governance of China with *tianming*, the mandate of heaven, also explained the imperial state's interest in astronomy. As with many cultures, the Chinese had observed lunar eclipses and other heavenly events for centuries. However, few societies or governments had refined the observation and prediction of these celestial movements to such an extent, and with such a political goal in mind. While Western astronomers viewed the cosmos with purely scientific interest, in China, it was widely believed that the movement of the planets and the moon could have very real effects on the governance of their empire. Interestingly, Staunton suggests that some of the mandarins knew very well that this was simply superstition, but that having a thorough understanding of astronomy was vital because the general populace believed that the stability of the state depended on signs from heaven. The incredible importance of getting astronomical predictions precisely correct was one of the reasons the Qing had allowed some Jesuits into the court, given their ability to forecast exactly what the heavens would say.

On the night of 21 August, Macartney and his men witnessed first-hand the impact of such an eclipse. As the moon disappeared, 'we heard a frightful commotion', wrote Johan Christian Huttner, a German musician who accompanied the mission. 'Bells, gongs, clappers and drums made a noise so dreadful that the dragon who held the moon in his claws, might be frightened and thus abandoned his prey'.[21] Of course, such a mass panic helped bind the populace to the emperor, who warned them such a calamitous attack on the natural order was about to come to pass, allowing the populace to rush to the moon's 'defence'.

Despite these examples of the strength of Chinese state institutions, the Qing realm was not without major organisational faults. The emperor had to expend vast sums on public works, just to ensure that enough money actually made it through the web of venal officials to have an effect on the ground. Indeed, one official told the British that a position dealing with foreign visitors was particularly sought after by the greedier mandarins. Not only was there the opportunity to fleece the foreigners, but Qianlong spent so much on hospitality for these guests that no one noticed a little lifted off the top.

On 16 August, having travelled 90 miles from Tianjin, the embassy disembarked at Tongzhou to travel the final 12 miles to Peking by road.

Storehouses had been specially erected as temporary refuges for the gifts, the two halls running over 200 feet in length each. Labour drafted in from the surrounding towns and villages loaded the contents of over thirty-seven barges and yachts into the warehouses within a day. Observing the workforce required for such a task led Macartney to remark, with phrases so often repeated since that they now rest firmly in the realm of stereotype:

> The removal of so great a number of packages in a few hours cannot, I believe, be paralleled or procured in any other country than China, where everything is at the instant command of the State, and where even the most laborious tasks are undertaken and executed with a readiness and even a cheerfulness which one would scarcely expect to meet with in so despotic a government.[22]

We can perhaps forgive Macartney for these words; lazy generalisations though they may now seem, he was at least one of the first English-language commentators to observe such mobilisation of labour. Yet it is striking how the concept of the hard-working Chinese, cheerfully subservient to a despotic state, is a trope that has endured among Western commentators throughout the nation's imperial, colonial, republican, and communist eras.

With the official gifts packed safely away in temporary storage, the embassy members themselves settled into their accommodation in a Buddhist monastery. Despite the fact that their quarters were requisitioned at short notice, the lodgings at first appeared to be very comfortable. Located on a slight rise, and surrounded by a high wall, the embassy was easily guarded by their accompanying Chinese escort, both against infiltration but also escape. Amid the varnished red pillars of the temple, a small band played to entertain the foreigners, and canvas sheets strung over the courtyard provided some respite from the overbearing sun. This homeliness was shattered somewhat by the discovery that some of the rooms were infested with scorpions and centipedes; while the more seasoned travellers were used to such creatures from India, the Mediterranean or the Caribbean, the less worldly members declared that should such horrors inhabit China, it was reason enough to write the country off. The adventurous nature of some of the British was wavering now that they were away from the European setting of HMS *Lion* and the rest of the fleet.

While the danger posed by the local wildlife was more imagined than real, the risk of disease was a constant. While staying at the monastery, 'an event took place which gave the (Chinese) an opportunity of seeing an European ceremony of religion in the funeral of a person belonging to the Embassy'.[23] A metalworker called Eades, who had joined the mission despite his advanced age, succumbed to the exhaustion and stress of the journey only a day away from Peking. Having decided on accompanying Macartney to China so that he could research new metalworking techniques, he was hoping that he might be able to use what he had learned in Asia to ensure the prosperity of future generations of his family. The ambassador had noticed that Eades had been suffering from the moment of their departure, and by Madeira, he was pressing the man to return home. His refusal, and the fact that Staunton nonchalantly notes that many younger men had already died *en route* before Eades passed, highlights just how finely balanced risk and reward were for such expeditions.

Between disease and the very real danger of shipwreck, travelling in the eighteenth century, even on the equivalent of a high-level state visit, posed serious perils. That so many Europeans were willing to accompany Macartney in the face of these challenges shows that they felt the potential fortunes which could be won merited facing the prospect of death. As the case of Eades shows, this desire crossed boundaries of age, rank, and position.

The mission pressed on over the final few miles to Peking. Macartney and a select few travelled in sedan chairs, each carried by teams of eight. The remainder went by horseback or rode in the wagons carrying the gifts, depending on their rank. While the sedan chairs proved to be a pleasant form of transportation, those in the carriages were in for a rough ride as these were 'fixed on wheels without springs, and having no seats in the inside, they are to a European, who must sit on his haunches in the bottom, the most uneasy vehicle that can be imagined'.[24]

Pausing for breakfast at a roadside inn, they eased their aches eating 'a most sumptuous [meal] of roast pork and venison, rice, and made dishes, eggs, tea, milk, and a variety of fruits served up on masses of ice'. Even with the hardships of the road, there was no suppressing the building excitement, the 'momentary expectation of entering the greatest city on the surface of the globe'.[25] Down another bumpy stretch of unpaved road and over a well-made bridge of smooth marble they travelled, before entering the outskirts of the city. They passed for fifteen minutes through the masses of shops, houses, and small factories that made up Peking's suburbs before the walls of the city came into view, 40 feet high and brick-built, with portions faced in stone. They entered through the Chaoyangmen Gate, under a tower soaring 100 feet above them. The Macartney mission had arrived in the capital of China.

At this time, the city was divided into four major zones. The Outer, or Chinese, City, taking up most of the south of Peking, was where the bulk of the populace lived and was dominated by the Han. Here was the city's economic heart, with the major marketplaces and shopping areas, as well as the vast bulk of the residential housing. This zone also housed Tiantan, the Temple of Heaven, and Xiannongtan, the Temple of Agriculture, which were the sites of some the most important religious rituals led by the emperor. To the north was the Inner City, referred to by European observers as the Tartar City, reflecting that this was where the Manchu elite resided, along with senior Han Chinese officials and religious figures. In effect, this zone was the government district, with ministerial offices, tribunals, and accommodation for visiting embassies, as well as recreational areas such as Xihai and Beihai Parks, where Peking's upper classes could relax. The Inner City surrounded the Imperial City, where the highest functions of government resided and where the imperial court met. Within this exclusive area was the Forbidden City, the private residence of the emperor and his family, accessible only to the highest officials, retainers, and eunuchs.

In total, Staunton estimated the entire city of Peking to cover only 14 sq. km, just a third larger than contemporary London in terms of area. However, their minders told the embassy that the city's total population was around 3 million (more than three times more modern estimates, although it does seem that the greater metropolitan area around the city may have had this many people).[26] In contrast, the 1801 census found that the whole of the greater London area was home to a population of just over 1 million.[27]

Churlishly, the visitors were initially underwhelmed by the capital. Today, soaring architecture and imposing edifices are common in China generally, especially in Beijing. From the intricate web of the Bird's Nest Stadium, commissioned for the 2008 Olympics, to the lunging arch of the CCTV Headquarters, home of the state television network, a visitor to the modern city is constantly having their gaze dragged upwards. Yet Macartney and his colleagues found a city of predominantly low-rise, single- or two-storey buildings. The roads beneath their feet were unpaved and needed constant dampening to keep down the dust of summer. Compared to contemporary European cities, Qing-dynasty Peking was perhaps a little too understated for the tastes of the British, who sniffily suspected that the Chinese would be overawed by London.

Staunton was struck by how Peking had developed almost purely for political and administrative reasons, with little commercial reason for its establishment. It did not lie on the coast, nor on any great river or other artery, and the surrounding area was not abundant in natural resources. While a settlement had stood on the site since the eleventh century, it had only become China's primary capital during the Mongol Yuan dynasty, with construction of the new city they would call Dadu beginning under

Kublai Khan in 1264. Peking lacked the engine of trade and commerce that would have been immediately apparent in one of China's great port cities like Canton. Similarly, Staunton felt that the Qing court did not provide the same level of demand for luxuries and entertainment that would have typified similar institutions in Europe. In essence, he described the city as being almost an artificial capital, in terms reminiscent of a Qing-dynasty Brasilia or Canberra.

Heading west, the procession made its way towards the outer wall of the Forbidden City, the great palace complex already in view, ochre roof tiles shining over the red walls. To their left, elevated on a platform above the rooftops, was the imperial astronomical observatory. Originally built in 1442 during the Ming dynasty, the Qing had expanded it with the help of the Jesuit missionary Ferdinand Verbiest. Modern visitors can still see the extensive array of instruments he installed on site, although now the observatory overlooks Beijing's second ring road motorway, which replaced the city walls.

The embassy passed onward, through a number of *paifang* ceremonial gates, which divided the city into its different neighbourhoods. The streets were thronged by a great procession, all dressed in white, in the midst of which were a number of women being carried in veiled sedan chairs. At first, the foreigners thought this must be a wedding party, but they discovered it was in fact a funeral, white being the colour the Chinese associated with death and grief.

When it reached the eastern wall of the Forbidden City, the embassy proceeded north before turning west again to skirt the northern edge of the palace compound. To their left was the moat that surrounded the imperial residence, while on their right was the hill of Jingshan park, and behind that the Drum Tower and Bell Tower, used to alert the populace to important events and to mark the passing of the hour.

Moving to the north-west, they proceeded past the lakes of Beihai Park, carpeted in lotus flowers, and on towards the Haidian district of the city, where the Yuanmingyuan, or Summer Palace, was located. The road became paved with granite and the populace more diverse as they passed deeper into Qing Peking's embassy belt. Russians, members of China's own Muslim minorities, and representatives from Central Asian states, as well as numerous members of the Manchu ruling class, milled around them. The shops along the road were no longer selling the staples of daily life, but specialised in the toys, curios, and trinkets that the British had heard were so popular at the imperial court.

Leaving the city walls behind them once more, Macartney and his people finally found rest at one of the palaces put aside for their use. Set amid a landscaped garden featuring a stream flowing among manmade islands, the many pavilions of the residence were decorated with delicate watercolours of landscapes from throughout the Qing realm. Despite this outward beauty, the facilities 'had been now empty for some time, and wanted repairs'.[28] Zhengrui came to see how they were settling in and was asked about the prospects of the embassy moving into the other palace set aside for them just inside Peking. For once, the Manchu legate proved accommodating, saying there should be no issue with this.

The following morning, Zhengrui called again, accompanied this time by a number of missionaries. Among them was Bernando Almeyda Rodriguez, whom Macartney realised was the Portuguese Jesuit he had been warned was agitating against the British mission. Rodriguez had been in China for many years and had become a member of Peking's College of Mathematics (despite, as Macartney witheringly notes, having 'a very limited knowledge in that science'). More impressive was his skill in surgery, which allowed him to treat a minister's hernia, resulting in him acquiring some rank in the emperor's court. The trust placed in him by Qianlong resulted in Rodriguez being appointed the Macartney embassy's official interpreter.

Unfortunately for Rodriguez, he could not actually speak English. The legate immediately recognised this failing, realising the priest was incapable of conversing with the British in their native language. Perhaps cruelly, Zhengrui made this quite publicly obvious, deeply embarrassing Rodriguez, who in a fit of temper 'expressed very unfavourable sentiments of the Embassy to an Italian missionary who stood near him' in Latin.[29] Of course, Macartney understood every word, but he did not reveal this.

His negative impressions of the Jesuit were only strengthened when the issue of moving into quarters in Peking was again raised with Zhengrui. Rodriguez immediately said this was a bad idea, and that it would be an easier journey to Rehe from their current location. Despite his earlier agreement to the move, Zhengrui was open to accepting this argument, when Jin Jian, the mandarin in charge of the Summer Palace, intervened, decisively shooting down any suggestion that the embassy would be better off remaining outside the city. The other missionaries were openly appalled at the conduct of their Portuguese colleague, and his clear hostility led Macartney to mark him as dangerous and unpredictable: 'it will be right to cultivate and make use of him, if possible, but it would be egregious folly and dupery to confide in or depend on him'.[30]

Rodriguez's underhand behaviour would also harden Macartney's opinion of the Portuguese as Britain's primary competitors for the favour of the emperor. Despite its imperial status wavering elsewhere in the world as it slid down the rankings of European powers, there was much for Lisbon to play for in China. Being the only Western power with a permanent foothold on the Chinese coast, and with considerable experience and representation at the Qing court through the presence of numerous Portuguese Jesuits, there was an understandable desire for Portugal to try to frustrate the entry of any potential competitors into this lucrative market. It was clear 'that the Portuguese have formed a sort of system to disgust and keep out of China all other nations. Between them and the rest of the missionaries there appears to be great jealousy and enmity'.[31] This went against the grain of common Western identity that one might expect would bind Europeans who found themselves alone amid a culture very different to their own. Macartney was told by another priest that, 'all the missionaries except the Portuguese were our warm friends, but that the Portuguese were friends of nobody but themselves'.[32]

With the issue of accommodation dealt with, the mission was now able to turn to assembling the many wondrous items of European technology that were to be installed in the Summer Palace. Jin Jian was a senior member of the emperor's council (indeed, he was Qianlong's cousin). He was thus eager that the gifts would be arranged in an appropriate manner around the throne in one of the reception pavilions, and so he brought Macartney and his key personnel on a tour of the palace.

Set in gardens that stretched for 18 sq. miles, the magnificent audience hall was 150 feet in length and 60 feet in width. The entire pavilion stood on a platform of granite, so that it loomed 4 feet above the courtyard before it. At the far end stood the imperial throne, carved in mahogany, and flanked on either side by pheasant tails spread out into fans. Above their heads, a canopy rested on varnished red pillars topped with carvings of dragons and scrolls, while beneath their feet the floor was of chequered grey and white marble. The pavilion was guarded by a fine golden mesh to prevent birds, swooping in great flocks over the palace grounds, from entering the enclosure. Staunton noted that the whole space was set aside to receive tribute—the vast hall was largely empty, apart from a few vases and, curiously, a clock 'by George Clarke, of Leadenhall Street, London'.[33] Tellingly, the only other furniture was a small table set before the throne, on which was placed offerings of tea and fruit for the spirit of the absent emperor. On either side, incense burned in small tripods, giving the throne room the atmosphere of a temple or shrine.

This semi-religious nature belied a major challenge that Macartney would now be forced to face. From the Western perspective, he was representing one sovereign to another. Power resided in the secular realm, based on trade, economic heft, and troop numbers, not divine intervention. From the Chinese perspective, at least in theory, only one ruler had the mandate of heaven—that was Qianlong. George III was merely a fortuitous barbarian that had risen to the top of a savage realm. In comparison, when Macartney reached Rehe, he would learn that Qianlong declared descent directly from Manjusri, a holy figure in Buddhism, and that his own success, and the prosperity of the realm, depended in large part on these innate ties to higher powers.

Regardless of the relative power of the Qing versus the British empires, for the Chinese, only one ruler was divinely ordained, and hence they could not be equals. The emperor was *huangdi*, supreme lord. All other rulers were simply *fanwang*, lesser lords. As a result, his hosts expected the British ambassador to recognise the implicit subservience of his sovereign to Qianlong by rendering every mark of respect. This included *koutou*—the kowtow. It was this piece of court etiquette, an element of ritual symbolism, that now threatened to derail Macartney's diplomatic mission entirely before he had even met the emperor.

6

The Kowtow: An 'Ingenious Vehicle'

Can a red carpet ever be too short? Many would assume that if it is of sufficient length for an honoured dignitary to walk along it for a noticeable period, the carpet is long enough. However, in June 2014, a red carpet at Heathrow Airport was found to be definitely too short—by 3 m exactly. The luminary who had to tolerate such shoddy treatment was Chinese Prime Minister Li Keqiang. We know that the carpet was too short because, according to *The Financial Times*, the Chinese ministry of foreign affairs complained about its length directly to Ed Llewellyn, Prime Minister David Cameron's chief of staff. Of course, the issue of how long Premier Li's red carpet should be was only part of a wider tiff over the ceremonial aspects of his visit to the UK. Other areas in which the UK disappointed their guests included not allowing Li to meet with Queen Elizabeth II (the refusal of which led a Chinese Government-controlled paper to call Britain a 'narrow-minded', 'prejudiced', 'petty' 'declining empire').[1] Even in this age of social media, regular state visits, and permanent, professional diplomatic services, the role of ritual is key in diplomacy, particularly in the way China engages with the world.

Under the Qing, this respect for ceremony was even stronger. The centre point of their framework for diplomatic engagement was the kowtow, a formal series of 'three kneelings and nine bows' before the Chinese emperor.[2] By design, an act of deliberate obeisance, the use of the kowtow in courts throughout Asia was driven by a very different view of international relations to that held in the West. For a start, whereas an ambassador to a European court was the embodiment of the sovereign he represented, from the perspective of Asian rulers, particularly the Qing,

George Macartney, 1st Earl Macartney, 'ambitious and arrogant, honest but prejudiced, interested in, but ignorant of, China'. (*Wikimedia Commons*)

Above: George Macartney and Sir George Leonard Staunton. (*National Portrait Gallery*)

Below: George Thomas Staunton pictured with his mother, Lady Jane Staunton, and a Chinese attendant holding a chest of tea, after the Macartney embassy. (*Wikimedia Commons*)

'Affable and affectionate to his subjects, vindictive and relentless to his enemies'—the (Young) *Qianlong Emperor in Ceremonial Armour on Horseback* by the Jesuit Giuseppe Castiglione. (*The Palace Museum, Beijing*)

'A man of great parts, learning, and application'—Portrait of the Qianlong Emperor in court dress. (*Wikimedia Commons*)

Right: Emperor Qianlong inspects paintings by Giuseppe Castiglione. (*The Palace Museum, Beijing*)

Below: The East Indiaman 'Hindustan' at anchor, possibly off the rocky coast of the Canary Islands. (*Royal Museum Greenwich*)

The civil mandarin who accompanied the Macartney embassy, Qiao Renjie, 'a faithful and benevolent discharge of his duty seemed to be the sole and simple object of his pursuit', drawn by William Alexander, draughtsman of the Macartney embassy. (*Wikimedia Commons*)

Right: 'He had signalized himself in battle, and received several wounds', the military mandarin Wang Wenxiong, who escorted the Macartney embassy, by William Alexander. (*Wikimedia Commons*)

Below: The Chinese military drawn out in compliment to the British ambassador by William Alexander. (*Wikimedia Commons*)

A fort near Tianjin on the Hai river by William Alexander. (*Wikimedia Commons*)

A temporary building of mats in Tianjin, which was erected for the reception of Macartney embassy, by William Alexander. (*Wikimedia Commons*)

Above: A Chinese military post by William Alexander. (*Wikimedia Commons*)

Below: Chinese gamblers with fighting quails by William Alexander. (*Wikimedia Commons*)

A Chinese soldier by William Alexander. (*Wikimedia Commons*)

A traveling cargo junk, 'exceedingly convenient—more so, indeed, than any I have ever seen on our canals in England' by William Alexander. It was vessels like these that transported the embassy personnel on the riverine portions of their journey. (*Wikimedia Commons*)

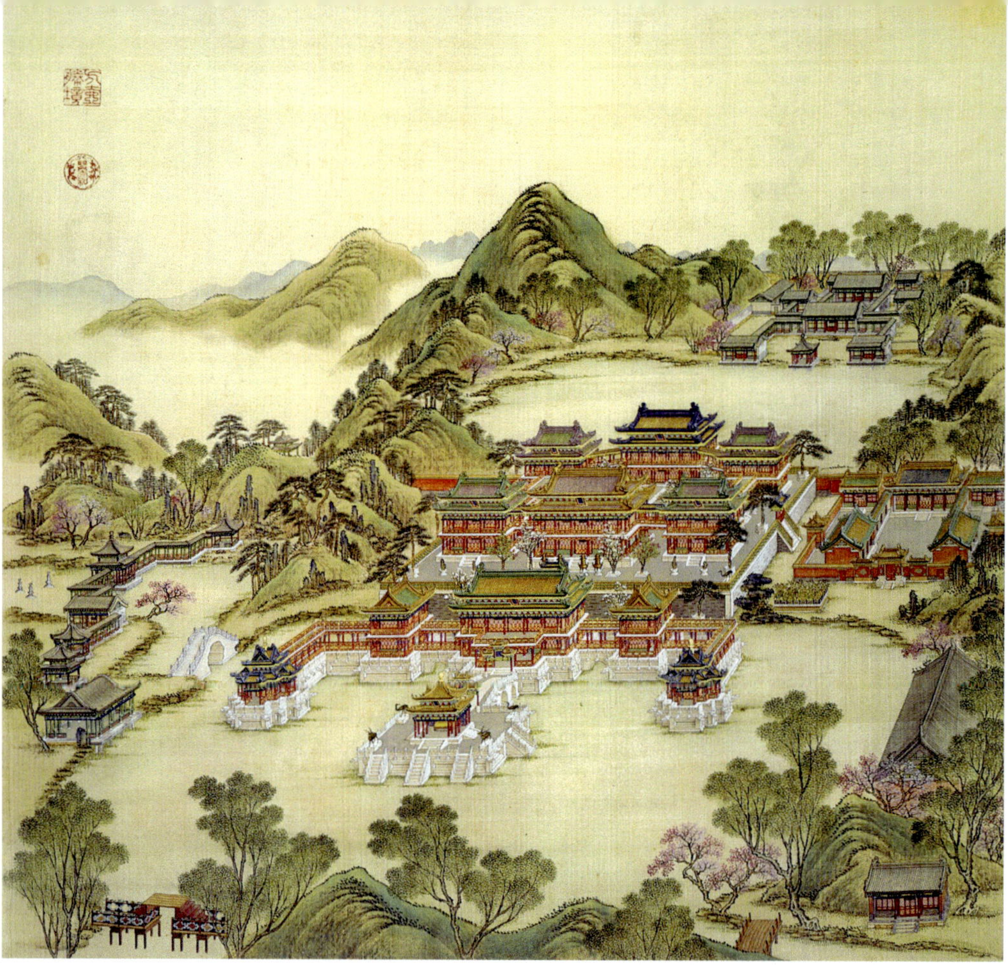

Above: A scenic view of part of the Old Summer Palace, or Yuanmingyuan, the complex where the Macartney embassy assembled the gifts which were too sensitive to transport to Rehe. The estate was sacked and largely destroyed by British and French troops in 1860. (*Wikimedia Commons*).

Below: A banquet given by the Qianlong Emperor for the leaders of Mongolian Dörbet (Choros) tribes in Rehe in 1754. (*Jean Denis Attiret*)

King Solomon in all his glory—Macartney's first meeting with Qianlong. The boy on the right is eleven-year-old George Staunton, who impressed the emperor with his spoken Chinese. (*The British Library*)

Drawing by William Alexander of the city of Yangzhou, through which the embassy passed on its journey south. (*Wikimedia Commons*)

A view of Canton *c.* 1760–70, roughly contemporaneous to the Macartney embassy (*British Library*)

The most noxious weed—two Chinese opium smokers reclining in a booth watched by a woman with bound feet. Wood-engraving, late nineteenth century. (*Wellcome Images*)

Above: The opium ships at Lintin in China, 1824 by Edward Duncan. (*National Maritime Museum*)

Below: The century of humiliation—the 18th (Royal Irish) Regiment of Foot at the storming of the forts of Amoy, 26 August 1841, during the First Opium War. (*Wikimedia Commons*)

The mandate of heaven refashioned? British Foreign Secretary Philip Hammond welcomes President of China Xi Jinping to London, 19 October 2015. (*Foreign and Commonwealth Office*)

the ambassador was merely a messenger. To Chinese eyes, in no way was Macartney a manifestation of his own sovereign; thus, by definition, he was inferior to the ruler he was visiting.

Added to this was a further gap in understanding between Chinese and Western approaches to diplomacy. While two European sovereigns, despite the difference there might be in the relative power of their respective states, would afford each other broadly equal courtesies, the same was not true of those kings or emperors who sought to engage with the Chinese court. As the 'Son of Heaven' (*tianzi*), the ruler of China was, obviously, superior to all other rulers, and they could at best hope to engage with him as respected inferiors. Their lower position was reinforced by ceremonial elements guided by a complex set of rites known as *binli*, the guest ritual.

The use of multiple locations to receive foreign embassies helped project an image of the emperor as global sovereign. Visitors from the south, from locations such as Siam, Burma, and Annam, always paid homage in Peking, while Mongolian, Turkic, and Tibetan missions were welcomed to the imperial summer retreat of Rehe, to the north of the capital.

The delegations from Korea were sometimes received there as well, but were also often met in Shenyang, the old Qing capital of Manchuria, perhaps reflecting the fact that ties between Korea and the Qing predated the latter's conquest of China. The diversion of different delegations to various reception points helped to underline the vast breadth of the Qing's influence; so great was the empire that it needed many locations to host its wide variety of foreign tributaries.

At root, these fundamentally different approaches to the dignity of ambassadors and the nature of monarchy were reflections of the contrasting civilizational foundations of Chinese *v.* European society. The best illustration of this is how the Macartney mission responded to the confusion of the legate when he learned of their reluctance to engage in the kowtow. Zhengrui explained that this was a necessary and non-negotiable part of engagement with the Qing court. In response, Macartney drew on western history to explain his reservations. He told Zhengrui of the fate of Timagoras, the Athenian ambassador to the court of the Shah Artaxerxes II, who was executed by his countrymen in 367 BCE for engaging in *proskynesis*, the habitual bow of supplication before the Persian throne.[3]

Needless to say, Zhengrui had never heard of Timagoras and was perplexed as to why the ancient emissary had suffered death at the hands of his fellow Greeks. What better symbol of the cultural gap over the kowtow could one ask for—Chinese confusion at the tale of vengeful Athenians, the original democrats who helped formulate Western understanding of the contract between state and citizen? In Qing China, there were no citizens, only subjects with an obligation to whoever held the mandate of heaven.

As well as the kowtow, another key element of the guest ritual was the offering of tribute to the emperor. The British now discovered that even the language used to discuss the gifts they had brought represented a diplomatic minefield. To the Chinese, these items were described using the word *gong* (tribute). The British insisted that the items they would present to the Qianlong Emperor were in fact *songli* (gifts). Time and again, the Chinese lapsed into describing the packages brought by the British as tribute, and on each occasion, they had to be corrected—these were gifts, given in good faith between equals, and not in a measure of supplication.

For the Chinese, however, the value of what was being laid before Qianlong was less in the actual monetary worth of the gifts themselves and more in the fact that they did, indeed, represent a tribute and acknowledgement of China's superior position. It was for this reason that tributary envoys to the imperial court presented gifts that symbolised their homeland and were specific to its culture. With previous Asian missions to the Chinese court, this led to the somewhat ridiculous situation where embassies often returned home with cargo more valuable than that with which they had arrived, having received gifts from the emperor superior to the tribute they had offered. The commodity exchange signified less to the Chinese than the power relationship expressed by the transaction. It was rather a public display of how the foreign state was willingly subjecting itself to the power of the Chinese emperor (even if, in reality, the emperor had little direct control beyond China's borders). More crucially, however, the ceremonial and literal prostration of the kowtow also displayed for the domestic audience in China that the emperor was divinely ordained. It was therefore crucial that European barbarians be seen to bow before him; if they did not, questions of how Qianlong could really claim to be worthy of ruling China could arise.[4]

As such, we must recognise that the requests placed on the British to perform the kowtow stretched far beyond simple ceremonial protocol. Elements such as the kowtow were the language of diplomacy for the Chinese, playing the same role for Qianlong that written treaties and official, permanent embassies performed for Western sovereigns. The kowtow, and the tribute system in particular, had become in the words of the historian John King Fairbank an 'ingenious vehicle' for handling foreign relations and international trade.[5] More than mere symbolism, these ceremonies acted as a conduit for wider engagement on diplomatic and commercial ties. They also had very real security implications, offering a clear sign of the supremacy of the Son of Heaven over those who came before him. When a Mongol or Tibetan leader bowed before the emperor, it not only meant that they had accepted the Chinese view of the proper order of the cosmos, but it was also reasonably substantial proof that China need no longer fear attack from that corner. The Chinese method of engaging with foreigners was different to the European approach certainly, bringing with it a number of challenges for the inexperienced. Yet it is also clear that it was more than an archaic ritual, performed only because things had ever been thus.

At the same time, the Chinese themselves recognised that there was something different about the foreigners who came from the 'Western Ocean' compared to dignitaries from more familiar territories. For example, the engagement with Macartney's team was handled through an unusual bureaucratic channel. Ordinarily, the ministry of rites handled all embassies from Korean, Vietnam, and the Ryukyu Islands, and it was traditionally the primary agency for foreign affairs in Imperial China. Between 1637 and 1881, Korea sent a total of 435 embassies to Peking, while the Ryukyu islands are believed to have sent annual embassies. These were dispatched to offer thanks to the emperor for any support he had provided the local ruler, to offer congratulations on the emperor's birthday, offer condolences on the death of leading court figures, and to request the formal bestowal of titles which were the prerogative of the imperial court. Given that these tributary rulers were themselves engaged in similar rituals with dependents and vassals at their own courts, it is not hard to see why the Qing believed themselves to be atop a cosmological power structure that defined order throughout the world, with legitimacy flowing outwards from their throne.[6]

A special department, the *lifan yuan* (ministry of outer dependencies), was established in 1638 to deal with what might have been seen by the Chinese as 'common or garden' barbarians from Central Asia, such as the Mongolians or the Tibetans. This ministry's staff exclusively contained Manchus and Mongols loyal to the Chinese emperor, providing a body of specially trained experts familiar with the language and culture of the region. By contrast, the Macartney embassy was handled by the *junjichu* (the Grand Council), which under Qianlong was operating as a central privy council.[7] That such an elevated body directly managed the British visit suggests that the Qing well understood how fraught with difficulty dealings with the Europeans could be.

The British were not the first Westerners to tussle with the trials posed by Chinese court etiquette, and indeed, they would not be the last; it was only in 1873 that the Qing court publicly began to receive foreign envoys without requesting the kowtow. As early as 1248, a French friar sent by Louis IX to Karakorum, capital of the Yuan dynasty, was told he must prostrate himself before the imperial throne. Even at this early point, the people of China believed that such prostrations were proof that the Westerners were subject to the emperor. Given that the Yuan dynasty were descended from Genghis Khan, it is perhaps understandable that this claim did not appear outlandish.

In 1654, a Russian envoy, Feodor Iskowitz Backhoff, arrived in Peking and from the start made clear that he would offer the emperor no further honour than a bow, which was all that the Russian tsar expected. Backhoff found himself under house arrest until he agreed to leave Peking, with the Chinese even returning the gifts he had brought.

The same year saw the Dutch arrive; perhaps surprisingly given that they represented a republic, they proved more flexible when it came to matters of personal dignity. No doubt they immediately felt on the back foot when the Chinese asked whether they were related to royalty, hinting that only diplomats with such heritage would be admitted into the emperor's presence. In fact, this was only a ruse by the Chinese to encourage tributary states to send royal relations as envoys; the representatives of Korea and the Ryukyu Islands at the court were both princes. Again, this magnified the sense of greatness which surrounded the Chinese emperor.

So eager, in fact, were the Chinese to highlight the exalted nature of the embassies sent bearing tribute that according to some accounts, neighbouring states regularly dispatched five or six ambassadors together. This was because, allegedly, their hosts would regularly poison one or two of these royal diplomats so they could inter them in Peking as concrete, eternal proof of how even the most regal of foreigners bowed before the Qing.

Along with the challenges arising from their comparatively humble origins, the Protestant Dutch also faced the opposition of the Jesuit missionaries of Peking, who were determined to convince the Shunzhi Emperor 'to confirm [his] favour to us, and interclude all ways to these Hereticks [*sic.*]'.[8] Despite these hurdles, they were able to secure a brief audience with the emperor, in part through agreeing to carry out the kowtow before the royal seal in a preparatory ceremony. As it transpired, they then had to wait weeks before finally being brought into Shunzhi's presence, when they again performed the kowtow in the reception hall, and once more directly in front of the emperor. In return for all this bowing, the Dutch got fifteen minutes of imperial time and attention, during which Shunzhi never spoke to them directly. They also achieved the somewhat limited success of securing the opportunity to bring a trade mission, containing not more than 100 people, to Canton once every eight years.

While representing his homeland, one of Europe's pre-eminent powers, a French Jesuit visiting in 1689 was recorded as the ambassador of a 'tributary vassal'.[9] In 1720, the Russians were back with Count Leoff Ismailoff, who hoped to win the Kangxi Emperor's favour by appearing in Peking between a man of 'gigantic stature' and 'a dwarf'.[10] Whether or not this novel tactic was directly responsible for Ismailoff's success, his mission did produce results. More likely, it was the Russian's ability to parry and thrust with the Chinese over questions of protocol, raising objections and requests before tactically giving way to reach an acceptable compromise, which involved the performance of the kowtow.

Looking at this long history of European attempts at diplomacy with China, it is clear that it was vital for the British that nothing should discredit the position of their sovereign as a major world figure, nor to undermine Britain's claim to being a great power. They were already having to battle Qing assumptions that their ambassador did not represent a sovereign equal in stature to the emperor, but it was rather just the latest in a long line of humble envoys dispatched by minor tributary states to seek Chinese favour. This view of foreign nations was so ingrained among Chinese officials that Macartney had to turn a blind eye to the fact that the carriages carrying the mission from Tongzhou to Peking were adorned with banners that proclaimed their passenger to be 'The English Ambassador bringing tribute to the Emperor of China'.[11]

What is more, the British could not even be certain that submission to the requirement for the kowtow would yield results. In a line of argument still occasionally made today, some questioned whether the Chinese in fact responded better to those who refused to engage with China's assumed position of superiority. Tellingly, a Dutch embassy the year after Macartney's visit did submit to the kowtow and felt themselves subsequently ignored and belittled by the Qing, with little to show for their flexibility on matters of protocol. In truth, the Dutch may have also suffered because of their faith. Whatever effect their acquiescence in ceremony may have had on the emperor, they were allegedly cut down to size by Catholic missionaries (wanting once more to undermine these Protestant interlopers) who showed Qianlong a map of Europe, pointing out how tiny the Netherlands was.

The effects of Macartney's decision on the kowtow were not limited to the diplomatic realm, however. In their hesitancy to engage fully in Qing court ritual, as we have seen, the British were also falling foul of internal political dynamics within China. At this point, the Qing dynasty had been ruling China for nearly 150 years; yet they were still cultural interlopers. Manchu by ethnicity, they had originally been themselves foreign barbarians who had raided the borderlands and peripheries of the empire they now ruled. With the instability that came with the last days of the Ming dynasty, the Manchu had seized the opportunity to become more than merely transient ransackers and instead seized the greatest prize of all—China itself.

Some members of the Manchu political and military elite suspected these newly arrived foreigners might now want to displace them in turn.

Staunton suggested that the arrival of the British, coming hot on the heels of the garbled reports of revolution the Qing were receiving from France, also resulted in some sections of Chinese officialdom viewing all European embassies with caution. This tendency was particularly pronounced among the ethnic Manchu, who were no doubt painfully aware of their somewhat precarious position, governors so out-numbered by their subjects. Ironically, with his Ulster Protestant background, the British ambassador might have found significant grounds for empathy with the Qing.

Added to these internal security concerns, the intransigence of the British would have very personal consequences for the mandarins they dealt with. Zhengrui in particular was keenly aware that whatever impact Macartney's willingness to carry out the kowtow might have on relations between the two empires, it would be a very personal failure if he could not convince the British envoy to agree to standard court protocol. The pressure on him came not from the emperor so much as from mandarins of more senior rank. After all, Qianlong could no doubt be quite pragmatic when it came to matters relating to his own divinity (who better knew the truth about his nature, heavenly or otherwise, then the emperor himself?).

For those in the inner circle, however, the narrative of a divine presence on the imperial throne reflected a sanctified glory from which they benefitted. China's most senior ministers would take a very dim view of a junior official allowing a mere foreigner to undermine the holiness of their sovereign (and in consequence their own position). Heshen himself had laid out very clearly what was expected. One of his letters to Zhengrui read:

> When the tributary envoy arrives in Jehol [the Machu name for Rehe] he will have to respect the etiquette ... You are to instruct him in all the details. He will be shown into the audience only after being versed in the salutations of the kowtow.[12]

The legate and the mandarins Qiao and Wang were therefore determined to convince the ambassador to give in. Despite the tensions, Macartney was at heart such a diplomat that he could not help but be impressed by how the Chinese slowly ratcheted up the pressure. To start, the topic was broached by a number of seemingly innocent questions about English dress, which led to the innocuous observation that the tight clothing worn by the British must make 'the genuflexions and prostrations' required at court very difficult. Perhaps the ambassador would prefer to dress a little differently when he met Qianlong, it was suggested, if only for his own comfort? This was batted away by Macartney, who thanked them for their concern, but promising that he would be fine; after all, he pointedly noted, he assumed the emperor 'would prefer my paying him the same obeisance which I did to my own Sovereign'.[13]

Of course, replied the Chinese, that was precisely what the emperor wanted:

> They supposed the ceremonies in both countries must be nearly alike, that in China the form was to kneel down upon both knees and make nine prostrations or inclinations of the head to the ground.[14]

This requirement was, regrettably, indispensable. What is more, they told Macartney, the emperor wanted to cut short his hunting and return to Peking as soon as possible after their initial meeting in Rehe. The implication was clear; if Macartney kowtowed, the emperor would be prepared to return to the capital early to spend significant time in discussion with Britain's envoy.

So eager were the trio of officials to secure Macartney's agreement that they even performed the kowtow before him themselves, as if to suggest that, really, it was all just for show. Yet the ambassador understood what was really at stake and still refused. Even when they suggested that perhaps Macartney's translator, who was after all Chinese himself, might perform the act, the British remained steadfast. No member of the embassy, in any capacity, could submit to an unequal display that suggested any subservience towards the Qing. If nothing else, the readiness of his Chinese opposite numbers to claim that the kowtow was only symbolic worried Macartney even more. The fact that they could prove so slippery on its significance suggested to him that he had to be extremely wary of doing anything that could be spun as a sign of submission. He was dealing, he felt, with counterparts who were 'wonderfully supple, and though generally considered as most respectable characters, are not very scrupulous in regard to veracity, saying and unsaying, without hesitation, what seems to answer the purpose of the moment'.[15] There was a need to tread very lightly indeed.

An elegant answer to the quandary might prove possible, however. Rather than try, like so many Westerners before, to remove the need for ritual, Macartney sought to extend it. He would be quite happy, he announced, to carry out the kowtow, or indeed any ceremony, before Qianlong—as long as a mandarin of equivalent rank was willing to perform the same display before a portrait of George III. This represented a neat piece of diplomatic compromise. The question of the divinity of the Chinese emperor was not at issue for the British; given Macartney's agnostic leanings, no doubt he could not care less whether he had to pay lip service to the holy elements Qianlong claimed to represent. What did matter to George III's representative was that there should be no implied submission by the British crown to the Qing Emperor.

Such a proposal would have to be put to the Chinese in a manner at once sufficiently formal to satisfy the requirements of court, but also subtle enough to gloss over the fact that this represented a face-saving fudge for all concerned. Macartney wrote a letter explaining in a respectful but clear manner his proposed solution, but this now needed to be translated into the courtly Chinese of the imperial mandarins. This task was beyond the abilities of even the most accomplished European student of the language. Indeed, this called for such a complete and confident mastery of sophisticated official Chinese that even Father Li doubted his own ability to fulfil the commission. Another trawl for translators began, with the embassy reaching out to Peking's community of foreign missionaries, traders, and diplomats, all the while wary of the fact that by asking for help from potential competitors, they might leave Britain's interests dangerously exposed.

Eventually, a sympathetic Catholic priest introduced them to a Chinese Christian, who had regularly provided high-quality translations in support of the missionary's own activities. Now a new problem presented itself; this was the first time this translator had ever been asked to prepare a communication to the imperial court. When he discovered the destination for Macartney's letter, he immediately baulked and with good reason. In Canton, another translator, helping the English merchants there to make a petition to the imperial court, had been put to death for daring to help the foreigners contact the emperor. Fearing that someone at court might recognise his writing, this Chinese Christian refused to help.

It was at this point that Thomas Staunton's efforts in the language bore real fruit. The translator could rewrite Macartney's letter in court Mandarin, which Staunton would then copy in his own hand. This would guarantee that the language used would be sufficiently fluent to make a good impression at court, while ensuring the nervous translator was safe from association with the British mission. The letter was duly written up and presented to Zhengrui, who seemed satisfied that it would not be inappropriate to present such a communique to Heshen for the emperor's attention. It announced that Macartney was willing to 'conform to every exterior ceremony practised by his Imperial Majesty's subjects, and the tributary princes attending at his court', promising he would reflect 'the high and just sense universally entertained of his Imperial Majesty's dignity and transcendent virtues'. In return for this slavish adherence to Qing court etiquette, he requested:

> By his Imperial Majesty's order ... one of the officers of his court, equal with the Embassador [*sic.*] in rank, should perform before his Britannic Majesty's

> picture at large ... the same ceremonies which should be performed by the Embassador [*sic.*] before the throne, of his Imperial Majesty.[16]

All in all, a reasonable request, and while Zhengrui was as negative as usual about whether the suggestion would be accepted, Qiao and Wang felt that this could provide a way forward. In fact, they were so convinced that they immediately offered to kowtow to the portrait of George in Macartney's own quarters. Recognising the potential issues that might be caused if he were seen to undermine Zhengrui, this offer was politely declined by Macartney. Instead, the matter would have to wait until the imperial court decided on his proposed compromise.

Along with displaying Macartney's imaginative approach to overcoming obstacles, this incident also shows that the accepted narrative of Western arrogance derailing this first official contact between Britain and China is a little unfair. The ambassador was interpreting his instructions from London in as flexible a manner as possible in an effort to please his hosts, while not diminishing his own position. This agile approach in handling the kowtow question extended so far, Staunton claimed, that Macartney even offered that he would kowtow to Qianlong in a public ritual before the imperial court, while in return, his Chinese equivalent could pay the honours before George III's portrait in private. The agreed trade-off would never need to be made public (in China, at least), thereby protecting the emperor's aura of superiority.

No doubt, to Macartney, this seemed a rational solution. It also reveals that the British understood that what truly mattered to Qianlong's officials was not whether the British were tributary states, but that the sense of the Qing's pre-eminence on earth was maintained among their Han subjects. Yet they were still underestimating the psychological distance they were asking Qianlong, and perhaps more importantly, his advisors, to travel. This was not simply a request to acknowledge an equality between the emperor and the British monarch; what Macartney saw as the middle ground between the two positions had the potential to call the whole basis of Qianlong's legitimacy into question. While the general populace might remain ignorant of this implicit downgrading of the emperor's status, court gossip would ensure that China's elites, political and military, would hear of how Qianlong's semi-divine status had been tarnished. For a ruler that depended on the mandate of heaven, that would be too a heavy price for establishing relations with a barbarian kingdom.

7

'Treated Too Favourably, a Barbarian Becomes Arrogant'

Every night during the summer, the city of Chengde in northern China plays host to the 'Kangxi Ceremony', a performance commemorating the construction by Qianlong's grandfather, the Kangxi Emperor, of his summer resort in the area he knew as Rehe. The show is less ancient tradition and more multimedia extravaganza, featuring lights, lasers, and Broadway production values. There are displays of equestrian brilliance, as stage Manchu riders gallop across the display square. At one point, the emperor studies astronomy with a Jesuit missionary; at another, he is receiving an oath of fealty from a Tibetan cleric.

The (predominantly Chinese) audience is left with a clear impression that the Chengde site ties many strands of Qing history together. There is the nomadic nature of the dynasty, their hunger for knowledge in key, politically sensitive areas such as the study of the heavens, and the deep ties between the Qing and the Tibetan school of Buddhism. Thousands of kilometres from Tibet, Chengde looks as if a chunk of Lhasa was lifted from the foothills of the Himalayas and dropped into north-eastern China. One of the most striking features is the Putuo Zongcheng Temple, blood-red walls brilliant against the trees of the slopes above, and modelled on the Potala Palace, the traditional residence of the Dalai Lama in Lhasa. Despite the modern focus on Kangxi in the glitz and glamour of the nightly extravaganzas, this slice of Tibetan culture represented not only by the 'Little Potala' but also by a number of other buildings inspired by sites in Tibet, is actually the product of his grandson, Qianlong.

Whether called by its modern name of Chengde, its Qing-dynasty name Rehe, or its Manchu name, Jehol, this site represents the flight of

Qianlong's imagination and ambition, the realisation in physical form of his worldview and belief system. A palatial faux-nomadic camp, fit for the descendent of tribal chieftains who now ruled over one of the most sophisticated civilisations on earth, in its exclusivity and removal from Peking, it reminded the emperor's subjects of the superiority of the Manchu ruling class over the other ethnic groups in China. The heavy emphasis on Tibetan Buddhism developed in Chengde speaks of the semi-mystical origin of the Qing, who claimed descent from an incarnation of the Buddha. In journeying to what they knew as Rehe, Macartney and his embassy were travelling to Qianlong's very soul.

That they were able to progress along this path at all was at least, in part, down to their communique to Heshen. While the imperial court prepared a response to the suggested concession around the kowtow, no mandarin, not even the emperor's favourite, was willing to take the risk of impeding the embassy, in case he suddenly found himself at odds with official policy. As they prepared to leave for the north, the British had left their assigned quarters near the Summer Palace and were rehoused within the city walls in the palace of a wealthy mandarin who had made his fortune in Canton. This official had been responsible for collecting taxes and customs duties on foreign trade; he had also slyly overcharged the visiting merchants, redirecting the excess take into his own pockets. Having been caught, tried, and imprisoned, his palace now lay empty and available for the visiting embassy. The irony was not lost on Staunton, who, when viewing the delicate woodwork and colonnaded architecture, realised they were built with levies corruptly extorted from British traders.

It was decided that James Barrow, Dr James Dinwiddie, and the Swiss engineers Petitpierre and Tiebault were to be left behind to assemble and care for the various scientific pieces and gadgets that would be presented to the emperor on his return to Peking. They had already installed terrestrial and celestial globes on either side of the throne in the audience room in the Summer Palace, while crystal chandeliers now hung from the ceiling. The planetarium had been set up at the northern end of the room, while the southern end played host to clocks, a barometer, and a clockwork model of the solar system. A variety of Derbyshire porcelain vases and figures were dotted about the space. Macartney was certain that this was 'an assemblage of such beauty as is not to be seen collected together in any other apartment, I believe, of the whole world besides'.[1]

As the heavier gifts were unpacked and assembled, a number of items caught the eye of the attending Chinese observers, including three of the emperor's own grandsons. The portraits of King George and Queen Charlotte in their royal robes drew considerable attention, and Macartney had to ask the mandarins accompanying the mission to regulate the crowds pressing to get a glimpse of these images of alien royalty. The greatest admiration, according to the British at least, was reserved for some ceramics by Wedgewood; although how likely it was that the foreigners could impress in that field where China reigned supreme, the manufacture of delicate vases, is an open question.[2]

Those gifts sturdy enough to survive the road had been brought to the centre of Peking in preparation for the final leg to Rehe, but they now fell under the suspicions of the ever-wary legate. He was particularly eager that a team of six brass cannon, which had accompanied the mission both as part of its protective escort, but also to provide Qianlong with a display of firepower, should not travel north. Ostensibly, this was over security concerns, but the British willingly offered up the guns and their powder for inspection on request, to prove how safe they were. Staunton believed that the real reason was that, having seen the redcoats drilling with these weapons, the legate realised that any British display of their prowess with artillery would paint Chinese gunners in a poor light, even if the mandarins 'pretended to think lightly of them, and spoke of such things as being no novelties in China'.[3] Easy though it is to dismiss this as the innate British sense of superiority, proof of whose weaponry was best came just under fifty years later in the First Opium War, when the Qing were made painfully aware of how far behind their opponents they lagged.

Other military technologies, however, did earn the open admiration of Macartney's hosts. 'Flexible swordblades, of Mr Gill's manufactory at Birmingham', received particular esteem. Wang, the military mandarin, was very happy with the blades he received as a gift and 'seemed more pleased with them than if I had offered him any other present of a hundred times the value'.[4] This response caused Macartney to hope that such items would form a key export opportunity for Britain, if only Qianlong could be convinced to allow greater access to this demand among China's military.

More pacific items also elicited interest. Macartney's team received visits from numerous mandarins and other members of the Chinese upper classes, who called either on official business or out of sheer nosiness. One of the most intrigued visitors was Qianlong's director of music, who was amazed at the range and quality of the instruments that the mission had brought with it. Not wishing to pass up such an opportunity to expand the musical repertoire available to his master, this mandarin sent for artists to sketch 'the clarionets, flutes, bassoons, and french horns' in intricate detail.[5] Detailed notes accompanied these illustrations, recording how each instrument was played and their general construction.

Despite his curiosity, he refused to take the instruments as gifts when offered; instead, he hoped to have copies reproduced successfully in China. A cynic might comment that this was an early forerunner of the sort of reverse engineering that Chinese industry has been regularly accused of in more recent years. However, this interaction also highlights the deep intellectual curiosity that pervaded among of Qianlong's most educated subjects, also giving lie to the claim the Chinese were blinded by their own sense of exceptionalism. When they saw something that truly impressed them, Chinese intellectuals were very capable of recognising foreign ingenuity.

A carriage provided as a gift for Qianlong was less well-received, however, with the Chinese demanding that significant alterations be made before it could be accepted. The European norm, where the coach driver was elevated above the passengers in the carriage, was deemed completely unacceptable; how could anyone, let alone a mere driver, be elevated above the emperor? When they initially saw the carriage, the Chinese presumed that the finely embroidered driver's seat must be for the emperor, while the compartment itself would be reserved for his wives and concubines.

Macartney's own four-horse carriage nonetheless drew considerable crowds as the ambassador toured around Peking before his departure. Clattering through the city, with red-coated British guards at the front and the back, drawn by small Tartar horses only twelve hands high, it must have made for quite a sight. It was this carriage that, at 6 a.m. on 2 September 1793, led the embassy convoy out of Peking, and north-east into the plains surrounding the city. On board, Macartney was accompanied by Wang and Qiao, who were at first alarmed at their mode of transportation. Compared to the lower Chinese carriages, this European vehicle seemed very high, unstable and liable to topple over, and 'the fearlessness ... with which (the) postilions drove it along almost petrified them with astonishment'.[6] Once they had experienced the (comparatively) smooth ride provided by its sprung suspension, Wang and Qiao were more comfortable, quickly becoming distracted by 'increasing or diminishing at pleasure the openings of the Venetian blinds'.[7]

Young Thomas Staunton sat beside Macartney, so his language skills could be drawn on when needed, while his father travelled separately in a palanquin, as he was suffering from gout. Behind them, seventy other musicians, artists, servants, soldiers, and officials were transported in a host of carriages, while more than 200 porters were needed to carry the baggage.

After travelling about 20 miles, the relatively fertile soils surrounding Peking gave way to thinner clay, and the groves of willow trees that spotted the countryside began to peter out. They ascended into hillier terrain, spending the night at a small palace usually set aside for the emperor to break up his journey between the capital and his summer hunting grounds. The next morning, they continued, passing through fields thick with tobacco plants, the land around them becoming more mountainous all the time, the hills starker now and bare. The countryside had 'a very Alpine appearance, much resembling Savoy and Switzerland'.[8]

On the third day's journey, having passed the night in another rest-stop palace, the population around them began to change with the landscape. The balance between Han Chinese and Manchu became more even the further north they went. The latter were easy to spot, according to Staunton, with the women in particular standing out as their feet were unbound. It was easiest to discern who were Manchu by their manners; they were less given to courtesy, as no doubt befitted their position as the conquerors of China.

The tensions between the Manchu overlords and the Han Chinese, who still formed the bulk of China's administrative and military management, crops up regularly in the first-hand accounts of the mission members. We have seen how the Manchu Zhengrui and the Han Chinese mandarins, Wang and Qiao, were not on easy terms. Macartney himself noted that while their superior was around, the normally chatty Wang and Qiao were almost silent. In the presence of other, even relatively low-ranking, Manchu officials, the garrulous and confident Wang refused even to sit. When Zhengrui was out of earshot, it became plain that Wang and Qiao did not 'seem much to like their colleague the Legate, who is a Tartar ... and whom they consider a sort of crazy and morose man'. Indeed, the disgruntled Han officials even congratulated the British on their dealings with him, as the foreigners had 'seemed very early to have discovered his character'. The cowed and browbeaten Wang and Qiao 'admired us much for the complaisance and patient attention of our deportment towards him'.[9] Macartney's ability to put up with the Manchu was proof enough for these Han Chinese of his diplomatic skill.

These ethnic tensions were mirrored in the lands through which the embassy now trekked. This was, historically, the frontier zone between the settled Han Chinese and the nomadic raiding Manchu. They passed a fortified town, surrounded by a sturdy wall but undefended by cannon. Here the taxation, tribute, and food supply for the region had once been secured against the Manchu raiders, until they themselves became China's rulers and the threat of violence was removed. Typically travelling light on horseback in their pillaging days, they would not have had the artillery necessary to punch a hole in such a wall. Neither would the Chinese have needed much firepower to defend this fortified location. To British eyes, however, it seemed that the strongpoint would have posed little challenge to a company of redcoats equipped with even light field guns.

The most striking proof of this area's troubled past then appeared before them, strung across the mountainsides, on the fourth morning of the journey. At first, the British took it to be a seam of quartz in the slopes above, but as they drew closer, the long grey line above them resolved itself into battlements and sturdy towers—the Great Wall. It stretched both east and west, as far as their eyes could track. Even today, at the sanitised locations where most tourists brave the mobs of hawkers to clamber up its steps, the Wall can be breath-taking.

Built of bluish-coloured brick upon a stone foundation, where the embassy crossed, it measured 26 feet high. At its base, the outer surfaces on either side were 5 feet thick, at the top, 1.5 feet. The space between these exterior shells was filled with earth and paved with cobbles on top, leaving a roadway 11 feet across—space enough for two coaches to pass along. Every 150 to 200 feet, there was a bastion, from which a small garrison would have defended their portion of the fortification.

By the time Macartney arrived, with the Qing in firm control both to the north and to the south, the wall was militarily irrelevant. Still, the British were in awe, not only by its scale, but also by its antiquity. The more educated members of the mission understood just how far back in Chinese history construction of such fortifications began, and recognised that the strength and robustness of Chinese historical enquiry ensured that the tales of its origins were more than mere myth. Some of the fitter visitors found a breach in the wall and scaled the tumbled-down brickwork to reach the battlements above. Here was something of China's that the West simply could not equal. 'If the outline of all the masonry of all the forts and fortified places in the whole world besides were to be calculated, it would fall considerably short of that of the Great Wall of China,' Macartney wrote.[10]

The psychological symbolism of the Great Wall is revealing, and this did not escape the British. It aimed to keep the barbarians out, but militarily, that was an impossible goal. In defensive terms, these battlements in China's north and west were only ever intended to slow an invader, not stop them entirely. Perhaps more significantly, it also represented, in bricks and mortars, a tendency to look inwards. As Staunton noted, the Chinese were for the most part, especially compared to rapacious European imperialists, never terribly interested in conquering foreign peoples. Indeed, their greatest subductions of outsiders came not through conquest, but defeat, when the Chinese internalised their foreign rulers, be they the Manchu Qing or the Mongol Yuan.[11] The Great Wall was the ultimate icon of the contemporary Chinese belief that there was little foreign worth having.

Onwards they pressed to the north, and as they travelled, Macartney noticed another road running parallel to theirs. This was the private route taken by the emperor himself when travelling between Peking and Rehe, and it was now undergoing maintenance in preparation for his return to the capital. In total, the British estimated that 23,000 soldiers were working on the 136 miles of this restricted route, getting it in perfect condition. Towers guarded its whole length, battlements bedecked in yellow flags, each housing garrisons of between six and fifteen soldiers. These turned out on parade as the embassy's convoy passed along the public route, welcoming the British with the clash of gongs and firing of small cannons.

Then, on Sunday, 8 September 1793, they found themselves amid the pine-clad hills of Rehe, at the gates of the emperor's *Bishu Shanzhuang* (Mountain Estate for Escaping the Heat). The estate was designed to represent the Chinese empire in miniature, with thirty-six gardens mimicking scenic views from across Kangxi's imperial domains. Not to be outdone, Qianlong had added thirty-six more scenes upon ascending to the throne. These joined five temples—three Buddhist, one Daoist, and one Confucian—constructed in the grounds to reflect the *sanjiao* (three cornerstone creeds of China). On a plain in the centre of the estate, elegant pavilions with simple grey tiles were interspersed with yurts and ornamental lakes, a neat fusion of Manchu culture with the tastes of the emperor's Han subjects. Indeed, Rehe was something of a waypoint between the Qing dynasty's nomadic past and its more sedentary present. Within easy reach of Peking, so that it could be easily supplied with the luxuries required for court, the estate was also in good hunting grounds.[12] There, surrounded by a garrison of 100,000 troops, the emperor could enjoy a facsimile of the nomadic life his ancestors once led.

In such a grand setting, the British would have to work hard to make a good impression. They deployed dignified ceremony to the full to impress on Qianlong's court that the empire embodied by Macartney's embassy was no tributary nation, but rather a global power. Their arrival was choreographed down to the last detail; led by 100 mandarins on horseback, the first British personnel to enter the imperial grounds were four light dragoons on chargers, their ceremonial armour polished to a gleaming shine. There then came a section of fife and drums, providing the glorious scene with a martial soundtrack, while marching behind came a team of artillerymen and then a platoon of infantry. These were followed by the servants and couriers attached to the embassy, along with some of the German musicians. There then followed the embassy's own officials, the first two clad in scarlet-embroidered uniforms, the second pair in uniforms stitched in gold. Finally came Lord Macartney's own gilded carriage, in which he travelled with Sir George and Thomas Staunton, with servants in a livery of green and gold in attendance. After voyaging many miles, and many months from home, the British had arrived in Rehe, and aimed to impress.

Only now, at the threshold of an imperial audience, would the issue of the kowtow ceremony be finally resolved. Zhengrui informed Macartney that the British would have to make the case for compromise over the kowtow directly to Grand Councillor Heshen. In preparation for this final reckoning, a sense of optimism began to filter through into the British camp. The ever-encouraging Qiao and Wang suggested that Macartney's arrival had greatly impressed Qianlong, the display of gilt and foot drill having achieved the desired effect. The two mandarins also revealed (with what one can imagine was a large degree of *schadenfreude*), that the legate had been caught out lying to the imperial court. Evidently, when the emperor's chief officials were able to form a first hand-impression of the British, they felt that the Zhengrui had been inaccurate in his reporting on the foreigners.

His position worsened further when it was discovered that only Qiao and Wang had gone aboard HMS *Lion* to greet the ambassador at Tianjin. Zhengrui's desire to remain aloof now appeared to be dereliction in carrying out the emperor's orders to offer the British all reasonable hospitality. These perceived failures were reason enough to demote him by three ranks; when the embassy members next saw him, he no longer wore the phoenix feathers that denoted a senior mandarin, but instead sported crows' feathers, allegedly a sign of his disgrace.

In the legate's defence, he had found himself in a very trying position. While he now found himself censured for not showing sufficient hospitality, he had earlier been under pressure for precisely the opposite reason. At first, Qianlong felt that given Zhengrui had never held a position of power in Canton and was thus inexperienced in dealing with Europeans, there was a considerable risk of the legate being overawed by the foreigners, with their bold claims of technological prowess. During the wrangling over the issue of whether the gifts should be transported directly to Rehe or assembled in Peking, Zhengrui was under pressure from court to stand up to the British, in particular the ambassador, and challenge the claims being made about the complexity of the gifts being offered. In part, this might explain Zhengrui's confrontational manner. Unfortunately, court perceptions overtook his instructions, and failing to change tack in time, he left himself open to criticism.

Zhengrui's fall from grace gave some hope that the suspicious mindset he personified was now also out of favour and that a more open-minded approach on dealing with the embassy might prevail. Amid this air of optimism, Staunton was dispatched to convince Heshen of the need for flexibility in person. Before formally accepting the letter outlining Macartney's suggestions at compromise, the grand councillor pushed hard to convince the British to abandon the ridiculous notion that their sovereign was in some way equal to Qianlong. Would the British not consider changing their written request before it was delivered? Nevertheless, Staunton was insistent on submitting the communiqué as it was, asking that it be given to Qianlong personally, so that he may decide on a response. In itself, this piece of administration was as much theatre as anything else; it was quite clear that Heshen and Qianlong were already well aware of the compromise suggested by the British and were seeking to avoid the difficult position of having to give a direct reply. Covertly nudging the British to an acceptable agreement behind the scenes would be far seemlier.

When finally delivered to the imperial hands, this letter was to prove deeply unsettling to Qianlong. The emperor wrote to his officials, both locally and in Peking, describing the crisis that had resulted from the British progressing so far without developing an understanding of how they would fit in to court ritual. Qianlong placed the blame for this squarely on the shoulders of the officials who had accompanied the embassy; they had not been sufficiently measured in how they handled the foreigners, and Macartney had thus become arrogant. The latest example of this hubris had been how Staunton, a mere vice-ambassador, had delivered the letter outlining Macartney's compromise on the issue of the kowtow.

Despite the vitriol directed at his mandarins over this lapse in standards, Qianlong forgot to apportion blame to one very culpable party—himself. Confronted with what appeared to be a very presumptive British ambassador, who was taking for granted the flexibility of court ritual, the emperor had forgotten the role his own words might have played in creating such a situation. When the British had first baulked at the suggestion of the requirement for the kowtow, on arrival in Tianjin, Qianlong had airily declared that 'if the English do not submit to the ceremonies, let them simply observe then customs of their own land. There is no point in forcing them to kowtow'.[13]

Allowed to become too bold, these ignorant foreigners now needed to be cut down to size. The emperor decided that, whatever decisions were made about an imperial audience, the British would have their provisions reduced for their return journey to Peking. The programme of entertainment laid on for them in the capital would also be reduced.

Luckily for Macartney, he never sensed the chill developing between himself and his hosts, and so pressed on in happy oblivion. Suddenly, on what would appear to be mere imperial whim, Qianlong's mood softened. It is hard to say why. Did the emperor decide there was value to meeting the British even if they were not locked into the prescribed court ritual? Was it mere curiosity? Did he want to check that what his officials reported was tallying with the experience of the foreign traders? Whatever the reason, he decided there would be no need for the kowtow. Rather, despite being wary of the fact that 'treated too favourably, a barbarian becomes arrogant', Qianlong could still condescend to perhaps allow the British to follow their own 'vulgar practices', in place of the more usual, refined ceremonies.[14] Consideration would be given to allowing Macartney to bow before the Chinese emperor in the same manner as he would in front of any European sovereign.

Qiao and Wang arrived on the morning of 10 September, asking Macartney to describe, in detail, how he would pay homage to his own monarch. Quite simply, they were told, he would go down on one knee before the king and kiss his hand. The two mandarins departed with this answer and Zhengrui arrived shortly afterwards, announcing that it may be possible to allow the British custom to be used. Macartney could perhaps bow, and go down on one knee before the emperor, as he would before George III. Even at this late stage, though, the legate sought to win some further concession; would it not be possible, he asked, for Macartney to kneel on both knees? When this was answered with a firm no, he pushed back in the only way he could. The ceremony might proceed in the English manner, but Macartney would definitely not be allowed to kiss the emperor's hand. Despite the British protestations that such a gesture would only pay further respect to Qianlong, Zhengrui was clear.

With this fresh movement on the Chinese side, Macartney had high hopes when he was finally called into the presence of the grand councillor. Flanking Heshen on his right was his deputy, while to the left were two further officials, one of whom was in charge of the imperial finances, while the other had responsibility for court rites and ceremonies. Illustrious company indeed, these officials were senior enough to give Macartney a final, concrete answer on how he would greet the emperor. More than this, they also had enough experience to judge for themselves whether the British had developed notions above their station and to deliver a rebuke, should one be necessary.

Thankfully, Heshen proved flexible in his thinking. He sensed a humility in Macartney's demeanour (something which does not come through in the ambassador's own account of this meeting) and decided that a more conciliatory approach to the foreigners was indeed appropriate. Given the distance and hardships suffered by the embassy, just so that they could reach Qianlong's court, it would be entirely understandable if British customs were followed, Macartney was told. In particular, Heshen noted, the splendour of the gifts brought by the embassy highlighted the deep respect held for Qianlong by George III. As such, the ambassador would be allowed to go down on one knee before Qianlong and would place the letter from his king directly into the emperor's hands.

No doubt, the minister's confidence in his decision was strengthened by Macartney's response to questions about Britain's place in the pecking order of European powers. On Britain's relationship with Russia, the ambassador explained that they were at peace:

> But that there did not seem to be the same cordiality at present as formerly, on account of the King of England (who is a lover of peace and justice, and a friend of the distressed) having once interfered to repress a spirit of encroachment shown in some of her measures with regard to Turkey.

Heshen was also told that the relationship between London and Lisbon was strong as 'the King of England had often afforded them protection and shown them marks of his friendship'.[15] If these reported comments reflect the actual answers provided by Macartney at the time, they both reflect his diplomatic skill and perhaps offered the Chinese another reason for flexibility on the issue of the kowtow. Macartney had given obvious hints that Britain was not an ally of Russia (and hence might be open to action against Catherine the Great) and was of such a magnitude of power greater than Portugal that the latter benefited from British protection. Given the existing Chinese relationships with Russia (including some thorny border disputes) and with Portugal (through Macao), this neatly situated Britain in the middle of the Qing's existing experience of the European powers.

Heshen later reported to Qianlong that Macartney, and the sovereign he represented, were both sincere in their desire to engage with the Qing Empire, and that the foreigners recognised their rightful place in the cosmic order. Again, it is worth remembering that nothing in the British accounts of the meeting suggests they had displayed such modesty. At the remove of more than two centuries, it is hard to know whether Macartney had simply won Heshen over with deliberately ambiguous language, whether something was lost in translation, or whether Heshen himself recognised the importance of ensuring that the audience between the emperor and ambassador went ahead. Perhaps he felt this was the ideal opportunity to incorporate the British into the wider international order the Chinese had assembled in Asia. Whatever the reason, Qianlong was sufficiently pleased with reports that not only did he agree to meet Macartney, he even cancelled his previous orders regarding the harsh treatment the British were to receive on their journey back to Peking. The diplomatic tussle over the kowtow was thus resolved, even if the underlying issues that caused it were not.

8

'King Solomon in All His Glory'

When President Richard Nixon boarded Air Force One on 17 February 1972, bound for China, he did not know for certain who would meet him in Beijing. The American public assumed, of course, that he would be greeted by Chairman Mao Zedong, the man who, despite shying away from almost all public appearances, still held sway over China. In the face of constructive ambiguity on the part of their Chinese hosts, American diplomats and officials simply deployed an unshakeable faith that Mao could not refuse to meet with the leader of the most powerful nation on earth. As Winston Lord, special assistant to Nixon's national security adviser, Henry Kissinger, said, 'We knew in our gut that Mao would meet Nixon'.[1]

Some 180 years earlier, only similar confidence in the inevitability of success ensured Macartney, like Nixon, lasted the course and found reward in an audience with the ruler of China. After so much diplomatic toing and froing as well as innumerable bureaucratic hurdles, the moment had arrived. In the predawn chill of 14 September 1793, Macartney, Staunton, his son Thomas, and the interpreter Father Li were escorted by Qiao and Wang to the emperor's tent complex, travelling in palanquins with their train of musicians and guards. The ambassador was in 'spotted mulberry velvet, with a diamond star and his ribbon, over which he wore the full Order of the Bath, with the hat and plumes of feathers'.[2] Lacking robes of state, Staunton was bedecked in rich velvet and the flowing silk robes of a doctor of laws at the University of Oxford. In this final reckoning, the British were determined to enter into the emperor's presence in as fine a manner as possible.

At the imperial encampment, they were led into a large tent, in effect a waiting room, before which was a green carpet. There they were to remain for three hours, until at seven o'clock the banging of gongs and cymbals announced the arrival of Qianlong. Macartney and his three companions went outside, going down on one knee as the emperor passed, while all the Chinese around them performed the kowtow.

In contrast to the British, Qianlong was wearing a simple dark silk outfit. Carried in a palanquin by sixteen attendants, around him were guards, flag-bearers, and pages proclaiming his greatness. On his head was 'a velvet bonnet, in form not much different from the bonnet of Scotch Highlanders; on the front of it was placed a large pearl, which was the only jewel or ornament he appeared to have about him'.[3] In appearance, he was 'a very fine old gentleman, still healthy and vigorous, not having the appearance of a man of more than sixty'.[4] The British were likely unaware that Qianlong was dressed in the robes he would wear for any regular court audience; his guest today obviously required no special sign of ostentation.

The British delegation then followed Qianlong into a grand pavilion, 26 yards across, which acted as the throne room in Rehe. The throne itself sat amid a forest of varnished and gilded pillars, while draped all around were fine tapestries and rich carpet. After the emperor had ascended the throne, Macartney climbed the steps to place in the imperial hands a delicately gilded box, encrusted with diamonds, which held the letter from George III. This was quickly passed to a waiting minister, who placed the box on a velvet pillow before Qianlong. In return, Macartney was presented with two sceptres (*ruyi*), one in marble for the British monarch and one in jade as a personal gift to the ambassador. Once Staunton was introduced as Macartney's *chargé d'affaires*, he too was presented with a jade sceptre. The emperor expressed his hopes that these gifts would be symbols of the peace and friendship that existed between the two nations. To the British, they seemed like unremarkable items, and they were perplexed as to why the Chinese felt that such objects were due considerable reverence.

As personal gifts to the emperor on his own behalf, Macartney offered a number of watches, each enamelled and set with diamonds, and a pair of pistols; again, these were passed to the minister, who placed them on a velvet cushion. The ambassador had rustled these presents up at the last minute from among the private possessions of the embassy members, just prior to the departure from Peking. Macartney had not realised that he was expected to offer the emperor a personal gift as well as the official items presented by the British state. Thankfully, a number of his colleagues had brought fine watches with them, hoping to sell them at a considerable profit to the Chinese; these entrepreneurs were convinced to forgo commercial opportunity in the national interest.

All throughout this exchange, Qianlong remained completely impassive. The only moment where the emperor betrayed obvious satisfaction was when Thomas Staunton was invited to display his skills in the Chinese language and duly obliged; for this, he was rewarded with the gift of a yellow silk purse. Macartney and his colleagues were now bid to sit at low tables to Qianlong's left, where they were served warm rice wine and food, while all around them, the mandarins and officials of the imperial court were seated in order of importance. The British were not the only diplomats present; embassies from the Kalmyks and other Central Asian peoples were also present, 'but their appearance was not very splendid' as far as Staunton was concerned.[5] Appearances notwithstanding, the British should have perhaps recognised the significance of Qianlong receiving them in a job lot with other embassies, rather than in a private audience.

From time to time, the emperor sent Macartney dishes from his own table, in a sign of hospitality. Qianlong then motioned for Macartney and Staunton to approach the throne again, so that he could hand them both a cup of warm wine, which they drank in his presence. Throughout this meal, the room was hushed, with no chatter among the guests, nor any noise from the servers; 'the commanding feature of the scene was the solemnity and silence with which the whole business was conducted'.[6] Despite the grave atmosphere, the diners were entertained with wrestling, acrobatics, tightrope walking, and plays, with the whole event lasting five hours.

The audience certainly left an impression on the British. To capture his awe in words, Macartney had to return to the wide-eyed innocence of his youth:

> Thus, then, have I seen 'King Solomon in all his glory'. I use this expression, as the scene recalled perfectly to my memory a puppet show of that name which I recollect to have seen in my childhood, and which made so strong an impression on my mind that I then thought it a true representation of the highest pitch of human greatness and felicity.[7]

The British believed they had received from Qianlong the recognition that was their due. Staunton claimed that the concessions Macartney had won in relation to the etiquette surrounding the occasion, in particular the waiving of the kowtow, were 'significant of a change of opinions of their government in respect to the English'. The adaptation of the ceremonial requirements expected of the embassy 'was considered by the Chinese court as particularly honourable and distinguished; Embassadors [*sic.*] being seldom received by the Emperor on his own throne, or their credentials delivered into his own hands'.[8]

The Chinese, on the other hand, believed that the magnificence of this engagement slightly overawed Macartney. Court documents suggest the usually bumptious ambassador showered praise upon the emperor and his court, expressing in the deepest terms his own loyalty and respect for Qianlong. The imperial mandarins felt that the British had been transformed by this audience, from ignorant barbarians to vassals who now understood their place in the cosmic order.[9]

The graciousness of Qianlong's welcome to Macartney did not end with the feast. After returning to his own lodgings, the ambassador received further presents; tea, porcelain, and silks embroidered 'with the four-clawed dragon or imperial tiger, and some with the Chinese pheasant'.[10] Clearly, Qianlong was pleased by what he had seen. Further rewards arrived the next day, when, at 3 a.m., Macartney and Staunton were summoned again to the emperor's compound. The early start was once more a lesson in patience, as the two diplomats had to wait three hours before Qianlong appeared, again carried in a palanquin. He explained that he must go to conduct the religious rites required each morning, but that he had instructed his ministers to give the two guests a tour of the gardens at Wanshu Yuan (Ten Thousand Tree Park).

The sightseeing party rode out through 3 miles of parkland, in country 'much resembling the approach to Luton in Bedfordshire'. Accompanying the two diplomats was Heshen, a vice-minister named Fuchang'an, his brother, Fukang'an (who was the former viceroy of Liangguang, the province that contained Canton, and was now viceroy of Sichuan), and a mandarin called Songyun, who had previously led negotiations with the Russians on fixing the northern border of the Qing's territories.

The party came upon a massive lake, where a magnificent yacht waited for them. The vessel was so luxuriously appointed with porcelain, furnishings, and 'every kind of European toys and singsongs; with spheres, orreries, clocks, and musical automatons of such exquisite workmanship ... that our presents must shrink from the comparison and hide their diminished heads'.[11] For the first time, a slight concern awoke in Macartney's mind. Perhaps the bounty offered by the British was not as awe-inspiring as originally hoped?

Given Macartney's own diplomatic experience in Russia, his confidence was restored somewhat when pressed for his thoughts on international affairs by Songyun, and he settled easily into a discussion on that nation's foreign policy. Nevertheless, he knew he was being tested and that Songyun was measuring his responses against his own impressions formed in boundary talks with the Qing's northern neighbours.

In part, this may have been to ascertain if Macartney was trustworthy, but it may also have been a way to divine just how far British knowledge reached. Songyun was impressed with the depth of Macartney's understanding, but other Manchu officials viewed the breadth of British information with suspicion, especially when it came to their intelligence on China. While touring the gardens, Macartney deployed what he believed to be an artful compliment, noting that the creation of such a paradise in the wilderness of Rehe was a sign of the genius of its builder, the Kangxi Emperor. No doubt, he was expecting Heshen to be pleased by the research he had carried out. Instead, this comment was greeted with open suspicion; how did Macartney know that Kangxi had built the gardens? Who had told him this?

While Heshen proved wary of the foreigners, the former viceroy of Liangguang, Fukang'an, was openly hostile, no doubt due to his experience of governing the southern trade entrepôt of Canton. Macartney suspected that the viceroy's aversion to the British was perhaps down to an 'unintentional slight' that he had received at the hands of English traders. He was probably closer to the truth when remarking that this official had possibly observed 'with regret and indignation, that superiority which, wherever Englishmen go, they cannot conceal from the most indifferent observer'. The question of whether that sense of superiority was justified never seemed to have occurred to the ambassador.[12]

This bad feeling towards the British manifested itself in many petty, harmless ways. On one occasion at yet another imperial audience, as he approached Qianlong, Macartney found his elbow grabbed by the same viceroy, who began gesturing at his head. Clearly, he was demanding that the foreigner doff his hat in respect to the throne; notably, this was purely a European custom and not something the Chinese did themselves. From his experience in Canton, the viceroy knew how Europeans paid genuine respect. Similarly, when the envoy tried to win the same truculent mandarin over by appealing to his martial interests, through offering him the opportunity to see the embassy guard drill, the offer was rebuffed. The Europeans had little that would be of interest to him in military matters, the viceroy baldly replied, and in any case, he had already seen everything that their soldiers could do.

Word now reached Rehe that the *Lion* and the *Hindoostan*, last seen at Tianjin, had been forced to restock at Zhoushan. However, the crews were beginning to suffer from disease, delaying the fleet's departure on its Asian tour. Macartney hoped that Captain Mackintosh, having paid his respects to the emperor as protocol demanded, would be able to depart directly to re-join his ship, allowing him to oversee preparations for departure. He asked Heshen whether this would be possible, but before an answer could be given, Fukang'an intervened, saying that such a thing would be improper and completely forbidden. It was not in the habit of the Celestial Empire to let foreigners traipse across the countryside. Despite Macartney's protests that this would simply be a matter of making the logistics of their return a bit easier, the viceroy waved away his entreaties.

The British sources portray this disagreement as another example of the suspicious, authoritarian streak in the Qing Empire's mandarins. Yet despite the claims of innocence in his own diaries, Macartney provides little support as to why Mackintosh should have been allowed to proceed directly to Zhoushan. As an employee of the East India Company, we know that Mackintosh was tasked with collecting commercial knowledge during his time in China, particularly in relation to goods of great commercial interest to the Company, such as porcelain and tea. In the absence of any evidence as to the necessity of his cross-country trek, it is easy to understand the lack of enthusiasm displayed by the Chinese for what sounds like an attempt at commercial espionage.

In the teeth of all this, Macartney was aware that the real meat of his mission had yet to be tackled. While he had navigated, with some success, the challenging waters of court etiquette and had received an apparently warm reception from the emperor, key issues like the opening of the Chinese market to British goods or the establishment of a permanent embassy had not even been broached. In an effort to begin what would surely prove to be a protracted and difficult conversation, Macartney sought a private meeting with Heshen.

One does not, however, ascend to the position of first minister of Qianlong's government by blithely walking into the sort of career-ending discussions that the British were seeking to have. Suddenly, the ministerial diary became very busy, what with the upcoming imperial birthday and a host of attendant administrative and ceremonial tasks. It would be better to discuss this matter when they had all returned to the Summer Palace in Peking, the ambassador was told. In the meantime, Heshen did condescend to receive a note from Macartney outlining any issues he sought to raise, including the necessity for a quick exit for Captain Mackintosh via Zhoushan. Macartney set to making his argument in writing.

Heshen's busy schedule was flexible enough to accommodate certain British guests, however. While reluctant to see anyone on official embassy business, he was very eager to discuss at length a wide variety of ailments with the mission's Dr Gillen. Suffering from 'violent pains which affected some of the lower points of the arms and the legs', as well as an 'excruciating pain in the lower part of the abdomen', he was willing to try anything to ease his agony, even the medicine practised by the Europeans.[13] Immediately upon beginning his examination, Gillen realised that his approach to medical practice differed greatly from the patient's previous experience. While the Scot was satisfied taking Heshen's pulse only at the wrist, the Chinese doctors in attendance argued that multiple pulse readings were necessary, from across the body, to accurately gauge the patient's health. According to Staunton's account, Gillen encouraged Heshen to feel his own pulse, with one finger at his temple, and another at his ankle. To the astonishment of the Chinese, the heartbeats were in time. No doubt, this anecdote is a little unjust in its portrayal of medical knowledge in Qing China, and the argument over the importance of taking the pulse at various points in the body may have been a garbled description of the acupuncture practised by Chinese doctors.

Nonetheless, Gillen's treatment produced immediate results where traditional means had failed. Diagnosing Heshen with a serious hernia, the Scot fitted his patient with a truss. According to Staunton, the mandarin began to feel better shortly after the consultation; this must have helped to improve perceptions of the foreigners, who were now extended enough trust to be allowed roam beyond the boundaries of the city, although Macartney decided that for reasons of propriety he should stay put. Staunton and a number of others rode out into the countryside, accompanied at all times at a discreet distance by a party of mandarins and soldiers. Again, the British thought this further evidence of the proto-surveillance state nature of the Qing Government, but they may have been closer to the mark when observing that should anything untoward happen to the visitors, it was 'a maxim of the Chinese Government never to excuse an officer for any accident that may happen in his department'.[14]

By now, Macartney's note to Heshen, clearly outlining what Britain hoped would result from the strengthening of ties between the two nations, had been translated into Chinese. How could they now get it to its intended recipient? Zhengrui could clearly not be trusted to pass it on, but a common messenger would imply a slight to the grand councillor. Wang and Qiao, despite wanting to help, would not dare undercut Zhengrui. The ever-resourceful and clearly brave Father Li volunteered to courier the message to the Heshen's quarters. Despite, or perhaps because of, his Chinese origin, dressed as he was in European clothing, he faced serious harassment as he made his way alone across the city. Upon reaching Heshen's compound, he was met by a secretary, who agreed to deliver the message and quickly get Macartney an answer. To ensure the communication got through, Father Li offered the man a substantial cash bribe, but this was refused; all the servant wanted was some little souvenir from the Europeans.

With their petition delivered, the embassy now simply had to wait. No response had been received by the emperor's birthday on 17 September, the formal reason for the mission's visit, and an occasion that required another early start and patient waiting. Setting out for court at 3 a.m., the British delegation had to take comfort from the tea, warm milk, and fruit they were served during the usual two-hour wait for the object of celebrations to arrive. Finally led into a large garden, they found the chief mandarins, all dressed in yellow silk, drawn up in ranks before a pavilion, within which Qianlong sat, hidden by a silk screen. A dreary ritual of solemn music followed, featuring muffled drums and deep-toned bells, accompanied by chants of 'Bow down your heads, all ye dwellers upon earth; bow down your heads before the great Qianlong, the great Qianlong'. With each chant, the assembled officials performed the kowtow while the British remained standing. To Macartney's mind, the ritual was unique; he could not think of any other ceremony even from the ranks of the world's religions that was so exhaustive in its honouring of deity. Yet here so many were venerating a mere mortal ruler.[15]

With the official birthday celebrations completed, Macartney and his entourage endured another garden tour, led once more by the same four mandarins. The day featured meals of a 'collection of petits pates, salt relishes, and other savoury dishes, with fruit and sweetmeats, milk and ice-water', gifts of 'several pieces of silk and porcelain, which we were told were presents to us from the Emperor', and even a puppet show.[16] Throughout all this, Macartney tried to speak to Heshen on the actual work of his diplomatic mission, including the contents of his petition. As always, the mandarin brushed off his enquiries, turning the conversation to the points of natural beauty around them, promising that there would be plenty of time yet to discuss business. By 3 p.m., all hopes of achieving anything productive that day were dashed when Heshen excused himself. Macartney and his fellows were left in the care of Songyun, who was tasked with showing them a local pagoda.

Only a few days before, the Chinese court had seemed to accept the British refusal to kowtow, but now it appeared that the embassy was to be thwarted in all its efforts. From our perspective today, it is obvious that Macartney's second letter to Heshen, clearly laying out Britain's demands, had changed the tone of the bilateral engagement. While the imperial court had been willing to make concessions on issues of ritual, the mandarins had assumed that Macartney at least understood Britain's relative position to China was that of an inferior. The British were now, the mandarins believed, part of the Sinocentric international order presided over by Qianlong; this did not give them the right to start setting the agenda.

With the arrival of Macartney's second letter seeking more rights for British traders and the establishment of a sovereign enclave, it had become undeniable that the ambassador was still ignorant of where his nation figured in a Chinese-led world. That he had presumed to express an opinion on an internal Chinese matter, the authorisation of Mackintosh's journey across the interior to Zhoushan, only served to deepen the impression that the British were upstarts who did not know their place. Indeed, the insistence that Mackintosh be allowed to make his way south separate to the rest of the embassy increased suspicions that the foreigners were intent on spying on the empire (which in many ways, of course, they were).

This change in Chinese perceptions can be seen in the news filtering back from Rehe to junior mandarins in Peking. Barrow, who was still assembling the larger gifts for Qianlong's arrival in the capital, was able to observe first-hand how Macartney's refusal to kowtow was interpreted as word of it spread through the Qing bureaucracy. 'The great officers of State in Pekin, in the Tribunal of Ceremonies, were mortified, perplexed, and alarmed at an event unprecedented in the annals of the Empire,' he records.

While in Rehe the actual implications were still being digested, there was immediate concern in Peking that 'the Emperor, when he began to think more seriously over the subject, might possibly impeach before the criminal tribunal those who had advised him to accede to such a proposal, on reflecting how much his dignity had suffered by the compliance'.[17] The mandarins in Rehe might be far less pessimistic than their colleagues in Peking, but they must also have shared some of that instinct for caution. After all, Qianlong might be willing to indulge the strange notions of the foreigners now, but who could say how he might view their obstinacy in a few weeks or months? The prudent official in such circumstances would make sure the hospitality extended to the British was warm enough to be above reproach, but also that there were no concrete promises in terms of policy changes or new approaches until it was known for certain how the emperor would wish to engage with these foreigners. Given this backdrop, it is no wonder Heshen was less than eager to begin discussions on the actual nature of bilateral engagement.

Of course, this official caution probably mirrored Qianlong's own state of mind. The day after his birthday, the emperor invited Macartney and his retinue to watch a comedic opera in the imperial compound. As a good diplomat should, the ambassador used his time with the emperor to try to steer the conversation towards weightier matters. Qianlong, however, avoided any such entanglements by making a fuss over giving Macartney another gift for George III, small pieces of agate, noting that 'though the present may appear to be small, it is, in my estimation, the most valuable that I can give, or my Empire can furnish', as they were handed down through many generations of Manchu leaders.[18] No doubt, this provenance story represents a historical flourish, but the gift highlights that, while the emperor did not want to accede to Britain's demands, he did not wish to dismiss them entirely yet.

With no chance to press his case further that day, Macartney mingled among the audience, trying to learn as much as possible about the court. He noted that the men in attendance were almost entirely Manchu—clearly, this event was of such exclusivity that the ethnic Han Chinese were largely left out. However, other ethnic groups who had a common steppe origin with the Manchu were in evidence. Falling into conversation with one, a Kalmyk, Macartney was asked if he could speak Persian or Arabic, before being told how this particular tribe had come into Qianlong's service. Having fallen into conflict with the Russians in Central Asia, these Kalmyks had migrated east, and upon reaching the borders of China, they had asked for the emperor's protection. That Qianlong acceded to this request might seem odd; after all, at first glance, it would seem strange to risk antagonising the Russians by aiding their fugitive enemies. Given the Qing's own nomadic origins, however, it made good strategic sense for Qianlong to bind the Kalmyks to his service. After all, his own dynasty was once dismissed as shiftless barbarians, but they had seized control of China—who was to say it could not happen again? It was better to bring the Kalmyks inside the tent.

Despite the press of the crowds, it was again striking how solemn and quiet everyone was, even in the midst of a fireworks display 'a dead silence was rigidly observed, not ... even a laugh exploded during the whole of the performance'.[19] It is quite possible that the attendant mandarins were quiet so as not to risk any embarrassment in front of the foreigners, but one also wonders if such a taciturnity was a natural reaction to the presence of the emperor. Foreigners regularly observed that the events that Qianlong attended were remarkably mute and reserved in atmosphere; did he spend his entire reign in a bubble of drab sobriety?

As they left the theatre, Wang took Macartney aside and told him that the emperor would be returning to Peking on the 24th. As a result, the British would have to leave on the 21st to greet him on his return to the Summer Palace, as was traditionally expected of ambassadors. The pressure was now on; Macartney needed to firm up with Heshen how and when discussions could take place on the future of British relations with the Qing Empire before this departure date. He was uncomfortably aware that if no firm engagement had been promised before the emperor reached Peking, the time lost might tempt the more conservative factions in the Chinese court to press for the embassy to be sent home before these delicate matters might be raised. If they succeeded, Macartney would fail.

9

'Tremblingly Obey and Show No Negligence!'

In 1982, crunch talks between the People's Republic of China and the UK over the future of Hong Kong seemed to be going nowhere. In the face of British efforts to shape the future path of their colony ahead of its return to Chinese rule in 1997, Deng Xiaoping, pre-eminent leader of the People's Republic, had reportedly told Margaret Thatcher that his troops 'could walk in and take Hong Kong back later today if they wanted to'.[1] Despite the prime minister's warnings that such a move would make China an international pariah, Deng remained inflexible on matters such as capital controls on Hong Kong and the management of the colony's economy. So taken aback was Thatcher that she privately began to moot the possibility of granting Hong Kong self-rule. Yet despite the negativity surrounding negotiations, the two sides had taken the first steps towards signing the 1984 Joint Declaration in Beijing, which would lead to the peaceful transfer of sovereignty over Hong Kong from Britain and China in 1997, with a Chinese guarantee that the region's institutions would remain untouched for fifty years.

Nearly 190 years earlier, the Iron Lady's forerunner in Anglo–Chinese negotiations was similarly bogged down in stalemate. Perhaps Macartney would have taken heart if he could foresee that future British leaders would also face challenging negotiations and yet still achieve compromise in the end. Had such knowledge been available to him, he might have had more optimism in September 1793, as it rapidly became clear that his mission was in serious danger of abject failure. As the day of departure loomed closer, Zhengrui, Wang, and Qiao were back, finally bearing Heshen's response to Macartney's petition. Refusing to hand the note over, Zhengrui read the much-anticipated words aloud. The grand councillor had decided that Mackintosh must stay with the embassy until all the foreigners headed for home. To soften the blow, the *Hindoostan* had leave to take on board a cargo of tea at Zhoushan, with all duties waived, which would at least give the Company some concrete return on its investment in the mission. On the major questions, though—such as a permanent embassy, the ceding of a small island, or market access—the note was silent.

The tide of court opinion was clearly turning against the British. Macartney heard rumours that Heshen had convened a special council to discuss whether further engagement was prudent. Not only was Fukang'an, the Anglophobic former viceroy of Canton, invited to contribute to this forum, but the disgraced former Canton Hoppo, or customs inspector (in whose palace the British had stayed in Peking) was actually released from prison to give his thoughts on whether the foreigners were worth listening to. From Macartney's perspective, this was not exactly a sympathetic audience.

The embassy now seemed beset by bad luck and was constantly the focus of negative attention. The day before they departed for the capital, 20 September, one of the mission's gunners, a man called Reid, passed away. A tragic occurrence in any circumstances, it was viewed as much more than this by the hosts. Permission to bury the body within the limits of Rehe was refused. Macartney suspected that it was feared that the death of a foreigner on imperial grounds would embarrass the emperor. Others in the embassy wondered if the relevant mandarins feared they would be blamed for the death of this soldier. Of course, the most likely reason is that the Chinese feared the dead man might have contracted an infectious disease and wished to limit the chances of contagion. Regardless, the next day, Reid's remains were loaded into a palanquin with drawn curtains and accompanied the embassy down the road to Peking. A mile into their journey, the body was removed and hastily buried in a roadside grave, at which point the death of the unfortunate Reid finally became official.

As they proceeded further south, another glaring manifestation of official suspicions about the British loomed before them. Approaching the Great Wall again from the north, many of the more adventurous mission members hoped to climb it once more, as they had done on the journey out. However, the collapsed section near the roadside that had earlier allowed them access to the top ramparts had since been filled in with debris and rubbish. The sight of the foreigners scrambling to the top of the fortifications had been a cause for concern to the local officials, who made sure that the scene would not be repeated.

Arriving in Peking at midday on 26 September, the embassy staff found themselves under pressure to finally complete the arrangement of the emperor's gifts as quickly as possible. While likely due to the imminent arrival of Qianlong, it speaks to the low mood now gripping Macartney that he assumed that this was because they were to be sent home. His uneasiness grew when he learned of the treatment received by his colleagues who had remained in the capital during his absence. Confined to their quarters, with a guard posted at the gate of their lodgings to prevent both unauthorised entries and exits, their only relief from the tedium of their house arrest came in visits by the missionaries who were resident in the city. Even these were subject to close observation by Chinese officials, who sat in on the meetings to eavesdrop, despite not understanding a word of the conversations, all of which were held in Latin or French. Eventually, the officials decided that even such harmless contact was risky and put an end to these social calls.

The British position seemed so insecure that despite suffering from a case of rheumatism, it was felt Macartney could not risk the emperor's disappointment by crying off sick from greeting him in person at the city outskirts. Fatigued and shaky, Macartney waited many hours at the side of the road for a momentary salute from the passing Qianlong. Blessedly, a message soon arrived from the emperor noting that, as he was ill, Macartney should head back to Peking and was not expected to visit the court at this moment. No sooner was this message gratefully received than the patient was hurrying back to his bed.

While the ambassador fought off illness, his officials continued to wait for word from the court on where things might progress. The emperor had now viewed the gifts awaiting him in Peking, but his first impressions were not good. Far from being bowled over by the advanced nature of Western science, Qianlong dismissed the wonders assembled for him, scathingly commenting that 'these things are good enough to amuse children'.[2] The mandarins attached to the Summer Palace had themselves been astonished at how long the British had taken to assemble what now seemed quite basic technology, adding to the sense that the foreigners were crude and unsophisticated.

As is often the case in such trying circumstances, dark rumours began to circulate, and in the absence of hard information, the anxious British seized on this gossip as truth. Word reached Macartney that a number of ministers had been pushing to have the embassy expelled forty days after its arrival in Rehe. In an attempt to extend the mission's time in China by as much as possible, and to allow for the opportunity for the imperial mind to change on the topic of a permanent embassy, the ambassador once again wrote to Heshen. Expressing gratitude for the emperor's graciousness in allowing the *Hindoostan* to load cargo at Zhoushan, Macartney wondered if, now they were in Peking, it might not be acceptable for Captain Mackintosh to proceed directly to his ship. The ambassador and the remainder of the embassy, he informed the grand councillor, were hoping to proceed home via Canton. They would be happy to leave Peking, sometime in the New Year would be perfect, weather permitting (i.e., he hoped to stay until the spring). If this ruse proved acceptable, the intervening months would give him valuable time in which to try to change the emperor's mind.

While Macartney's efforts to extend his period in China through honeyed words and loaded suggestions are laudable, his note was met with a predictable response. The next day brought a summons to meet with the empire's senior mandarins, and Macartney once more found himself facing the daunting trio of Heshen, Vice-Minister Fuchang'an, and his brother, Fukang'an. Such an audience bode badly for British hopes. Heshen presented Macartney with communications from the commander of the *Lion*, Sir Erasmus Gower, stating that he was preparing to leave Zhoushan as soon as possible, as the threat of disease now proved overwhelming. The *Hindoostan* would wait for its own captain, Mackintosh, to arrive before it would head south.

Heshen wondered, pointedly, whether Macartney would not be eager to re-join his ship, and with it the comforts of home? After all, as soon as he was aboard, he could begin the long journey back to England. Indeed, the grand councillor added, the emperor himself had noted that, given the number of mission members who had succumbed to illness during their time in China, staying the winter in Peking would be a very bad idea. Foreigners did not really have the constitution for such cold weather, the envoy was bluntly told. There was no need to wait until spring. Macartney was not yet facing forcible expulsion from China, but he was being shown the way to the exit, with steadily diminishing subtlety.

Still, the Irishman used the audience to press his case. It was his own sovereign's dear wish, he replied, that he be allowed to reside in China, at the British Crown's expense, 'for the purpose of cultivating and cementing a firm friendship between two such powerful monarchs'.[3] In exchange, the British Government would be delighted to host Qianlong's own ambassador in London. The ministers ignored this, but once more suggested a rapid departure might suit Macartney's health. What the British did not know was that the emperor had put pressure on his officials to firm up the schedule for the embassy's exit. Qianlong was awake to the possibility that the foreigners might attempt to extend their stay in the capital. He even predicted that the ambassador might feign ill health (hence Heshen's apparent interest in ensuring Macartney's well-being and his encouragement to take to the seas).

By the time he had returned, deflated, to his quarters, word had reached Macartney that Qianlong's personal reply to George III's original letter of introduction had been completed and sent to a missionary for translation into Latin. The ambassador's usual optimism, so ardent in the face of so many trials, now finally deserted him; this was 'an infallible indication of the Court's intentions and as a signal for us to take our leave'. The next day, his pessimism increased when Zhengrui called early in the morning. He brought news that the most senior British officials were summoned to a ceremony at Heshen's palace. He immediately assumed that this audience would merely be the start of his formal expulsion from China. As Macartney was still battling illness, and given the bitterness he must have felt at receiving this news from the ever-sour Zhengrui, it is scarcely surprising that his diary notes 'I do not remember ever having received a more unpleasant message in my life'. The spectre of failure now loomed large over the whole mission.[4]

As usual, the British were kept waiting for three hours once they arrived at the appointment; if such a delay had been irritating before, it seemed cruel mockery now. Eventually, they were led through several courtyards, over a number of ornamental bridges, to the foot of a grand staircase in an audience chamber. There, they were faced with a line of yellow silk armchairs, on the centre of which had been placed Qianlong's response to George III's letter. Once they had bowed to this manifestation of the imperial opinion, they then processed up the staircase, led by a mandarin holding the letter aloft. Above, Heshen met them, along with his usual retinue, who showed them a number of items, all wrapped in yellow silk, which were personal gifts from the emperor to the British sovereign. The letter and the gifts all confirmed a simple fact—they were no longer welcome in China.

The entire interaction was handled 'not only without the Minister's usual graciousness of manner, but with a degree of constraint and stiffness that appeared to me not natural, but assumed for the occasion'.[5] The Chinese officials all refused the gifts that Macartney offered by way of thanks for their help, such as it was, over the course of his time in China. Unsurprisingly, when he reminded Heshen that so many important issues had not yet been addressed, the response was non-committal; perhaps the ambassador could lay out exactly what was sought in yet another note, he was told. With waves of fatigue washing over him, and eager to return to his sickbed, Macartney agreed to this, assuming it would be a pointless exercise. Later that afternoon, suffering through his illness, he laid out once more in exact terms what he, on behalf of the British Government, expected from the Qianlong's officials. In Macartney's own words, his requests were as follows:

> First ... to allow the English merchants to trade to Cheusan [Zhoushan], Limpo [Ningbo], and Tiensing [Tianjin]. Second, to allow them to have

> a warehouse at Pekin for the sale of their goods, as the Russians had formerly. Third, to allow them some small, detached, unfortified island in the neighbourhood of Cheusan as a magazine for their unsold goods, and as a residence for their people to take care of them. Fourth, to allow them a similar privilege near Canton, and some other trifling indulgences. Fifth, to abolish the transit duties between Macao and Canton, or at least to reduce them to the standard of 1782. Sixth, to prohibit the exaction of any duties from English merchants, over and above those settled by the Emperor's diploma, a copy of which is requested to be given to them, as they have never yet been able to see it for their unequivocal direction.[6]

This represented a last roll of the dice by Macartney, the one remaining chance that he would return home with something to justify his voyage. Yet even as he drafted this communication, the emperor's own letter to George III arrived at his quarters, conveyed in great fashion by sixteen mandarins. His diaries do not mention when Macartney took the liberty of seeing what the Qianlong had written to his British counterpart, but it seems unlikely that he would have waited long to open the golden scroll. Once read, this letter would have finally sunk his hopes of success.

From the opening lines, Qianlong made it clear he refused to see this as an engagement between equals; the British were to be commended for their humility, not for their potential as partners in trade. He began:

> You, O King, live beyond the confines of many seas, nevertheless, impelled by your humble desire to partake of the benefits of our civilisation, you have dispatched a mission respectfully bearing your memorial. Your Envoy has crossed the seas and paid his respects at my Court on the anniversary of my birthday. To show your devotion, you have also sent offerings of your country's produce... I have perused your memorial: the earnest terms in which it is couched reveal a respectful humility on your part, which is highly praiseworthy ...[7]

George III was an impressive supplicant, but nothing could change his innate inferiority to the Son of Heaven:

> As to your entreaty to send one of your nationals to be accredited to my Celestial Court ... and to be in control of your country's trade with China, this request is contrary to all usage of my dynasty and cannot possibly be entertained ... Your proposed Envoy to my Court could not be placed in a position similar to that of European officials in Peking who are forbidden to leave China, nor could he, on the other hand, be allowed liberty of movement and the privilege of corresponding with

> his own country; so that you would gain nothing by his residence in our midst.[8]

The very concept of a permanent embassy proved so alien to the Chinese court that rejection was inevitable. The only experience Qianlong or any of his officials had of permanent European residents in Peking were those who were in his service. Indeed, Qianlong found the role of a permanent diplomatic mission so confusing that he points to some remarkably petty reasons to deny permission for an embassy:

> Supposing that your Envoy should come to our Court … his language and national dress differ from that of our people, and there would be no place in which to bestow him. It may be suggested that he might imitate the Europeans permanently resident in Peking and adopt the dress and customs of China, but, it has never been our dynasty's wish to force people to do things unseemly and inconvenient …[9]

This letter is a pure, unfiltered example of how the Qing were unable to understand the direction the global economy was taking and the consequent inevitable shifting of international political power. The age where the might of an empire depended only on its vast scale and the multitude of its population was at an end. Trade, and the control of commerce, would be the defining elements of hegemony in the long nineteenth century. In this light, what is particularly glaring is Qianlong's lack of appreciation for how the multitude nations of Europe, comparatively small though they might be, represented future global actors:

> Besides, supposing I sent an Ambassador to reside in your country, how could you possibly make for him the requisite arrangements? Europe consists of many other nations besides your own: if each and all demanded to be represented at our Court, how could we possibly consent?[10]

The idea that China would be expected to engage with all the states of Europe seemed ludicrous to the emperor. Yet while it was British power that came to be felt most keenly in China in the century following this dismissive assessment, the imperialism that rent the country to pieces was a multinational effort. As well as Britain and France, by the start of the twentieth century, even second- or third-tier European powers such as Austro-Hungary, Italy, Belgium, and Portugal had a colonial presence in what was once the unfettered domain of the Chinese emperor. In Shanghai's international settlement, a self-governing enclave established in

1863, the citizens of fourteen foreign powers were exempt from Chinese law. The Qing were used to guarding against the usurper overthrowing the ruling order through blunt force; after all, that was how their dynasty had arisen. However, to secure China against nations that achieved dominance through the application of commercial pressure, sly diplomacy, and carefully targeted force using superior technology was a new challenge, against which the Qing did not have the breadth of strategic understanding necessary to form a defence. The imperial court simply did not know how to engage in diplomatic exchanges in which other states were equals. The traditional tributary relationships with their near neighbours meant that any approach based on a parity of respect or esteem upended the Chinese view of the international system. 'How can our dynasty alter its whole procedure and system of etiquette, established for more than a century, in order to meet your individual views?' Qianlong asked George in his letter.[11]

Unfortunately, it was not simply the desires of the British that were alone pressing for a change in China's relationship with the outside world; the cold, unyielding logic of the global economy, and its attendant realities in terms of power relations, had already decided that China would be opened up to foreign influence. Qianlong had no choice as to whether this would occur; in reality, he had control only over how this process would take place. Yet this truth was too blunt to pierce the carapace of Middle Kingdom superiority. Not only, in the eyes of the Qing, were the foreigners culturally unworthy of bilateral relations with China, they seemed even incapable of acquiring the societal refinements needed to achieve such a position.

> If you assert that [you] desire to acquire our civilisation, our ceremonies and code of laws differ so completely from your own that, even if your Envoy were able to acquire the rudiments of our civilisation, you could not possibly transplant our manners and customs to your alien soil.[12]

As these dismissive lines might suggest, Qianlong remained unconvinced that Europe generally, and Britain in particular, had civilisation and culture on a par with his kingdom. Given the historical tendency for successive Chinese dynasties to assume the centrality of their nation's role in the world, this is not surprising. A far greater failure was Qianlong's inability to divine what the Macartney embassy represented in technical, scientific and engineering terms. In the gifts they presented him, with the items they carried with them (such as mass-produced watches and steel swords), and through their modes of transportation from Europe, the British offered numerous indications that, in some areas at least, China had fallen badly behind. How could any responsible emperor—either witnessing first-hand or hearing through his officials of the power of the British telescopes, of the quality and low-cost of their blades, of the ease with which the *Lion* and its squadron sailed off-shore—not recognise the threat that such a technologically advanced state might pose to the empire if not appropriately handled? Yet Qianlong's reply to all this evidence of scientific achievement was simply to state the following:

> Strange and costly objects do not interest me. If I have commanded that the tribute offerings sent by you, O King, are to be accepted, this was solely in consideration for the spirit which prompted you to dispatch them from afar ... We possess all things. I set no value on objects strange or ingenious, and have no use for your country's manufactures.[13]

If only such confidence in China's technical superiority, especially in matters military, had been justified. At times, subsequent history refracts the self-assuredness with which Qianlong addresses the British sovereign as an inferior, revealing simple naivety behind the hubris.

> It behoves you, O King, to respect my sentiments and to display even greater devotion and loyalty in future, so that, by perpetual submission to our Throne, you may secure peace and prosperity for your country hereafter.[14]

China was in no position to play any role in securing peace in Europe, but Britain was most definitely able to create havoc in the lands ruled by the Qing dynasty.

This short-sightedness is even more apparent in a second communication sent by the emperor shortly after the initial letter, addressed again to George III and replying to the specific requests made by Macartney. In this document, it becomes clear that the Chinese understand the relative commercial strengths of their position, due to the trade imbalance between east and west, given that 'the tea, silk, and porcelain which the Celestial Empire produces are absolute necessities to European nations and to yourselves'.[15] However, there is no recognition that this enviable state of affairs could change if trade relations were not actively managed and if trading partners were not treated with respect. Once more, Qianlong rapidly dismissed each of the British requests, rejecting even the suggestion that further ports be opened to British trade, noting that, 'until now trade with European nations has always been conducted at Macao ... For the future, as in the past, I decree that your request is refused and that the trade shall be limited to Macao'.[16] That the emperor simply lumped

Macao and Canton together shows just how unimportant foreign trade appeared from the perspective of Peking.

Tellingly, in this second letter, Qianlong again completely fails to grasp what the British are actually looking for when they request a permanent embassy in Peking, which in the view of the emperor 'is the hub and centre about which all quarters of the globe revolve'. He assumes that, rather than a diplomatic mission, what they are actually seeking is only 'a repository in the capital of my Empire for the storing and sale of your produce, in accordance with the precedent granted to Russia'.[17] It is simply too much of a shift in his worldview to understand that British want to go beyond mere commercial concerns and are aiming to forge stronger bonds between the two empires. Unsurprisingly, then, the request for the ceding of a small island to Britain is completely unacceptable to Qianlong. In language foreshadowing modern China's view of its claimed maritime possessions (but lacking Beijing's current ability to back up words with force), he warns that 'every inch of the territory of our Empire is marked on the map and the strictest vigilance is exercised over it all: even tiny islets and far-lying sandbanks are clearly defined'. The request is nothing but 'a flagrant infringement of the usage of my Empire and cannot possibly be entertained'.[18]

At times, perplexingly, Qianlong retreats from blind superiority and deploys carefully reasoned logic, rather than hauteur, to oppose British requests. A trading base in Macao and access to the markets of Canton should more than suffice the foreign traders, after all 'European nations have been trading with Canton for a number of years and, as they make large profits, the number of traders is constantly increasing'.[19] If the commercial opportunities on the ground were so attractive to Western traders, he notes, clearly China was already offering them an enticing deal. What was in it for the Qing to open up their markets further? Similarly, Qianlong claims that accepting British arguments on abolishing tariffs would hand them a competitive advantage over the other European nations, as the British controlled the bulk of foreign trade through Canton. Even this argument carefully ignored one simple fact, however; Macartney was not seeking special treatment for the British. They sought no preferential treatment; it was always intended that whatever concessions were won could apply to all European nations.

Strangely, Qianlong also refused the British the right to spread their religion in China, where there 'has been no hankering after heterodox doctrines ... your Ambassador's request that barbarians shall be given full liberty to disseminate their religion is utterly unreasonable'.[20] At no point did Macartney make this request; indeed, to push for such opportunities for proselytization went against his own personal beliefs. This caused the ambassador considerable concern and was a misunderstanding he was determined to clear up before returning to London.

Oblivious to the damage that Britain could wreak on his nation, Qianlong ended his second communication in a tone that, given subsequent developments, rings down through the centuries as one of history's great miscalculations. Commending the British king for having 'shown your submissive loyalty by sending this tribute mission', he warns George that should the British seek to force entry into the Chinese market through any port but Canton, they 'will be subject to instant expulsion. In that event your barbarian merchants will have had a long journey for nothing'. He closes with an order more fit for one of his mandarins, a line that would appear devastatingly hollow within fifty years of his writing it: 'Tremblingly obey and show no negligence!'[21]

10

'An Opportunity of Knowing Us'

In 1992, Deng Xiaoping's ambitious reform programme was stalling. Following the Tiananmen Square protests in 1989, conservative factions within the Chinese leadership were seeking to roll back the economic liberalisation and political reforms championed by Deng. China's former paramount leader now needed to fight to keep his nation's process of 'opening-up' on track. To shore up support for this policy, Deng travelled to the area of the country that had already benefitted most from the turn to market economics and access to global trade—the south. Visiting Guangzhou (Canton), Shenzhen, and Zhuhai, Deng drew attention to those cities that were already enjoying the fruits of increased contact with the wider world: bustling factories, expanding skylines, and increasing wages. Indeed, in the case of Shenzhen, the city had only truly developed after it was designated a special economic zone in 1980 under Deng's reforms.

On this 'Southern Tour', Deng was laying out a roadmap to China's future. Yet ironically, he was also tracing a path set by China's past, especially by its 'Century of Humiliation'. The very reason that these southern metropolises were able to so easily reach out to the outside world was because they were close to Hong Kong, a relic of Britain's imperial ambitions. By touring the south, Deng was visiting those places where the imprint of Western activity in China had been pressed most indelibly. He was also following in the footsteps of George Macartney after his failed meeting with Qianlong. Setting out from Peking, Britain's ambassador was about to begin his own tour of the south, heading towards the theatre where the consequences of his failure to win over the Chinese ruler would be most keenly felt. It was in the south of China, where Britain's traders were forced to find their Chinese partners, that success on Macartney's part would have had the greatest effect. Indeed, it was in the same area that the terrible consequences of the failure to reach Anglo–Chinese accord over the issue of greater market access would in time levy the heaviest human costs.

The stark truth was now undeniable; Macartney was no longer welcome in Peking. One remaining hope was that somewhere between the capital and their departure port of Zhoushan, Qianlong might be convinced to let the British stay on for a while longer, allowing further attempts at diplomacy. Wishing to retain some dignity by pre-empting any formal action to expel his mission, the ambassador wrote to Heshen, suggesting that now was an appropriate time for him to make for his ships. In the spirit of hope rather than expectation, Macartney also asked the mandarin for permission to travel to Canton in the event that the *Lion* had already departed. A letter was duly sent ahead to try to catch Gower before he decided to set sail. In the meantime, Macartney prepared himself and his team to leave China in failure.

For Macartney's outbound journey, the emperor assigned two further senior mandarins as escorts. One of these was Songyun, the official with whom Macartney had discussed Russia during his tour of the parks of Rehe. Zhengrui would, thankfully, only accompany them as far as Tianjin, but the far friendlier Wang and Qiao promised to make every effort to remain with the British for as much of the journey south as possible.

Thus, on 7 October 1793, the first British Embassy to the court of the emperor of China began its long journey home. In a final farewell ceremony at the palace of the grand councillor, Macartney was presented with two large scrolls, placed on a table covered in yellow silk. One was a list of the presents that Qianlong was sending to George III, the other was the second formal reply from the emperor to all of Macartney's outstanding requests (the text of which we saw in the last chapter). A mandarin was called forward and bowed before the assembly. The two letters from Qianlong were fastened to his back with yellow ribbon; mounting his horse, this official then rode before the embassy all the way to Tongzhou, where he dismounted, bowed, and allowed the letters to be removed from his back before the British boarded their yachts on the river.

Macartney wrote little of what must have been a very depressing journey from Peking to Tongzhou. With every mile travelled, his sense of failure must have become ever more crushing. For a man so ambitious and driven, this was a heavy blow. 'I cannot help feeling the disappointment most severely. I cannot lose sight of my first prospects without infinite regret,' he recorded in his diary.[1] The sense of promise that seemed almost tangible on his voyage out now contrasted cruelly with the shame that dragged at his mind through the many miles of flat Chinese countryside.

From Tongzhou, they sailed back down the Hai River, the weather now contributing to Macartney's misery as the temperature at night began to fall sharply, while the sky overhead was sullen and overcast. The one bright spot was his strengthening relationship with Songyun. Having impressed Macartney in Rehe with a shrewd and nuanced assessment of the Russians, Songyun now revealed himself a more fitting foil for the British than Zhengrui. His international experience left him far more flexible in his approach to foreign embassies. He willingly engaged with Macartney on trying to understand the British case and to make written representations on their behalf to the imperial court. Perhaps his own efforts in negotiating diplomatic deals made him understand Macartney's plight.

Songyun's candour was most apparent when he informed Macartney that, despite the promises he had received in Peking, the letter to Erasmus Gower requesting the *Lion* to wait at Zhoushan had not yet been sent. This was perplexing; after all, if the Chinese wished to be rid of the British as quickly and cleanly as possible, then allowing them to rendezvous with their ships at Zhoushan was the easiest way to do this. Songyun undertook to write immediately to Peking to ensure that Macartney's orders to Gower were now finally dispatched.

Their new chaperone also proved capable of explaining to the British, in accessible terms, the requirements of Chinese diplomatic protocol. Songyun confirmed for the first time that embassies were not supposed to stay in China for longer than forty days. He also revealed that the fears at court around adapting procedures for the British had less to do with suspicion of foreigners and more to do with internal concerns as to what it might mean if court ritual became less than immutable. Songyun also listened to Macartney's complaints about the treatment of British merchants in China and promised to relay these concerns to Peking.

His was the polar opposite attitude of that displayed by Heshen or Zhengrui. Where once Macartney's requests had received a polite rejection or open obstruction, here now was a mandarin willing to engage directly with his concerns and understand the reasoning behind them. Songyun even went so far as to clarify for Macartney why duties levied against foreign trade had increased steadily since 1782. Contrary to what many foreigners believed, this was not due to qualms about export trade; rather the Chinese exchequer was attempting to find some way of paying for wars in Tibet and Tonkin. Given that goods to Britain were flowing at the rate of more than a shipload a week, customs duties levied against this trade were a tempting revenue target. It was suddenly clear that what the

British perceived as a deliberate policy of targeting Europeans was nothing of the sort, but rather a mere side-effect of an entirely separate element of Qing foreign policy.

As the journey to Zhoushan continued, Songyun brought a steady stream of positive news that left Macartney feeling a little more upbeat, if not actually hopeful. The emperor had now decreed that the British and other Europeans in Canton should be given greater freedom and treated with more respect by the newly appointed viceroy, a mandarin named Zhanglin. The British felt they finally had a partner in the Chinese administration they could work with; indeed, Macartney regretted that Heshen 'had not appointed Songyun to attend to us from the beginning instead of the Legate [Zhengrui], as possibly we might have been able by his means or through his channel to enter into negotiations'.[2]

With the emperor now publicly announcing a lighter regime for the Western merchants, it would also become easier for Zhanglin to pass on to Peking the future complaints of the merchants trading in his city. Songyun revealed that the new viceroy was particularly close to the emperor; his appointment was therefore a positive sign for the British. Songyun stressed that Macartney would have to trust that the Chinese would deal with his hopes in their own manner, and in so doing, they would produce a fair and reasonable result. This new transparency impressed the British. They felt that by Songyun displaying 'a strain of liberality scarcely to be expected in a Tartar or a Chinese' he revealed 'an elevated mind, and ... most friendly and gentleman-like manner'.[3]

This change in the atmosphere between visitors and hosts was particularly heartening given that at least two other mandarins always sat in on the meetings between Songyun and Macartney. The British thus realised that Songyun was making these encouraging claims in the full knowledge that his words would be reported to the ear of the emperor. He must therefore have been confident that this was the direction imperial policy was taking.

The benefits of Songyun's more positive attitude were felt in even the smallest details. Reaching Tianjin, they were entertained with a dinner of the usual Chinese dishes, all of them excellent, featuring 'mutton, pork, venison, and poultry of all kinds, fruits in great variety—peaches, plums, apples, pears, grapes, chestnuts, walnuts, and several others quite new to me'.[4] To add to this local cornucopia, however, Songyun had acquired a number of dairy cows, so that the British might enjoy fresh milk on their journey. Macartney, who recognised how rare the consumption of milk was in China, was hugely impressed by this small gesture of human kindness.

This close relationship was to prove very important in overcoming yet another failure in communication. As we saw earlier, when Macartney had read the Latin translation of the emperor's letter to George III, it contained a refusal to allow British missionaries to enter China, something that had never been sought in the first place. More worryingly, the letter seemed to suggest that the requests made of the Chinese, such as a permanent base on the Chinese coast, had been Macartney's personal demands, implying that these were not the wishes of the British sovereign. While Macartney wondered if this was a Machiavellian attempt to blacken his name with his employers, Songyun explained that this was simply an artifice to allow Qianlong to turn down the British requests. It was impossible under Chinese court etiquette for one ruler to refuse the request of another (even if, of course, George III was Qianlong's inferior). It therefore followed that if Qianlong had to turn somebody down, it must be Macartney. From the Chinese viewpoint, George III had not requested something Qianlong was unwilling to agree to. Instead, his ambassador had simply over-stepped his brief and had asked for too much. By this reasoning, Qianlong's refusal was perfectly logical and could cause no offence to the British monarch.

Despite the awkward position this might put him in when he returned to England, Macartney was willing to let this language slide. However, he was still eager to disabuse Songyun of any notions that the British were eager to proselytise. Particularly given his self-image as a man of the enlightenment, his suspicion of religion, and his professional pride, Macartney was eager to set the record straight. He noted to Songyun:

> The English never attempted to dispute or disturb the worship or tenets of others, being persuaded that the Supreme Governor of the Universe was equally pleased with the homage of all His creatures when proceeding from sincere devotion.[5]

Indeed, he explained, this was an opinion that contemporary British missionaries lamented greatly. Many British subjects, including the Catholics and Presbyterians in Macartney's own homeland, might have been surprised to hear British attitudes to other faiths described as being so open-minded. As it turned out, these efforts to achieve clarity on matters spiritual proved very important. Songyun revealed that, in fact, no reference to religion appeared in the original Chinese letter written by the emperor. Instead, it would seem that the missionary tasked with translating the letter into Latin had inserted the reference himself. This may have been an attempt to blacken Macartney's reputation at home or pre-emptively to block the British from sending Protestant missionaries to China in future.

Despite Songyun's assurances that Anglo–Chinese relations were on a productive track, Macartney knew that once the letters from Qianlong reached London, it would be impossible for him to suggest the embassy was anything but a failure. Against the bald rejections that the emperor had committed to paper, Macartney's claims of open and useful discussions with this mandarin would count for little. Would it be possible, he wondered, if a third letter setting out some of these more constructive developments could be dispatched from Peking, bearing Qianlong's vermillion signature? Unfortunately, Songyun responded, as the embassy had already departed Peking, it would be inappropriate for the emperor to dispatch a letter now. Whether he was simply trying to let the ambassador down gently, or whether court ritual once again interfered, the end result was the same. Notwithstanding Songyun's assurances that the emperor was by the day growing more open to dealing with Britain, and regardless of how often communications flew by horseback between Peking and the embassy drifting gently southwards along China's waterways, there would be no concrete proof that Macartney had won Qianlong over.

They were now travelling south along the Grand Canal, the great artery of Chinese commerce and transport. Completed in the seventh century, but with sections dating back to the fifth century BCE, it was (and remains) the world's longest artificial waterway. Illness began to lay some of the mission's personnel low. This may have been down to a sudden drop in temperature as winter approached, but Macartney was a little less sympathetic in his explanation: 'their living in the midst of such plenty without much restraint or exercise may ... contribute also to their complaints'.[6] Not for the last time, expats in China were finding it difficult to avoid the temptations associated with the easy life offered by their host country.

On 25 October, word reached them that the *Lion*, along with the *Clarence* and the *Jackall*, had left Zhoushan; only the *Hindoostan* remained. Gower could no longer stand seeing his crews decimated by disease while waiting in port. What is more, he had also learned that Britain and France were at war, meaning that he could soon find himself under attack from French ships. Facing these double threats, he had elected to sail to Macao immediately to restock with supplies and to enjoy the protection of the Portuguese fortifications there, leaving the *Hindoostan* behind. As Macartney explained to Songyun, the more than sixty men who were accompanying him could not, along with all their cargo, cram into this vessel. Instead, they must now make for Canton, and the ambassador pointedly added that this was only necessary as the original letter he had sent to Gower in an attempt to hold the *Lion* had not been dispatched. The consistently reasonable Songyun promised to relay this request to Peking, and the route change was quickly confirmed.

Cargo, baggage, and anything that was not of immediate necessity would be loaded on the *Hindoostan,* accompanied by Captain Mackintosh, who was finally free to re-join his ship. The embassy members would continue south along the Grand Canal, via Hangzhou, to make their way overland to Canton. Even if the mission's diplomatic goals remained unfulfilled, this would at least give their artists and scientists the opportunity to make the most extensive foreign study to date of the Chinese interior.

By 2 November, the yachts of the embassy had sailed to where the Grand Canal joins the Yellow River, a waterway of immense symbolic importance for the Chinese people. The semi-mythological Xia dynasty, first of the great Chinese kingdoms, was said to have arisen here on the muddy riverbanks. The reverence that the mission's guides had for the spot was obvious. Before crossing, they sacrificed animals to honour the spirit of the river, with the blood daubed at various points along the hull of their craft. Cups of wine, oil, salt, flour, and tea were placed in the bows of each vessel, and when the midpoint of the watercourse's 3-mile span was reached, each vessels' captain tipped the contents of these cups into the muddy waters below.

Re-joining the canal on the southern bank, the flotilla made its way for Yangzhou, before crossing that other great Chinese river, the Yangtze. They then passed through three lakes, before arriving at Hangzhou, a city considered one of the most beautiful in the country, a reputation it still enjoys. The great West Lake, which dominates the city, is a sight that will be familiar to anyone who has visited modern China and will thus have inevitably handled a 1-renminbi note. The currency features on one side a painting of the stupas, or small Buddhist pillars, found in the middle of the West Lake. The fact that such a view was chosen for the most ubiquitous denomination in their currency speaks volumes about the place the city has in the hearts of the Chinese. This respect is not purely aesthetic either; Hangzhou is of immense economic importance as well. For Macartney, the city was the southern terminus of the Grand Canal and was within easy distance of the Qiantang River, making the city a major commercial hub. Today, Hangzhou's importance continues, as the home of Alibaba, one of China's most successful internet companies, and also hosting the G20 summit in 2016.

Macartney now finally had the opportunity to have an in-depth discussion with Zhanglin, the new viceroy of Canton, who proved to be every bit as cooperative as Songyun. It was surely a great relief, given that the British would now be saying goodbye to the latter mandarin, that he would be replaced for the remainder of the journey by a man who was 'perfectly well bred, [with] the whole of his manner candid and gentleman-like'.[7] Continuity would also be achieved through the ongoing presence of Wang and Qiao, who were now authorised to accompany the British all the way to their departure point.

Their new escort confirmed that Qianlong had ordered him to make life much easier for the British traders and that he should readily accept submissions from them by letter or in person. The viceroy stressed that the emperor was particularly pleased to have received an embassy that had travelled so far, and he presented to Macartney yet more gifts from Qianlong to George III—some pieces of silk, a number of purses, and a scroll inscribed in the emperor's own hand. This further round of gift-giving, while the embassy was still on their way to Canton, seems somewhat odd. One wonders whether Qianlong now regretted his earlier abruptness and hoped to smooth any ruffled feathers among the British before they left China.

Continuing through Hangzhou on the morning of 4 November, Macartney took in from his palanquin the views of the 'gentle hills' above the city 'cultivated ... with plantations of mulberries and dwarf fruit-trees, sheltered by oaks, planes, sycamores, and camphors'.[8] Along the shores of the West Lake, they came upon Leifeng Ta, the Thunder Peak Pagoda. Despite the claims of their local guides who said this was built over 2,000 years previously, it was actually constructed around 975 CE and was only a youthful eight centuries old. Modern visitors can still see its silhouette on the horizon above the lake, although sadly, this incarnation is not the original, which collapsed in 1924.

Some 6 miles east of Hangzhou, they took ship again, this time on the Qiantang River, famed for the great tidal bore waves, the world's largest, that crash along the riverbank near the city and have drawn crowds of onlookers for over 1,000 years. Thankfully, the river proved calm for the embassy as they moved upstream, at first under sails before being towed. Zhanglin proved every bit as engaging as his predecessor, and Macartney found himself able to discuss, in detail, Britain's trade relations with China. Having voluntarily raised the issue with the ambassador, Zhanglin asked for an in-depth explanation of where Britain's grievances lay; it was clear that he was keen to improve what was his already good handle on the commercial situation in Canton. He posed a number of informed questions and was eager to get a sense for how Britain's exports and imports through the port compared to that of other European nations.

Macartney was also impressed by how Canton's new governor understood the difference between ships engaged in trade with Britain directly, and those that were shuttling back and forth with India (whether he recognised that one of the main differences was that the latter often carried opium is not recorded). The viceroy also mentioned that it was common knowledge that officials in Canton were defrauding the emperor of his tax revenue. Tactfully, Macartney responded that, as he had never been to the city, he could not possibly comment. If he discovered, however, information from any British merchants that might be useful in tackling this, he would be sure to pass it on. Thanking him for this promise, Zhanglin suggested that Macartney put all of the main points of their conversation down in a comprehensive paper so that he could study these further.

This engagement created a degree of trust between the two men, and the viceroy was ready to take Macartney into his confidence. Stating that he was committed to easing the lot of foreign traders, he reminded the ambassador that it must be borne in mind that any attempts to change policy in this area would have to run the gauntlet of court politics. Despite the viceroy's connections to the emperor, there should be no illusions as to how many obstacles lay in the path of reform. In particular, the sour Fukang'an, Zhanglin's predecessor as viceroy in Canton, would fight hard against any moves that might be seen as retrospective criticism of his own term. It was suggested that Fukang'an had influenced his mentor, Heshen, who consequently proved more intransigent in dealing with the foreigners than he might otherwise have been. Zhanglin feared that this had given the impression that the British were not welcome in China, when the very opposite was true, he claimed.

Macartney might well have been floored with surprise at this outpouring, but he replied quite bluntly that he 'concluded the Court of Pekin to be indifferent, if not unfriendly, to Great Britain; and that I should have represented it so in my dispatches home,' were it not for the soothing interventions of Songyun and the new viceroy.[9] This freshly apparent respect for the British was, Macartney claimed, what stayed his hand from writing to London on the negative response he had received. Of course, it was also in the ambassador's own interests to leave it as long as possible before confirming to headquarters that his visit had been a failure, in the hopes that some turn in his fortunes might come to pass. The possibility of him being in a position to write a positive report, he now pointed out to the viceroy, lay in the ability of the Chinese to convince him that Britain's requests would be taken seriously.

Over the coming days, the viceroy would come back to this subject again and again, testing Macartney with questions and hypotheticals. Would Britain send another embassy soon? If so when? Would Macartney allow the viceroy to write to the emperor, confirming that George III 'would always continue in friendship with him, and in testimony of it would write to him'?[10] In response to all these requests, the British answer was firm; the ability to cement the Anglo-Chinese relationship lay in the power of the Qing court. If they would give ground in those areas identified by Macartney, then all was possible.

The viceroy forwarded to Peking a list of the challenges the British faced in trading through Canton. To this, he requested that Macartney add a note 'of general compliment and acknowledgment of the Emperor's attention to us, and anxiety for our welfare', which was duly written using young Thomas Staunton's skills in Chinese.[11] Importantly, the private reports that Zhanglin was also sending to his superiors described the British in positive terms. Coupled with the similarly upbeat assessment provided to Peking by Songyun, the stance of the imperial court began to soften. In part, this was due to their assessments that whatever differences might arise between the Chinese and their guests, the British were not likely to respond with physical force in the immediate future.[12]

Travelling now in a more relaxed atmosphere, the party set out overland, crossing between Zhejiang and Jiangxi provinces. The British took the opportunity allowed by their very gradual progress on horse and palanquin to study the local flora. Among the specimens gathered were a number of tea plants, complete with balls of earth clinging to their roots, which they carried back to Britain for assessment. Macartney hoped that this crop might 'transmit to Bengal, where I had no doubt that by the spirit and patriotism of its Government an effective cultivation of this valuable shrub will be undertaken and pursued with success'.[13]

Behind the professions of friendship and the outward diplomatic role of the mission, this acquisition underlines a hard truth behind the Macartney mission—a reality that the Chinese, with their focus on maintaining the existing order, missed. Of course, a major driver for the embassy's dispatch to Peking was to reduce Britain's trade imbalance with China, a deficit caused in part by the British thirst for tea. Ideally, this would have been resolved by improving commercial ties between the two nations and opening export opportunities. However, if Britain needed to use what was in effect industrial espionage to end its dependence on China for tea imports, then so be it.

Taking to the waterways again, the party now sailed south through a deepening winter fog. The late November nights became colder, and from the mist-shrouded landscape, temples and pagodas loomed over them in the darkness. From time to time, their vessels would collide with one another, causing delays and frustration. Yet, against this bleak background, the personal relationships between the Chinese and the British officials were growing warmer. More and more, Macartney and Zhanglin engaged as equals, without the barriers of office interfering in the way of honest discussion.

An observation that China seemed to have far more blind people than Europe was met with a frank admission that there were no facilities for the removal of glaucoma; nor was there anything like the Western standard of dealing with amputations or a host of other surgical issues. Hearing of the medical knowledge that engagement with Britain could offer, Macartney claimed, the viceroy 'and his companions seemed as if awakened out of a dream, and could not conceal their regret for the Court's coldness and indifference to our discoveries'.[14] Of course, this account of Chinese wonder at the marvels offered by Western science comes from Macartney himself and should be treated with a degree of caution.

Yet we have seen how the display of British gunnery skill on the road to Rehe produced little admiration from Zhengrui. Similarly, while at the imperial hunting grounds, when Macartney offered Heshen the opportunity to see a hot-air balloon in action, he was refused permission to launch the craft. In Zhanglin, the British were finally able to deal with someone who was able to recognise that both sides had much to gain from increased contact. Until now, whatever the relative merits of Western *v.* Chinese technology, the embassy members had reason to believe that their own intellectual curiosity outstripped that of the locals. Even if Chinese knowledge matched or surpassed the European equivalent, would it not at least be prudent for the Qing to see how advanced the foreigners were? To the British, only Zhanglin seemed capable of such breadth of thought.

In the intellectual lethargy he perceived in so many in Chinese officialdom, Macartney felt he could sense a deeper political failing in the Qing Empire. The desire among the Manchu minority to retain control, to ward off instability, was hindering their ability to innovate, adapt, and face a changing global environment in trade and increasing instability at home. An external observer, Macartney wrote, would find little to suggest that, 'all the authority and address of the Tartar Government will be able much longer to stifle the energies of their Chinese subjects. Scarcely a year now passes without an insurrection in some of their provinces'. While these rebellions were regularly quashed, 'the paroxysm is repelled, but the disease is not cured'.[15] The more the Qing tried to shore up the *status quo*, the weaker they became.

They had now reached Chenzhou. With only seven or eight days to go to Canton, the viceroy rode on ahead to make ready for their arrival. As he no longer had an outlet for his official representations, Macartney stole an opportunity to engage in some light-hearted tourism and went to view a temple not far from their route, which was carved into the cliff face overlooking the river. The excursion proved less relaxing than hoped. No doubt cursing his impulsiveness, Macartney and his companions were landed by small boat on a ledge:

> [The ledge was] so narrow that we could not stand upon it without difficulty. We were hemmed round with danger, the mountains frowned on us from on high, the precipices startled us from beneath. Our only safety seemed even in the jaws of a cavern that yawned in our front.[16]

Plunging into a tear in the rock face, they then faced innumerable rough steps gouged from the innards of the mountain, which led through the darkness to the temple above.

Scrambling upwards, eyes fixed on a single candle flickering overhead in the gloom, they were greeted at the top by a bald monk, who seemed to materialise out of the mountain. Apparently unfazed by the sudden arrival of these bizarrely dressed foreigners, he proceeded to escort them through the deep vault-like chambers hewn from the stone. A dining hall more than 25 sq. feet looked out over the river below, 'well-furnished in the taste of the country with tables and chairs highly varnished, and with many gauze and paper lanthorns of various colours, in the middle of which was suspended a glass lanthorn of prodigious size made in London'.[17] This latter odd discovery was the gift of a Canton merchant, who having acquired it, by means fair or foul, donated it to the temple.

Entering the temple itself up another flight of stairs, they faced what they were told was an incarnation of the Bodhisattva. Macartney, displaying his usual cultural sensitivity, described it as 'a gigantic image with a Saracen face, grinning horribly from a row of gilded fangs, a crown upon his head, a naked scimitar in one hand, and a fire-brand in the other'.[18] Unbelievably, he claims that the monks tending to the temple could tell him little of the origins of this deity. Surely, this was merely a case of poor translation rather than actual ignorance on the part of the clergy.

Assessing the religious practices carried out in the venue, Macartney returned to first principles, and his suspicion of outward piety is ill-concealed in his account. The monks, far from deserving respect for their sacrifice and asceticism, were to be pitied for being 'buried under a mountain and chained to a rock, to be incessantly gnawed by the vultures of superstition and fanaticism. Their condition appeared to us to be the last stage of monastic misery, the lowest degradation of humanity'. These scathing comments aside, the ambassador saw fit to make a donation to the temple, small by British standards, but 'so far above their expectations that I think it not unlikely they will insert a new clause in their litany, and heartily pray that the Chinese Government may adopt a more liberal policy, and open the country to the free inspection and curiosity of English travellers'.[19] Where statecraft had failed, perhaps divine intervention might succeed.

On 18 December, they reached Foshan, a 'very considerable town' on the outskirts of Canton.[20] For centuries, Foshan had been a major centre of ceramics production in China, and it was this industry that had led the town to develop to such significant size. That the British passed through the city was fitting and a harbinger of Foshan's future role. Although they could not know this at the time, two centuries later, Foshan would be one of the Pearl River delta cities benefiting from the policy of international reengagement engineered by Deng Xiaoping. The city is still a major manufacturing hub, with ceramics now having given way to electrical appliances. Here, the leading officers of the East India Company in Canton greeted them. Macartney was also introduced to the Chinese Hong merchants, who had imperial sanction to sell to the foreign ships that put in at Whampoa, just down river. His fellow-countrymen brought Macartney fifteen months' worth of communications that contained a wealth of information—most pressingly, confirmation of the fact that Britain and France were now at war.

The Hong merchants were eager to meet with Macartney and to offer him their support, with much exclamation of their 'regard for the English nation, and willingness to try experiments in trade'.[18] Behind their eagerness to support the goals of the embassy was a very concrete, commercial logic. Knowing that the British were dissatisfied with how things were in Canton, but also realising that their request for access to other ports had been turned down, for now, the Hong merchants understood that by giving a little bit of leeway to the foreign traders at this point, they might make the whole idea of bypassing Canton go away. This would ensure, of course, that they still held a monopoly on foreign trade between China and the West.

Resting for a day in Foshan, the British finally entered Canton on the morning of 19 December. Rowing down the Pearl River on the way to China's greatest port, they passed numerous fortifications and bodies of troops, drawn up as if for review. It was clear that 'the Chinese consider the province of Canton to be the most obnoxious to invasion from the sea', and this was a show of strength to dissuade the foreigners from any nefarious plans. The effect was ruined in Macartney's eyes by the soldiers being 'totally ignorant of our discipline, cumbersomely clothed, and armed only with matchlocks, bows and arrows, and heavy swords, awkward in the management of them, and of an unwarlike character and disposition'.[22]

Such an underwhelming display led Macartney to some quite breathtakingly callous calculations as to how costly, in human terms, an invasion of China would be. He recorded in his diary:

> The circumstance of greatest embarrassment to an invader would be their (the Chinese) immense numbers, not on account of the mischief they could do to him, but that he would find no end of doing mischief to them. The slaughter of millions would scarcely be perceived, and, unless the people themselves soon voluntarily submitted, the victor might indeed reap the vanity of destruction, but not the glory or use of dominion.[23]

That the mind of the ambassador was turning to the practicalities of invading a nation in which he was still a guest, and which had, protocol slights aside, treated him with great hospitality, betrays the exploitative core at the heart of British diplomacy of the period. One way or another, the aims of the British state and of the East India Company would be achieved, whatever the human cost.

Passing into the heart of Canton, they were met on the riverbank by Viceroy Zhanglin, the Hoppo (or head of the local customs administration), and all the principal mandarins of the city. In the conversations that followed (conducted in a format that is still beloved of Chinese officialdom today, with the two parties sat in a line of armchairs across an open room), it was apparent to Macartney that the new viceroy was making good on his promise of greater flexibility. HMS *Lion* had already received fast-track permission to come from Macao up the Pearl River to Whampoa, on the far side of the river, where foreign vessels were able to find safe berths. The very fact that the viceroy was treating these foreigners with any level of respect was surprising to the local officials; his subordinates were apparently 'totally unused to see[ing] foreigners treated with any attention'.[24]

Following a performance by a comedy troupe specially brought south from Nanjing for the occasion, the British retired to their quarters. The bulk of the embassy staff were housed in the British 'factory', or warehouse, located in the western suburbs of Canton, around what is now Shisanhang Road in modern Guangzhou. Macartney and his immediate entourage were given quarters on an island, half a mile across the river from the factory. This was almost certainly Shamian Island; if so, Macartney slept that night in one of the spots where the failures of his embassy would be most keenly felt in the late nineteenth century.

In the aftermath of the Second Opium War, a victorious Britain and France forced the humiliated Chinese to cede them territories in the major coastal cities, parcels of land known as 'concessions'. In Canton, Shamian was divided between the two foreign powers, with the British taking two-thirds of the island. In such places, Chinese law no longer applied, and the territory was a *de facto* colonial possession. Today, Shamian is still a Western bubble in the heart of modern Guangzhou, its mid-nineteenth century office buildings, churches, and warehouses complemented by a Starbucks, hotels catering to Western tourists and, until recently, the US Consulate. Had Macartney proven a little more convincing in his engagements with the Qing court, China may have been able to work with the Western economies on its own terms, and little imperial enclaves such as Shamian may never have developed.

The lead up to Christmas 1793 saw numerous visits from the viceroy and the other senior city officials. Zhanglin was still dropping hints of positivity to Macartney, but behind the scenes, the Hoppo, who feared such developments would erode his own position, thwarted all moves towards compromise. The furthering of British interests in China was out of the hands of Macartney and his colleagues; they now depended on the resolution of internal bureaucratic wrangling among their hosts.

For a man used to driving the agenda forward, Macartney found this effective helplessness galling. A despondency emerges in his diaries as he came to realise that he had no choice but to 'dismiss from my mind many flattering ideas which I had entertained at the commencement of my Embassy, of distinguishing it by some happy discovery, some signal and brilliant success, in the prosecution of our political and commercial interests in these distant parts of the world'.[25] This intensely human admission underlines how far below his original hopes the reality of engagement with China had fallen. With so little to show to date, and considering the possibility that any journey by sea now brought with it the risk of running into a hostile French warship, Macartney was also forced to abandon his long-cherished plan of proceeding on to Japan.

Instead, he set to work with Gower in establishing a convoy system to see the British ships at anchor in Canton, eighteen in all, safely back to Britain. Ironically, HMS *Lion* had already, during its journey south to Macao, managed to capture a French vessel—the very ship that was chartered to retrieve the seal hunters from New Amsterdam, who would spend a further three years in exile as a result.

Not all of the embassy members spent their last few days in China plagued by such anxiety. Freed now from most of the pressures associated with escorting the British, Qiao and Wang had decided to let their hair down, inviting Barrow to join them. The subsequent yacht-bound soirée was tactfully recorded by the latter in his diary. On arrival, he entered 'the great cabin, [and] found the ... gentlemen each with a young girl by his side, very richly dressed'. Greeted 'with a cup of hot wine from each of the ladies, who first sipped by way of pledging me', Barrow settled down to 'a most convivial evening, free from any reserve or constraint'. Just how convivial the evening must have been is perhaps best conveyed by the fact that as he was leaving, Barrow was 'particularly desired by [Wang] not to take any notice of what I had seen'.[26]

The festivities surrounding the Christmas celebrations among the British themselves that year were considerably less raucous, with the EIC factory playing host to a dinner for the embassy. Little note is made of this in Macartney's journal, beyond a scant record of the date. It would be surprising if he felt much in the way of seasonal cheer given how events had progressed. Thankfully, the dawning of 1794 brought with it some pretext for Macartney to portray the mission as a success for the audience at home. A letter arrived from Qianlong to the viceroy; its tone, at least, suggested that the emperor had become much warmer towards his foreign guests. According to Zhanglin, Qianlong wanted Macartney to be certain of 'the Emperor's satisfaction from the Embassy, his good disposition towards the English, and promises to them of his future favour and protection'.[27] These imperial sentiments had encouraged the viceroy to issue a number of proclamations, each of which promised to punish in the severest manner those who would do any harm to the Europeans or subject them to extortion.

A cynic might view this letter as remarkably convenient. Received by the local administration just before the British are to leave, no original copy of it was available in full to bring back to London. Only partially translated sections of the text survive. Indeed, the available text of the letter only references those British requests that were denied by Qianlong, where he tells Macartney to 'inform His Britannic Majesty, that what you came to ask was not refused in consequence of the Emperor's indisposition towards you, but merely as being incompatible with the Chinese customs, and consequently not in the Emperor's power to grant; neither has he at any time doubted of your good and benevolent intentions'.[28] However, members of the mission quickly spread the word that this fresh communique lifted some of the burdens to which the traders of Canton were subjected, despite providing no evidence to back up this claim. The sections of the letter supporting this claim were lost to history.

The letter as reported provided at least short-term respite for the embassy's reputation; any immediate improvement in the lot of the British in Canton could now be claimed as a direct benefit arising from Macartney's mission. In the longer term, however, the vanished paragraphs of the text created a considerable risk. If the British Government's view, informed by Macartney's claim, was that Qianlong had explicitly ordered that the Europeans receive better treatment in Canton, how would the Western powers interpret the situation should no serious improvement come to pass? Without documentary proof of what, exactly, the Chinese had promised, there was ample opportunity for misinterpretation by the British, and for the disappointment of hopes that were never justified in the first place. All of this would create a case that violence now needed to replace diplomacy.

On 2 January, and perhaps now in a lighter mood, Macartney took the opportunity to see at first-hand what the life of a foreign trader in Canton was like. Despite the modernisation that has taken place in the city since, one can still get a sense of the city Macartney experienced in the Xiguan district and along some of the backstreets near the river. Today, in the narrow canyons between crumbling shops and houses, shopkeepers hawk wares of every variety, from dried seahorses to remote control helicopters. For Macartney too, 'the streets are narrow and paved with flag-stones … full of shops and trades, and has in general a gloomy appearance, except in two or three large open squares'.[29] Qing-era Canton banned carriages from within the city walls, modern Guangzhou has done the same with motorcycles; the challenges of intense urbanisation have remained the same over the centuries.

Wandering the city, Macartney reflected on where responsibility for improving the Anglo–Chinese relationship truly lay. Professionally, he had been obliged to put the burden of improvement on the Chinese themselves, but in his heart, he knew this was a two-way challenge. Instead of engaging as equals with the Chinese and trying to learn their culture and language, 'we keep aloof from them as much as possible. We wear a dress as different from theirs as can be fashioned. We are quite ignorant of their language'. If the British could adapt to local customs and take a more open mind in their dealings in Canton, he felt this would the surest route to warmer relations between the two nations. Such an approach would bring considerable reward, as the British would 'in some few years be able to mould the China trade (as we seem to have done the trade everywhere else) to the shape that will best suit us'.

Of course, there would always be the temptation to prioritise short-term financial gain over a strategic viewpoint that would bring lasting rewards; 'there are many hasty spirits disposed to go a shorter way to work, but no shorter way will do it'. He also had sufficient self-awareness to recognise that the attitude of the British was contributing to the Chinese sense of 'jealousy' towards the foreigners. He asked in his diaries:

> Is there any country on the globe that Englishmen visit where they do not display that pride of themselves and that contempt of others which conscious superiority is apt to inspire? Can the Chinese, one of the vainest nations in the world, and not the least acute, have been blind and insensible to this foible of ours?

There had been signs enough during the embassy's stay in China that English exceptionalism was rubbing the locals up the wrong way.[30]

Perhaps this more empathetic approach to the Chinese is closer to Macartney's own personality—a snapshot of the man behind the cynical, calculating façade of the professional statesman. That honesty is in marked contrast to the dispassionate weighing of political advantage against human suffering that he also readily engaged in. Shortly after acknowledging the need for more cultural sensitivity on the part of the British, Macartney sets out in his journals the obstacles to British hegemony in China and precisely how these can be removed. The Portuguese position in Macao was, in this cold-blooded analysis, dependent on British naval power for security. Should Britain find no alternative trading hub to bring under direct control, 'it might easily be taken from them by a small force from Madras, and the compensation and irregularity be settled afterwards'. Alternatively, it may not even be necessary to force the Portuguese from their enclave; establish a British trading base on a small island such as Lantau (tellingly enough, now part of Hong Kong) and Macao 'would of itself crumble to nothing in a short time'.[31]

This could be followed by the slow strangulation of trade through Canton, where the river would be 'impassable without our permission'; militarily, Britain could easily ensure 'a whole track of Canton and its correspondencies [*sic.*] annihilated in a season'. The pressure brought to bear by the British would only increase as other imperial powers took advantage of this undermining of Chinese authority. To the north, Russia would see the predicament of the Qing and would not fail to seize the moment to expand as deep as possible into their territory.[32]

Chillingly, this speculative description of how the imperial powers could dismember China foreshadows much of what actually occurred in the nineteenth and early twentieth centuries. Macartney sets out with raw precision the path that would lead to China's 'Century of Humiliation' and to the prostration of the nation's economy to foreign exploitation. Even in 1794, it was obvious that despite the outward displays of state power, the Qing Empire was unstable and that 'the breaking-up of the power of China [no very improbable event] would occasion a complete subversion of the commerce, not only of Asia, but a very sensible change in the other quarters of the world'.

The destruction of Chinese sovereignty would lead to a power vacuum into which a disciplined foreign power could step. The supplanting of the Qing state by a Western interloper would see ports such as Ningbo, Tianjin and Zhoushan 'no longer ... barricaded; they would be attempted by all the adventurers of all trading nations, who would search every channel, creek, and cranny of China for a market, and for some time be the cause of much rivalry and disorder'.

In the middle of all the chaos, competition and confusion unleashed by the collapse of the Qing, the bounties bestowed by the China trade would go to the strongest.

> As Great Britain, from the weight of her riches and the genius and spirit of her people, is become the first political, marine, and commercial Power on the globe, it is reasonable to think that she would prove the

> greatest gainer by such a revolution as I have alluded to, and rise superior over every competitor.[33]

At the same time, Macartney was a diplomat, not some jingoistic, glory-hungry desk general; he was not blind to the costs of conflict. If the price of such adventures in human terms did not elicit his pity, he could at least appreciate the potential economic implications of the failure of the Qing state:

> Our settlements in India would suffer most severely by any interruption of their China traffic, which is infinitely valuable to them. To Great Britain, the blow would be immediate and heavy. The demand from Canton for our woollens alone cannot now be less than from £500,000 to £600,000 per annum, and there is a good reason to believe that, with proper care, it may in some years be stretched to a million.[34]

Certainly, the severing by war of commercial ties between China and India would be a heavy price to pay. Yet having weighed up the options, he still felt that a military intervention might be justified.

Still, it was not too late to guide the Anglo–Chinese relationship away from this most destructive of paths. Despite his recognition that the British must be more willing to adopt to China's culture, however, Macartney felt that the onus to avert a violent rupture was entirely on the Chinese. True, his conscience forced him to recognise that 'our present interests, our reason, and our humanity equally forbid the thought of any offensive measures with regard to the Chinese, while a ray of hope remains for succeeding by gentle ones'. Implicit in this, though, is that Qianlong and his court must allow the British to find what they felt was success. 'By my Embassy the Chinese have had, what they never had before—an opportunity of knowing us—and this must lead them to a proper way of thinking of us and of acting towards us in the future'.

From Macartney's standpoint, the British must learn about China to enable trade and their own commercial success; the Chinese, however, must come around to the British way of doing things to prevent disaster. This represents a remarkably lopsided apportion of risks and responsibilities between the two states.[35]

If consensus could be found, though, it would not be while the mission resided in China. On 9 January 1794, Macartney was rowed out to the *Lion*, accompanied by Wang and Qiao. They dined together one last time aboard the British warship. Tears were shed as the two mandarins bade farewell to the men that they had chaperoned for nearly six months. The sadness was not one-sided; despite the frustrations experienced in dealing with the byzantine ways of the Qing state, Macartney had always trusted in Wang and Qiao. Should he ever 'forget the friendship and attachment of these two worthy men, or the services they rendered us, I should be guilty of the deepest ingratitude'.[36] Deservedly, both received promotion on their return to Peking, subsequently going on to high ranks in Chinese officialdom.

The following day, Macartney and his mission sailed down the Peal river, leaving China behind to meet up with a convoy of British merchant vessels at Macao. Here, they finally bade farewell to the irrepressible Father Li, translator and fixer extraordinaire. His very service with the embassy had put him in danger of punishment by the Qing authorities, and on more than one occasion, he had exposed himself to further risk motivated only by the desire to help Macartney succeed in his mission. Even offered a position in England by his employers, he nevertheless chose to remain in the land of his birth. The British were obviously very impressed with him, a respect built on mutual affection; as late as 1802, Macartney and Li were still exchanging letters, the contact continuing as the latter spread the Catholic faith in remote corners of the Chinese interior.

Father Li's departure rounded off the embassy's activity in China. Another British diplomatic representative would not set foot in the Qing domains until 1816. By then, a new emperor would be on the throne, and the little progress made by Macartney would be entirely lost. The brief ray of hope that Britain's requests might be fulfilled through gentle persuasion had been extinguished. In the future, the demands of commerce would take precedence over those of common humanity, and the case for China accommodating British interests would be made not through diplomatic entreaties, but by force, vice, and smuggling. In this harsher environment, the possibility that the Chinese people might have the opportunity to engage with the West on their own terms, finding their own path to modernity, and being ungrudgingly afforded the respect their nation deserved, were all snuffed out. The nineteenth century would be one not only of humiliation for China, but also of shameful greed, callousness, and racism from the West, and most particularly Britain.

11

'An Old, Crazy, First-rate Man of War'

In October 2015, more than 220 years after Macartney left China, the word kowtow once more featured prominently in discussions of Anglo–Chinese relations, albeit symbolically. Newspapers, magazines, television reports, and blog posts felt this image of ceremonial submission best portrayed the attitude adopted by then-UK Prime Minister David Cameron and his government as they hosted Chinese President Xi Jinping. Britain's leaders were engaging, so many in the press claimed, in a modern-day kowtow, adopting a manner that was humiliating, subservient, and crawling. In a rare meeting of minds across the media ideological divide, *The Daily Mail* complained, 'David Cameron brings dishonour on Britain by kowtowing to China's despots', while *The Guardian* echoed, 'Kowtowing to China's despots is morally wrong and makes no economic sense'. *Fortune* magazine noted this newfound deference as an example of the UK's diminished role in the world, as 'a weakened Britain finally learns how to kowtow to Beijing'. *The Irish Times*, slightly gleefully, noted that the prime minister had 'all but kowtowed to [the] visiting Chinese leader'. Despite Cameron's best efforts to ensure a positive trade outcome for his nation, many in the press could not resist painting the episode as something of an embarrassment.

George Macartney might have feared a similar fate at the hands of the British press when he landed in Portsmouth on 5 September 1794, just under two years after setting out. Initially, he received what outwardly appeared to be a hero's welcome. George III bestowed the somewhat cumbersome title of 'the Earl of Macartney in the County of Antrim' upon his returning emissary. Such recognition signalled the readiness of British officialdom to accept Macartney's narrative about his time in China, which represented a strong defence of his mission and its results, such as they were. The failure of the embassy to achieve all its goals was pinned on the inability of Qianlong and his officials to grasp the opportunities offered by the British, due, it was claimed, to an inherent reluctance on the part of the Chinese court to embrace innovation.

Although there were some lazy cultural prejudices in this judgement, this point did reflect the political currents now swirling around the ageing Qianlong. In the twilight years of his reign, the emperor was suspicious of change; sensing this, those jockeying for power around him were anxious not to challenge the *status quo*. In such an environment, the chances of a foreign party convincing the Chinese to engage in a major policy shift on trade and international relations was always going to be unlikely. Stung by his inability to penetrate the layers of ossified tradition and complex court bureaucracy, Macartney's judgement on imperial China was petulantly damning:

> The Empire of China is an old, crazy, first-rate Man of War, which a fortunate succession of able and vigilant officers have contrived to keep afloat for these hundred and fifty years past, and to overawe their neighbours merely by her bulk and appearance. But whenever an insufficient man happens to have the command on deck, adieu to the discipline and safety of the ship.[1]

In his view, policy in China suffered from the classic flaw of autocracy, derived as it were wholly from the emperor's own views. When he was resistant to change, so too was the state. Moreover, should the emperor in future prove weak, so would China.

Cynical though one might be about Macartney's efforts to blame his hosts for the lack of meaningful progress, he had some justification in feeling aggrieved. Grappling with disappointment and trying to make sense of his confusing engagement with the imperial court, it must have seemed bizarre to Macartney that the Chinese flitted between warm hospitality and cold indifference, apparently on a whim. When he had arrived, Qianlong's officials extended great courtesy and respect to him, hosting his team and defraying all their expenses. Yet after only a few weeks, he found 'they wish us to be gone, refuse our requests without reserve or complaisance, precipitate our departure, and dismiss us dissatisfied'.[2]

In subsequent letters to Dundas, Macartney repeatedly points to these obstructionist tendencies among court mandarins as the primary cause of his failures. In particular, he pointed out Fukang'an as being a major agitator against engagement with Britain. Not only, Macartney reasoned, was his opinion of the British poisoned by his experience of engaging with foreign traders while viceroy of Canton, but in his new role as viceroy of Sichuan, he was engaged in combat with the Gurkhas over Tibet. The erroneous reports that the British had encouraged (either actively or tacitly) the Gurkhas to expand north were no doubt to the forefront of the mandarin's mind, regardless of Macartney's protestations of innocence.

However, this only made the emperor's softening stance shortly after the British departed Peking even more surprising. 'No sooner have we taken our leave of them than we find ourselves treated with more studied attentions, more marked distinctions, and less constraint than before'.[3] The mission had achieved some milestones very late in the day, but Macartney could not figure out why. What had caused this shift in mood? Had the more incalcitrant members of the court been sidelined?

In fact, the most likely answer is that as the embassy proceeded south to Canton, first Songyun and then Zhanglin were reporting back that Macartney was more respectful and less difficult than he had appeared in Rehe. As a result, Qianlong's attitude towards the British lightened. As a result, Macartney could now at least point to the slight easing of conditions for British traders in Canton to justify his mission. Yet this feat of persuasion, if that is what it was, could not be repeated. George III's ambassador had stumbled upon a result, almost by accident. Such a lack of clarity bode ill for the future of Anglo–Chinese relations.

Having dispatched the embassy, the British Government was also committed to portraying the venture as a success. Given the paltry return on the EIC's investment, it was vital that the politicians began to shape the conversation around the mission, to highlight successes and to dampen any disappointment among the merchants and consumers of England. Written accounts by the various members of the expedition, including Macartney, were collated together by Staunton, and in 1797, this work was released as the official story of the embassy. Painting a dignified picture of Britain's noble servants struggling against foreign intransigence, persevering and ultimately achieving significant success, the book was woven through with excuses to why some objectives, notably the cession of an island territory to Britain, remained unfulfilled.

Unfortunately, by the time this work reached the market, public opinion had already turned. Initially, the public had been enthralled by the dispatches sent back by Macartney, poring over descriptions of how warmly their representative had been welcomed on the far side of the world. As time passed, though, the news became more and more pessimistic, and in the relatively open press culture of eighteenth-century Britain, the downward trend in relations between Macartney and his hosts seeped unchecked into the public realm. From July 1794, when Macartney's communiques from his journey south began to feature, popular perceptions became increasingly negative. Each new report seemed to suggest a steady decline in the prospects of concessions from China. Feedback coming from the EIC's agents in Canton was also bleak. While the Company had no wish to publicly embarrass the embassy, its employees were numerous, well-connected, and lacked the sort of discretion typical of politicians or diplomats.

The *Gentleman's Magazine*, which had initially issued breathless accounts of the refinement and splendour of the court in Peking, was by this point portraying the whole venture as being little more than a disaster. Details about the spat over the kowtow were widely available as was news of the sudden departure of the embassy from Peking. When added to Macartney's failure to achieve any solid gains, and the reports of the tight controls over the members of the mission, the claims that the British had enjoyed a warm welcome rang very hollow.

As the years passed, many of the unofficial accounts of the expedition reinforced this initial panning in the press. Leaking out following the publication of Staunton's book, some of these were bluntly negative and contributed to increasing hostility in Britain towards China. Aeneas Anderson's *Narrative of the Voyage to China* was less than complimentary to the host nation, portraying a kingdom ruled by officials wedded to tradition and unable to innovate in even the smallest measure. In terms of assessing the embassy's own work, Anderson was similarly scathing, summarising their experience as having 'entered Peking like paupers; we remained in it like prisoners and we quitted it like vagrants'.[4]

This jaundiced view found echoes in the writings of Johan Christian Huttner, a German musician who accompanied Macartney. Unimpressed by the level of scientific knowledge in China, Huttner believed that the nation lacked even basic standards of expertise in areas as diverse as maritime navigation, architecture, sanitation, and leatherworking. He was sceptical, too, about the powers of the emperor; far from being the enlightened despot imagined by European philosophers, 'the old man who now reigns is deceived by his courtiers, much like any other sovereign'.[5]

A military officer accompanying the mission, Samuel Holmes, was equally scathing about China's military capabilities. Far from fielding a modern, capable army, Holmes claimed that the soldiers he had seen panicked when the British artillery had fired blank rounds as part of an exhibition. Clearly, His Majesty's Forces had little to fear from their counterparts in the service of the Son of Heaven.

Ironically, the most complete demolition of the notion of Chinese superiority came from the mission member who had most immersed himself in the nation's culture. After achieving a high degree of fluency in Mandarin, Thomas Staunton built on this experience through a number of posts with the East India Company in Canton between 1798 and 1816. Arguably, there was no one in contemporary Britain or its empire with a deeper understanding of China, its internal political forces, cultural norms, and economic trends. In 1800, Staunton began translating the *Da Qing Luli*, the Chinese criminal code, so that Britons operating in China might at least have some knowledge of the legal framework that constrained them. On publication, the preface to the work included a paragraph making clear what Staunton thought about the relative positions of Britain and China:

> The short residence in China of Lord Macartney's embassy … was amply sufficient to discover that the superiority over other nations, in point of knowledge and virtue, which the Chinese have long been accustomed to assume to themselves and which some of their European historians have too readily granted them, was in great measure fallacious.[6]

Some of the unauthorised accounts of the embassy were less bleak, however. Published in 1807, Barrow's *Narrative of the Public Life of Lord Macartney* did its best to paint the mission to China as a success. Barrow claimed that before the mission had left Britain, the home secretary, Henry Dundas, had 'concluded that if such an embassy should answer no other good purpose than that of procuring a due respect for the national character, and protection for the trading part of its subjects who might visit China, the expense would not be ill bestowed'.[7] By such measures, Macartney had been successful, but this was a remarkably low bar for an enormously expensive expedition, even accounting for the fact the EIC was to defray the costs. Such a goal would be the bare minimum expected from an embassy of this type, and it is questionable whether even this was achieved, to say nothing of the more extensive list of goals we know that Dundas had set Britain's envoy.

Barrow's attempts to cast the embassy in a positive light continue in his handling of the actual kowtow question. Claiming that whether a European delegation agrees to perform the ceremony 'may not materially affect the issue of the negotiations,' Barrow notes that Macartney was, through his own abilities and the flexibility of the instructions given to him, able 'to devise such means as might be satisfactory to the court of China, without compromising the honour of his sovereign'.[8] Lesser diplomats would have seriously embarrassed themselves, Barrow concludes, but Macartney was able to divine the ideal settlement.

This revisionism extended to the question of whether the British had offered the emperor a tribute. Despite the fact that Macartney acknowledged that banners announcing his arrival in China describe him as a tribute-bearing ambassador, Barrow's account challenges this. Admitting that their own translator told the British that the banner described the mission in such submissive terms, Barrow claims, despite lacking any skills in the Chinese language, that the translator was wrong. Attempting to reproduce the relevant characters in his printed account, Barrow breaks down his translation of the offending phrase, claiming it merely announced Macartney as 'The English Ambassador bringing precious things to the Emperor of China'.[9] Where (or whether) Barrow sourced the Chinese language skills to make this claim so confidently is not revealed, but this was a conscious effort to make the mission appear more resolute in their opposition to the Chinese demands for submission. After all, if so many years later there had still been no tangible successes that could be attributed to the mission, would it not be better if this was seen as the result of doughty British opposition to foreign arrogance, rather than a failure to win over Qianlong?

Such a tack helped Barrow gloss over even the most obvious of failings. Macartney's objective of securing an island as a trading hub for Britain, 'however desirable such an object might have been ... was not likely to be complied with at that time'. Again, it is claimed this was through no fault of the ambassador or his staff; rather Barrow pins the blame on one of the emperor's officials, never identified, 'in whose recollection were still fresh those unfavourable circumstances to the English character'.[10] If only the mandarins had not been so biased against the British, Barrow claimed, they would have been alive to the opportunities that ceding their nation's territory would apparently provide.

Beyond the post-mission spin and criticism, the embassy did have some concrete successes. Macartney's arrival in Rehe, and the positive impression he made on Qianlong, at least helped to differentiate the British from other European nations. This was particularly important in the context of the ongoing French Revolution, which caused great alarm when reports of its occurrence began to filter through to the Chinese authorities. Given that Britain and France were soon to be at war, this distinction would have proven vital should the naval forces of the two sides have come to blows in East Asian waters. Interestingly, Zhanglin was eager to make clear to Macartney that the Qing Empire now also recognised the difference between the British and Americans.

The duties on shipments between Canton and Macao were temporarily reduced, although it was made clear that this lower level of charges would not be permanent. Zhanglin undertook to ensure that Britain's merchants were treated fairly in Canton, and the idea of allowing the foreign sailors to establish a hospital in the city would be considered. So too would the possibility of the British being able to learn Chinese and to hire locals as teachers. British merchants were also now able to petition the emperor through the viceroy of Canton, meaning they no longer had to suffer mistreatment at the hands of the Hoppo without having an avenue for complaint. The arrival of the British in Peking had also increased demand for the textiles and consumer goods the foreigners had brought with them.

Most importantly, of course, the embassy established formal contact between the governments of China and Britain for the first time. Macartney could also point to the fact that his team had brought back samples of tea, mulberry, and silkworms, with the aim of allowing replication of tea and silk production in other regions, most notably India.

The expedition had collected information on the north China coast to an extent never before equalled and contributed greatly to the deepening of Western understanding of Chinese society and government. In military terms, the intelligence gathered highlighted how Asia's comparatively stable strategic situation, compared at least to seventeenth- and eighteenth-century Europe, had meant that armaments and other martial technologies in China had fallen far behind the West. Many accounts of the mission mention city fortifications, which were usually visually impressive, rising 40 or 50 feet into the air, and incorporating defensive towers and fortified gates. Yet against an army equipped with modern artillery, such brick-built strongpoints would not last long. Similarly, while the Chinese had muskets and other firearms, the bow was still very much in frontline use with the imperial military. So too was armour, which by the eighteenth century had been largely abandoned on European battlefields, offering little protection against musket fire.

To Macartney's mind, it was even questionable whether a senior Qing general had 'ever [seen] a firelock in his life'; it was certainly a fact that during his travels in Qianlong's realm, he never saw 'anything above a matchlock among all the troops in China'.[11] Those garrisons, which turned out in a show of strength during the embassy's journey south, had failed to impress with their discipline, the troops having a 'slovenly, unmilitary air ... their quilted boots and long petticoats made them look heavy, inactive and effeminate'.[12] Even the most highly trained soldiers, members of the Manchu elite, still held on to a romantic ideal of nomadic warfare and saw the bow as the weapon of a gentleman (despite Qianlong's own use of firearms). Manchu warriors were shocked when told that in Europe muskets were now ubiquitous.

Despite the sense of superiority they felt in relation to martial matters, the British still found much to admire in China, both in terms of culture and the arts, but also in how the country was managed and the advanced knowledge developed there in many sciences. While in the maritime sphere the Chinese were incapable of navigating the open sea, Staunton was struck by how delicate and finely worked their compasses were, revealing a deep reverence and appreciation of its role in seafaring. Indeed, not only did the Chinese lavish much attention and care on the devices themselves (which, Staunton noted, pointed south rather than north) but they also worked the compass into religious art, such as at the shrine of the god of the eastern sea at Taku. Staunton also provides numerous, and admiring, accounts of Chinese ingenuity and scientific enquiry in other areas, such as the use of alum to filter drinking water on the Hai.

The embassy also provided early observations of Chinese Buddhism from a foreign perspective. Although Britain had been involved in India since the beginning of the seventeenth century, the fact that Buddhism was by that point confined to only a few pockets on the subcontinent meant that the Macartney mission was largely ignorant of the faith when they encountered it in its adopted home to the north. Perhaps unsurprisingly, given the Irish background of so many of the mission's members, the similarities between the religion the Chinese knew as *fo* and Catholicism were striking. Viewing a chapel near the Sarira pagoda in Rehe, Macartney could not resist making a slightly disparaging comparison:

> The sanctimonious deportment of the priests, and the solemnity used in the celebration of their mysteries, have no small resemblance to the holy mummeries of the Romish Church as practised in those countries where it is rich and powerful.[13]

Seeing the faith's celibate monks, colourful temples, iconography, and extensive rituals, it is understandable that Staunton and other members of the mission would repeat a mistake often made by contemporary preachers working in China. They, too, assumed that the faith was the remnants of the early Nestorian church that had flourished in China for two distinct periods between the seventh and tenth centuries, and then again between the thirteenth and fourteenth centuries.

The pioneering contact between the two countries also produced a tiny but important spur to the study of the Chinese language and culture in Britain. When the embassy had set out, Mandarin translators were found only on the European mainland. Now, Thomas Staunton had developed significant skills in the language and had crucially shown that it was not impossible for a European to learn. His linguistic abilities were still being put to good use in 1806, when a letter written by him successfully argued the defence case for a British sailor facing the death penalty for an accidental death in Canton.

Whatever the value of the mission's observations on science, society, religious faith, political organisation, or economic activity, over two centuries later, it is the human element—the recognition of humankind's commonality across the widest of cultural divides—that is still most striking.

William Alexander surpassed his official role as mission artist, capturing not only the fortifications and palaces that provided the backdrop for imperial life, but also documenting the dress, hairstyles, tools, and accommodation for whole strata of Chinese society. Indeed, his depictions—which ranged across ages, incomes, and genders—provide a depth of observation that is rare even among contemporary Chinese sources. Through his watercolours and sketches, and through the many private diaries and published accounts his colleagues produced, the European public got a glimpse of everyday life in China, the country of peasants, merchants, bureaucrats, and foot soldiers.

Despite the obvious assumed position of cultural superiority that both sides adopted in this encounter, there are occasions when one can sense the surprise with which a shared humanity is suddenly recognised. During the voyage upriver from Tianjin, Macartney himself noted how he and his colleagues were subject to 'the great curiosity and attention' of a number of mandarins who 'were very inquisitive, lively, and talkative'. In that moment, as stiff ceremony melted away, he realised how his Chinese companions were 'totally void of that composure, gravity, and seriousness which we had been taught to believe constituted a part of the Chinese character'.[14] To the great surprise of the British, the Chinese mandarins were just as human as they were.

Sadly, for Macartney and his colleagues, but even more so for Anglo–Chinese relations, philosophical reflections meant little to a public more interested in consumer goods, export opportunities, or simple tales of oriental exoticism. With the mission's perceived failure came a substantial change in the views on China in British society. Where once China was seen as something of a utopia, particularly among the intelligentsia who imagined a compliant population overseen by a wise and benevolent despot, the experience described by the members of the embassy suggested a land steeped in superstitious ignorance, unwilling and unable to accept norms that the Western definitions of modernity required. For many, it was a stubborn aloofness on the part of the Chinese, sure of their superiority in science, culture, and in the very nature of their society, that had led Britain's efforts to fall so flat. The Qing, such reasoning went, felt themselves so sophisticated that 'if the court of Peking was to be swayed by splendour, much more ought to have been done to have accomplished it than was done'.[15]

For most, the response to the mission suggested only two things. The first was that China was clearly not an advanced paradise governed in perfect harmony, but rather backward and totally out of step with the West's vision of a modern state. The second was that Macartney's attempts at diplomacy had failed, and that Britain had, at the very least, been gravely insulted. Greater firmness would be called for in future.

Macartney's audience with Qianlong therefore represents one of those great missed opportunities that history tantalises us with from time to time. For the most part, the encounter seems to ask difficult questions of the British side and typically invites regrets at yet another example of Western arrogance. What if Macartney had not insisted on formal recognition of the very real power that his embassy represented? What if he had kowtowed? Would Britain have achieved its primarily commercial goals in China more smoothly, driving forward its free-trade agenda unblemished by the stain of violence that would later colour its activities in the treaty ports and Hong Kong?

This is a fair question. It is striking how obstinate the British were in refusing to follow the well-tread path towards acceptance taken by other Europeans, notably the Portuguese. Lisbon's stronghold in Macao, after all, had been secured through the provision of timely naval support for the Ming Dynasty, and the regular payment of rent. How much more valuable would the power of the world's finest navy have been, even to a power as land-focussed as China? Barrow noted that it was known the Qing were struggling with a piracy problem around the time of the Macartney mission. The island of Taiwan was also regularly rebelling, and the application of significant naval power there could have been extremely helpful to its mainland rulers. Yet no such offer was ever made or even contemplated. If the kowtow might have opened up China's markets, what rewards would have greeted the lending of only a few British warships and crew?

Such responses were never likely when the British failed to do even the most basic of diplomatic follow-up. When still in China, Macartney was encouraged, both by foreigners resident there and a number of the officials from Qianlong's court, to ensure Britain sent future emissaries. Macartney seized on such suggestions as proof of how his mission had indeed been a success. Failing a full embassy, it was suggested that a suitably authorised person might be dispatched by the Crown to take up residence in Canton or even Macao. This would allow for more rapid contact with Qianlong's court while not threatening the *status quo* accepted by the Qing, possibly increasing the likelihood of convincing the emperor of the merits offered by the British vision of Anglo–Chinese relations. The ambassador could see the value of such an appointment, recognising that 'nothing is more likely to contribute essentially to the promotion of our interests'.[16]

Yet it would be 1816 before a British ambassador next appeared in China. In the meantime, Qianlong had relinquished the throne, succeeded in 1796 by the Jiaqing Emperor. This new ruler faced steadily increasing instability throughout the empire, and against such a backdrop, the appetite for innovation and reform was low. The nation shied from further engagement with the outside world.

Yet against the wider backdrop of the historic rise of the British Empire, and the comparative decline of the Qing, Macartney's failure to achieve the goals set for him was of little consequence. The unrestricted access of British commerce to China was delayed by fifty years, and with it came the favourable trading terms and land acquisition that this first embassy had sought. The manner in which Macartney's goals were later achieved by his successors was in fact the greatest failing of his diplomacy. While their first mission had tried to employ negotiation and engagement, China would finally yield to British demands made down the barrel of a gun. The price for Macartney's failure was paid by the dead and injured in subsequent Anglo–Chinese conflicts, the wasting away of those addicted to Britain's opium, and the misery of the countless peasants and urban poor toiling away in conditions of economic exploitation created or strengthened by the activities of foreign imperial powers.

We must remember, though, that there were two parties involved in this diplomatic engagement. If Macartney's inability to swallow his pride and engage in the gestural diplomacy of the kowtow represented a dereliction in his duty, how much worse was Qianlong's failure to divine what the growth of British interest in East Asia meant for his realm? There has been considerable academic debate on what role court ceremony played in binding Qianlong to a set response, much of it tied with the question of whether Western observers are guilty of Orientalism when examining the approach taken by the Qing. Diplomatic protocol evolved in China through the channel of court rituals such as the kowtow; the Qing conversed with the outside world in this language of gesture and procedure. A key question then is whether by the time Macartney appeared in Rehe, this formalistic approach had led to a situation where, in the words of the historian James Hevia, 'law and economic activity collapsed into culture'.[17]

We must also wonder whether Qianlong was constrained by his need to use international engagement to shore up support at home. By the late eighteenth century, was the kowtow and the offering of tribute simply a means of displaying Qianlong's power to a domestic audience? If this was the case, by the time the Qing came up against the entwined opportunity and threat offered by contact with the West, the sophisticated structures for handling foreign engagement and signalling China's power had withered into meaningless symbolism. They were now for internal consumption only, devoid of concrete effects on the handling of foreign relations.

However, no matter how constricted Qianlong and his officials may have been, we should not, in examining the results of the Macartney mission, deprive the Qing state and its leaders of agency. After all, Qianlong ruled over a sophisticated realm, with a complex and efficient bureaucracy, a well-developed transport and communications network, and considerable military clout. Such a state and its servants could not fail to see the warning signs of Western ascendancy in the military and naval sciences or in the economic heft that European powers such as Britain now boasted. To suggest otherwise—that the Chinese simply assumed that the British were ignorant barbarians who could pose no possible threat—is to do the Qing a disservice.

Even the most insular mandarin would understand that the foreigners had sailed across the open ocean from the other side of the world. We know that as they sailed north from Zhoushan to Tianjin, the officials they met were astonished that they could have sailed beyond sight of the coast. As they travelled overland to Rehe, Chinese military officers had many opportunities to see the drilling of the British redcoats accompanying the embassy, to witness how their artillery teams handled modern cannon, or to test the edge of blades made with Birmingham steel. No competent military officer, Manchu or Han, could have possibly failed to understand the potential such technology offered on the field of battle. Although Zhengrui and others feigned indifference, this may have been a reluctance to publicly acknowledge what was privately recognised—China had fallen behind in feats of arms.

Similarly, in economic terms, there was ample evidence that the Europeans would increasingly tilt the nature of China's trade with the outside world. By the end of the eighteenth century, foreign traders had been buying and selling through Canton for nearly 200 years. Over the course of that time, China's rulers would have seen the nature of that trade change and the volume of exports increase. Even taking into account the traditional aversion for commerce among the empire's elite, even considering the scale of China's economy, the amount of silver that flowed through Canton and into the coffers of the state (despite the sums diverted into the pockets of corrupt officials) must have been noticeable and noteworthy. How could this growing trade with a new partner develop without any senior mandarins questioning what sort of political and military power underpinned the economy that could buy so much tea, porcelain, and silk?

The traditional view is that in splendid, arrogant isolation, China did not see anything of any value in Europe, and neither the emperor nor his officials could wrap their heads around the idea that the world abroad could offer anything of serious value. While Qianlong's own letters to George III support this view, it is an overly simplistic take on China's international economic ties, and it gives too much credence to a Sinocentric perspective that the Qing might have espoused but did not fully believe. Despite Qianlong's claims that the self-sufficient Chinese 'have no use for your country's manufactures', China did need, and indeed sought out, goods from abroad, things that could not be readily acquired at home. The nature of these products varied from the mundane, such as basic textiles like cotton, to the frivolous, like the clocks and 'toys' beloved of the imperial court.

This was not a recent development, either. Much of China's engagement with steppe tribes in Central Asia, not merely during the Qing period, but even stretching back to the Tang dynasty (618–690 CE, 705–907 CE), was driven precisely by a recognition that these areas offered something that China needed, particularly horses and certain crops. Indeed, Central Asian horses were so important to the Chinese that scenes of Qianlong receiving them as tribute feature in paintings from his rule. Trade with these peoples was bidirectional, with tea, among other items, going out into the steppes. If Chinese dynasties throughout history could see how engagement with foreign nations could sometimes be necessary, it seems unlikely that Qianlong and his mandarins could not grasp what was to be gained from trading with Europeans.

In this light, it is important to remember that court ceremonies, particularly the *kowtow*, were viewed as a guarantor of the security ties between the Qing court and a range of 'barbarian' peoples along China's borders. Perhaps then, when Macartney refused to engage in the prescribed ceremonies, this may have caused concerns among the more military-minded of Qianlong's officials? Yet if the British were identified as a potential threat, why was no consideration given as to how the Chinese military might deal with the superior battlefield technologies possessed by the foreigners, should the need ever arise? Did the Qing consider how they might convince the British to supply such advanced weaponry?

Outwardly, it would appear not. Instead, Qianlong's military officers and civil servants seemed to have pretended that the arrival of the British lacked any significance, that China's assumed position at the apex of global affairs remained unchallenged. Staunton notes that despite their many hours spent in conversation with the ambassador and his team, Qiao and Wang betrayed little interest in the outside world. While they were personally interested in the individuals who had travelled so far to visit China, they asked very few questions about Britain or Europe or about how other societies were organised or how other economies functioned. Goods and commodities imported into China became associated, in the minds of these mandarins, with Canton, not with the countries from which they came. What interest they did show in lands beyond China tended to be confined to the fantastic and the extreme, focusing on the exotic or fanciful, not the factual.

How could such intelligent men as Qiao and Wang, Zhengrui and Heshen, possibly see the capabilities displayed by the British, yet remain ignorant to what this meant for China's place in the world? They may well have known precisely what the Macartney embassy represented yet were reluctant to be the first to voice these fears. To do so would have brought into question the entire edifice of state power in China, by suggesting that Qianlong was not the apogee of global power and, by definition, the Son of Heaven. As such, he could not have a divine mandate, and every element of his legitimacy was thus undermined, as was the very structure of the Qing state.

In attempting to prolong this fantasy of Chinese exceptionalism, the mandarins had a willing accomplice in the emperor. He echoes the traditional views of foreigners in a poem he himself composed about the occasion of his meeting with Macartney. Noting that while the British had come in sincerity, Qianlong was unimpressed by the goods they brought in tribute, which were not precious, but rather curiosities whose qualities had been much exaggerated. Ultimately, the British were welcome to his court, but the unimpressive nature of the gifts they offered to him would seem, he claimed, to place them as inferiors to the Mongols or the Burmese in the context of a Chinese-centred international order.

Yet the engagement between the Qing and the peoples of the steppes or southeast Asia was nowhere near as fraught and complicated as the handling of Macartney's visit had been. In the sensitivity surrounding the occasion, it was clear that Qianlong recognised that the British were very different, and potentially far more dangerous. However, as his rule rested on the mandate of heaven, he could not explicitly acknowledge that China might be in danger of being surpassed.

Perhaps a more spectacular offering of gifts might have convinced him to acknowledge the necessity of dealing with the British. Certainly, there was a mixed message given by the embassy in the areas of trade and technology. As we have seen, a number of different perspectives informed the selection of gifts destined for Qianlong and the tenor of the mission as a whole. There was the 'best of British' approach favoured by the government, which sought to encourage the Chinese to buy more of industrial Britain's output, even if these were less glamourous, mass-produced items that commanded relatively low prices, such as steel blades and basic pots.

From the perspective of the East India Company, the emphasis was to be, in the first instance, on doing no harm to the current economic position it enjoyed in China. Further to this, greater commercial opportunities were to be welcomed, but only if they were for goods or commodities that the Company dealt in. Macartney's own position, in contrast, was far less commercial. He simply wanted to wow Qianlong with the best technology that the West had to offer, irrespective of source, and establish

Britain as an equal partner for the Chinese. The envoy's own starting point was to create an incredible spectacle for the Chinese court and, from this position of perceived technical brilliance, to build a strong political and commercial position.

By attempting to make all three arguments simultaneously, the mission failed to make any successfully. In retrospect, though, it is not difficult to see that Macartney's favoured approach was the poorest one. For a start, it is obvious that the items specially chosen to display before the emperor failed to astonish the senior members of the court. The clocks, the curios, and the lanterns were all things Qianlong and his mandarins had simply seen before.

The British were also prevented from deploying their most impressive tools. Clearly, the drill by British gunners was significantly better than their Chinese counterparts, but they were denied an opportunity to showcase these skills before the emperor or his inner court. The strength of European technology was thus never effectively communicated in a manner beyond all doubt, in particular to Qianlong himself. While Zhengrui, Qiao, and Wang could not have ignored the fact that their guests had a leading edge in a number of areas, the mandarins were reluctant to admit to the foreigners that there was any realm in which China's technology was bested by the equivalent from abroad. It is unlikely that they would have been more honest with the emperor, when such admissions essentially undermined the legitimacy of the state. Yet had Qianlong been confronted by this reality, it may have made the process of engaging with the British easier.

Ultimately, the embassy needed to personally impress Qianlong, to provide him with the conditions necessary to openly recognise that the West was equal to, and indeed pulling ahead of, China in a number of technological spheres. We know he was unimpressed in the displays that the embassy set up for his amusement in Peking. Did the emperor, returning to court, spend many hours considering the immense amount of research and study captured by the clockwork churnings of the model solar system? Did the skill and craftsmanship embodied in the lenses, set up for Qianlong to view the heavens, suggest to the emperor or his officials the advanced nature of European technology? It would appear not. Yet how could he? When the great lens was being installed in the Summer Palace for use in examining the heavens, even the attendant court officials could not understand why such care was being taken with this delicate piece of glass; after all, if it was damaged, could the foreigners not simply make another? Part of the problem with Macartney's approach was that the items he chose to display were not purely impressive by themselves; rather, they were symbols of the advanced nature of Western economic and productive systems. The lack of familiarity among Chinese officials with economies other than their own also meant that they failed to understand the role that automation and production technologies were beginning to play in European manufacturing. They thus fundamentally failed to grasp that the true advantage held by the British lay not in the product itself, but in the advances in production that created such a wonder.

Macartney must have known that he was gambling heavily on the showiness of the gifts he was presenting. Doubts about the quality of their wares undermined British confidence in their position from quite early on. All through the accounts of the voyage, there is a thread of concern that perhaps these items were a little sub-par. When the fleet arrived off Tianjin, Macartney, almost in a panic, rustled up some additional items of value from his staff to bolster the impact of their presentation for the emperor. A telescope was requisitioned from one of the embassy officials, while a powerful lens, 'Parker's Great Lens', 12–16 inches in diameter and brought to China by Captain Mackintosh of the *Hindoostan*, specifically for sale in the market there as a private venture, was bought at cost for inclusion in the diplomatic goody bag. Tellingly, Macartney included this latter 'object of singular curiosity' because he feared that if Mackintosh sold the lens on the open market, Chinese merchants might later present it to the imperial court, which would undermine the perceived quality of the British offering.

Indeed, it was the more basic items in the embassy's inventory, some brought to China for sale, but many simply carried as personal belongings, which fired the imagination of Chinese observers the most. Ironically, when the gifts destined for the emperor were first unpacked in the presence of a number of court officials, Macartney himself noted that special attention was paid to 'little articles of use and convenience that Europeans are accustomed to', with, as we have seen, swords, clothing, and musical instruments examined in detail.[18] Wherever the embassy went, officials sought gifts of the blades, watches, and pistols, which they saw British officers carrying.

During one of his long, freewheeling chats with Zhanglin on their journey south, Macartney casually moved to light his companion's pipe. To do so, he took a bottle of phosphoric from his pocket and kindled a match from it. This was astonishing to the viceroy, as 'the singularity of a man carrying fire in his fob without damage startled him a good deal'.[19] While this incident became almost a cliché in Western accounts of the mission, an example of how the West was harnessing scientific knowledge in a way that seemed beyond the Chinese, the commercial lessons offered in the exchange were missed. Simply put, Macartney did not structure his mission around the opportunity to sell the Chinese phosphorous fobs or other basic items of British manufacture.

Perhaps had they done so, the ambassador and his team may have created a more lasting impression on their hosts and a more comfortable channel for the Qing to engage with the West. Macartney admitted as much when he later pointed to an apparent uptick in demand for British woollen goods in China. He claimed this was due to his mission, failing to remember that he had eschewed focusing on such mundane products. By winning the respect of the Chinese in the marketplace, the British would have found a gentle entrée into the Qing state's consciousness. Even if the scientific advances represented by the telescopes and planetariums were ignored by Qianlong's court, they might recognise that Britain was far in advance of China in a wide range of key areas, from consumer goods to maritime navigation or, most clearly, military capability.

The technological gap was clear; all that was needed was a way to make acknowledging it politically acceptable to the Chinese. We know, despite his public words, Qianlong was aware of this deficit and could see how his own nation had fallen behind. Behind closed doors, he feared that the British might react violently to his refusal to allow an embassy to be permanently assigned to Peking. Given their brute strength, their lack of restraint, and their existing record of attacking their European opponents at sea, he could see cause for caution in his handling of these foreigners. There was a serious risk that, if disappointed, they might either seek to do harm to the empire directly or effectively muscle in on the trade between the other European nations and China, either cutting out the competition or charging protection money. It also did not escape the emperor's notice that in a confrontation with the British, his own troops may not fare that well. Writing to his officials in charge of coastal garrisons, Qianlong decried the poor training of troops in these key locations and their lack of discipline, demanding the situation be rectified. There was more to fear than future invasions; Qianlong was genuinely concerned that Macartney's embassy itself would have sufficient firepower to overwhelm any troops sent against it, should relations deteriorate to such a drastic extent.[20]

In fact, the audience between Macartney and Qianlong, far from convincing the emperor that the British were essentially harmless 'unsophisticates', merely stoked his fears about their potential threat. Not only did they have a martial edge, but the seemingly crafty way that Macartney had sought to handle the issue of the kowtow revealed what, to Chinese minds, was an inherent deviousness in these people from the Western Ocean. When Zhanglin and Songyun later reported that Macartney was more reliable than first assumed, Qianlong's decided that the duties owed by a particular British ship currently docked at Macao be waived. Giving some ground now would be likely to keep the British sweet in future.

The immediate threat was recognised, even if the British did not have the cultural nous to approach the emperor and his officials in terms that would be acceptable domestically. Why, then, did the Qing elite not at least develop a strategic approach for handling the British in the longer term? Could they really have hoped that these most demanding of foreigners would stay away? Macartney himself was probably close to divining what truly prevented the Chinese leadership from reacting to this emerging challenge.

> The personal character of the Ministers, alarmed by the most trifling accident, the aversion they may naturally have to sudden innovation, especially at the Emperor's late period of life, and some recent events ill understood, joined, perhaps, to a paltry intrigue, have been among the chief obstacles to my business.[21]

Unfortunately for Macartney, for Qianlong, and for China's future generations, the British embassy had arrived at an inopportune moment—a point where the space for innovation and reform in China was particularly constrained as the court waited for one emperor's reign to end and for another's to begin. Under such circumstances, none of Qianlong's officials was willing to risk unleashing the social and economic forces that real reform would bring, especially when change would be driven by the most unpredictable of engines, foreign contact.

Given these elements, perhaps we should resist the desire to portray the meeting between Qianlong and Macartney as a lesson in the need for cultural sensitivity. Viewed purely through the lens of power perception, this audience is seen for what it actually was—not the meeting of a coloniser and a colonised, but the collision of two empires, predominant in their own theatres, but also both constrained by domestic requirements. Following the Seven Years' War, with its ongoing gains in India, and with the simultaneous collapse of the old order in France, Britain seemed unfettered in its domination of the West. Napoleon was, at this point, still merely an artillery commander, fighting the Siege of Toulon. Future strategic rivalries with Russia and Prussia were not even on the horizon. The idea that anyone could have seriously challenged the British Empire would have seemed laughable to Macartney. He could not have possibly engaged in a ceremony that would have suggested to any potential critics at home that he had failed to maintain British dignity on the world stage.

Yet Qianlong and his court would have felt the same way about China, at least until the British had arrived. In its immediate strategic hinterland, China was unsurpassed. From Korea and Japan in the north-east, to Central Asia in the west, and Vietnam in the south, the primacy of the Qing dynasty was recognised, at least in theory, by all the other Asian states. The Europeans with whom they had developed official contact—the Portuguese, Dutch, French, and Russians—had all accepted the ceremonial requirements imposed when visiting the Chinese court, to a greater or lesser degree. For these foreigners, the kowtow may have been only an empty gesture, but for Qianlong and his predecessors, it allowed their guests from afar to fit into the overall structure governing China's relations with the wider world. The willingness of foreign dignitaries, both Asian and European, to conform to Qing court norms also helped to shore up the domestic legitimacy of the emperor. The British had failed to understand that by refusing to align with the ritual architecture Qianlong and his subjects imposed on the world, they were not simply providing a diplomatic challenge; they were also threatening the very stability of the Qing state.

The apparently all-powerful, divinely chosen Qianlong was not as splendidly isolated in his position of authority as was commonly believed in Europe. Rather, as Macartney understood, he was the leader of a 'tyranny of a handful of Tartars over more than three hundred millions of Chinese', and was dependent on his fellow members of the ruling caste.[21] This elite section of society was in turn basing its claim to rule on the norms and traditions that the Qing had inherited from previous Chinese dynasties, both Han and non-Han alike. These support structures rested on a very basic premise; that the person who sat atop the Dragon Throne was without equal. While the imperial elite knew that, in reality, the emperor was a man who needed the support of his civil servants and soldiers the same as any other ruler, the multitudes under his rule believed that as long as he had the mandate of heaven, he had a right to govern. This mandate was signified by success, in the reaping of harvests, in the victories of armies in battle, in the growth of the economy, and in the deference shown by barbarian ambassadors. Failure in these areas would suggest that divine opinion had shifted against the emperor, delegitimising him. Based on the inviolability of the emperor's power, the entire edifice that held up the empire depended on the belief, hollow thought it may be, that all people, Chinese and foreign, were subject to the Dragon Throne.

The irony, of course, is, by refusing to recognise Europeans not as barbarians, but as equals, the Qing helped sow the seeds of their own destruction. Revealingly, by the time of the next British embassy to China, in 1816, the Qing claimed that Macartney had in fact kowtowed. This suggests one of two things. Either the Qing court had simply not absorbed the institutional memory of the Macartney embassy, in which case they had failed to recognise the potential threat Britain posed. Given what we have seen above, that would appear unlikely. Alternatively, they were now hoping to simply bluff their new diplomatic guests into following accepted

Chinese court practice, in which case they greatly underestimated their counterpart's diplomatic capabilities.

Whatever risks engagement with Macartney might have brought in terms of undermining popular awe for the emperor, the Qing would suffer far worse from the path that their relations with Western powers would now take. Within a century, the fiction of the Qing's lonely superiority would be demolished, and a very different relationship with foreign states would come into being. As observed by the writer Lu Xun (1881–1936), the 'Chinese have never looked at foreigners as human beings. We either look up to foreigners as gods, or down on them as wild animals'.[23] If Chinese emperors had for centuries based their legitimacy on their claimed position at the pinnacle of global power, the shift in how their subjects would perceive foreigners—no longer as semi-feral barbarians but now as beings with almost unstoppable power—would sound the death knell for Qing power in China.

Each chapter of this book has started with an anecdote from more recent diplomatic engagements between China and the West, which I hope have mirrored the issues at the heart of the Macartney embassy and made them more relatable to a modern audience. It is fitting then to close with another historical snippet. This one, however, will be from a little closer to Macartney's time. In 1860, British soldiers stormed the Yuanmingyuan, the Summer Palace where, in 1793, Macartney's embassy had installed their most wondrous displays, hoping to dazzle the emperor. Nearly seventy years later, their countrymen were back, now with weapons levelled, in the Second Opium War. The causes of the war were depressingly familiar—the desire of Western powers to force greater access to China's markets for their goods, most particularly that most noxious of products: opium.

The course of this campaign was also wearily familiar, with the superior weapons and training of the British and French armies quickly putting pay to any Chinese resistance. With their enemies vanquished, the victorious raiders could indulge in that vice enjoyed by conquering armies since time immemorial, unbridled looting. Ordered by the British commander, Lord Elgin, to raze the Summer Palace, his troops quickly demolished the building, but only after scouring the estate for anything of value. Porcelain, bronze statues and even five royal Pekinese dogs (one of who would come to be the personal pet of Queen Victoria, who named him 'Looty') were taken as booty before the pillagers came across a sealed warehouse. Inside, they found the gifts brought by Macartney to Qianlong, including the golden carriage specially chosen for the emperor, crated up and ignored.

12

Conclusion

A byword for failure; a lesson in Western arrogance; and a symbol of Chinese insularity. The Macartney mission, and its experience in China, has passed from the realm of history into something approaching if not myth, then fable: a story with a clear moral lesson. Of course, such an approach to historical events is very common. We instinctively respond to the allure of a good tale far more easily than to reasoned argument or weighty facts. Yet forcing a complex interaction between individuals and societies into the narrow mould of narrative convenience, complete with heroes, villains, and a story arc, can blur the lessons of true value behind this early encounter between China and the West.

The Macartney embassy was indeed a study in eighteenth-century British arrogance, and this is what the traditional telling of the embassy's story gets right. What would have been the case if someone else had been called on to press George III's case in Peking? Perhaps another diplomat may have proven suppler in interpreting his instructions when it came to ceremonial matters such as the kowtow. Also, we have seen how Songyun, with his experience of negotiating with the Russians, and the newly appointed viceroy of Canton, Zhanglin, might also have proven better partners for Macartney then the perpetually suspicious Zhengrui. Rather than fodder for broad-brush moralising about Western hubris or Chinese exceptionalism, perhaps this is an example that sometimes specific individuals shape history, of how the interaction of particular personalities can set many millions of people on course to a century of famine, war, and strife.

Our fates as individuals, and indeed the fates of entire societies, rest on the personalities and abilities of those we choose (or have chosen for us) to represent our nations on the global stage. At a time when politicians in Europe and North America are derided for being 'all the same', part of the 'elite', or indeed mired in the 'swamp' of the establishment, the Macartney mission reminds us that whoever plies statecraft on our behalf, there are real consequences if they are not up to the task—consequences suffered by ordinary people in their everyday lives. Choosing the exciting outsider because they are untainted by the 'establishment', or indeed relying on the old hand because they have been at the job so long, can prove costly, and indeed fatal, for a nation. Nothing is so permanent, not even one of the greatest powers of an age, that it cannot be brought low when a single individual gives history a nudge at a critical moment.

Of course, from a Western perspective, one is naturally drawn to identify with the British—what did they do wrong? Was it innocent ignorance or colonial greed that prevented them from reaching an effective agreement with Qianlong? What should we, in the modern West, learn from this case to help us better engage with China today? All these questions are understandable and logical, but they miss a key point. The positions have now shifted. Today, China is the rising, emergent power who is attempting to crack the edifice (political, economic, and strategic) of an incumbent, possibly ailing, West. It is Beijing's leaders, diplomats, entrepreneurs, and military officers who are heralding the dawning of new approaches to international institutions and global norms.

How is the West reacting? Are we awake to this change and the challenges it brings? Or, like Qianlong and his court, are we refusing to accept that the international balance of influence is shifting? When we look at events such as Brexit, the election of President Donald Trump in the United States, and the somewhat reluctant response by the European Union to security questions on its southern and eastern flanks, we may be guilty of the same sin as the Qing dynasty. We expect, or at least hope, that the world will continue along the vein most familiar to us. That power will reside in the great capitals of the West, that we will continue to lead the world in wealth and living standards, without having to adapt to new economic global realities. Some of those who voted for Brexit want Britain to return to an age of earlier glory. President Trump promised his supporters to 'Make America Great Again', suggesting it was once, but is no longer. Many European leaders seem to wish that the continent could go back to the warm optimism of the early twenty-first century, when the EU was expanding.

Therein lies the danger for the liberal international order that underpins the Western view of the world. The West has led the world for so long and has dominated economic and diplomatic affairs to such an extent that the idea that it could face competition is scarcely believable. This was the very same position that Qianlong found himself in. For all of its recorded history, China had no rival for dominion over Asia, or indeed the known world. In 1793, however, an undeniable truth presented itself at Qianlong's court. With his technical displays, well-drilled troops, scientific advisors, and globe-crossing fleet, Macartney was the herald of the new competitive reality facing China. Yet Qianlong and his mandarins chose to withdraw into comforting illusions of Chinese exceptionalism, refusing to acknowledge that here was a trial that could not be ignored, but must be met. For decades, the Chinese had been receiving ever louder hints of Europe's increasing importance. Now, forced to look this reality in the eye, they chose instead to cling to a soothing myth. In fact, the dispute over whether Macartney would kowtow to Qianlong was simply a cypher for a wider truth—outside of court ceremony, in the realms of global trade, military power, and diplomatic reach, Britain would not bow to China.

What will we in the West do, now that we are facing fundamental shifts away from long-held assumptions around international affairs? What shibboleths has the advent of Brexit exposed? What path now for nations whose foreign and economic policies have long been pinned on the presumption of a globalist United States? Most importantly of all, how do we adjust to a world where China is a major player not only in Asia, but across the globe? After all, China will significantly change the dynamics of international affairs, away from the current established arrangements which mirror Western values.

For example, on the one hand, China prefers bilateral engagement over key issues such as sovereignty questions in the South China Sea, whereas the West has favoured multilateral approaches to solving disputes between nations. Yet paradoxically, China is also a major contributor of United Nations peacekeepers. This is a significant shift from the historical trend, where leading powers such as the United States and the Soviet Union/ Russia have avoided becoming too closely identified with the UN's peacekeeping operations.

It is vital that Western nations recognise that China's re-emergence does not mean that Beijing will be dominating the international economic and diplomatic structures that we have created. Rather, entirely new frameworks will be developed, or at the very least, existing institutions will be re-shaped beyond recognition. When Qianlong met Macartney, the Qing court failed to understand that not only did China have a new peer, but that the very way their nation engaged with the world was about to change. The British did not inherit the mandate of heaven. They made it redundant. Perhaps now it has been refashioned.

Endnotes

Introduction

1 'David Cameron all but kowtows to visiting Chinese leader', *The Irish Times,* 21 October 2015.
2 Why China insists foreign organisations kowtow to its nationalistic red lines', *South China Morning Post,* 29 October 2019.
3 'Stability of Gulf countries comes from within', *The Global Times,* 17 July 2019.
4 'HP again reject Xerox billion dollar acquisition offer', *E-News Telecast*, 25 November 2019; 'Tomi Lahren blasts "The Kaepernick Circus": Stop the "poor me" charade', *Fox Nation*; 'Nic Couchman: Athletes in the ascendant', *Sport Business*, 25 November 2019.

Chapter 1

1 Mercier, *L'An deux mille quatre cent quarante* (1772), p. 107.
2 Spence, *The Search for Modern China* (1991), p. 129.
3 Berg, 'Macartney's Things. Were They Useful? Knowledge and the Trade to China in the Eighteenth Century' in *GEHN Conference* (2002), Volume 4, pp. 3-5.
4 *Hansard's Parliamentary History*, March 30, 1790, and Peyrefitte, *The Immobile Empire* (1992), p. 10.
5 Wood, 'Closely observed China: from William Alexander's sketches to his published work' in *The British Library Journal*, 24.1 (1998), p. 101.
6 Hevia, *Cherishing Men from Afar: Qing Guest Ritual and the Macartney Embassy of 1793* (1995), p. 58.
7 Cobbett, *Parliamentary History of England* (1803), p. 650.
8 Peyrefitte, *The Immobile Empire* (1992), p. 10.
9 *Ibid*., p. 26.
10 *Ibid*., p. 26.
11 Smith, *Wealth of Nations* (1776), p. 30.

12 Staunton, *An Authentic Account of an Embassy from the King of Great Britain to the Emperor of China* (1798), Volume 1, p. 48.
13 Hevia, *Cherishing Men from Afar: Qing Guest Ritual and the Macartney Embassy of 1793* (1995), p. 77.
14 Pritchard, *The Crucial Years of Early Anglo-Chinese Relations, 1750–1800* (1936), p. 269.
15 Peyrefitte, *The Immobile Empire* (1992), p. 10.
16 *Ibid.*
17 Meyer, *Getting Our Way: 500 Years of Adventure and Intrigue: the Inside Story of British Diplomacy* (2013), loc. 1784.
18 Marshall, 'Britain and China in the late 18th Century', in Bickers (ed.), *Ritual and Diplomacy: The Macartney Mission to China 1792–1794* (1993), pp. 16-17.
19 Barrow, *Some Account of the Public Life, and a Selection from the Unpublished Writings of the Earl of Macartney*, Volume 1 (1807), p. 339.
20 Hevia, *Cherishing Men from Afar: Qing Guest Ritual and the Macartney Embassy of 1793* (1995), p. 77.
21 Morse, *The Chronicles of the East India Company Trading to China*, vol. 2 (1929), p. 236.
22 *Ibid.*, p. 236.
23 *Ibid.*, p. 235.
24 *Ibid.*, p. 240.
25 Staunton, *An Authentic Account of an Embassy from the King of Great Britain to the Emperor of China* (1798), Volume 1, p. 39.

Chapter 2

1 Robbins and Macartney, *Our First Ambassador to China* (1908), p. 7.
2 De Beer and Rousseau (eds), *Voltaire's British Visitors* Vol. 49. Institut et musée Voltaire (1967), p. 178.
3 Robbins and Macartney, *Our First Ambassador to China* (1908), p. 14.
4 Barrow, *Some Account of the Public Life, and a Selection from the Unpublished Writings of the Earl of Macartney*, Volume 1 (1807), p. 6.
5 Hill, 'Gleanings in Family History from the Antrim Coast. The Earl of Macartney (Continued)', in *Ulster Journal of Archaeology*, First Series, Vol. 9 (1861/1862), pp. 1-16.
6 Robbins and Macartney, *Our First Ambassador to China* (1908), p. 37.
7 *Ibid.*, p. 38.
8 *Ibid.*, p. 25.
9 *Ibid.*, p. 25.
10 Macartney, *An Account of Ireland in 1773 by a Late Chief Secretary of that Kingdom* (2010), p. 55.
11 Peyrefitte, *The Immobile Empire* (1992), p. 21.
12 Robbins and Macartney, *Our First Ambassador to China* (1908), p. 118.
13 *Ibid.*, p. 134.
14 *Ibid.*, p. 159.
15 *Ibid.*, p. 134.
16 *Ibid.*, p. 97.
17 *Ibid.*, p. 105.
18 *Ibid.*, p. 195.
19 *Ibid.*, p. 17.

20 Barrow, *A Voyage to Cochinchina* (1806), p. 94.
21 Robbins and Macartney, *Our First Ambassador to China* (1908), p. 195.
22 *Ibid.*, p. 100.
23 Boxer, *Four Centuries of Portuguese Expansion, 1415–1825: a succinct survey*, Volume 3 (1961), p. 87.
24 Barrow, Macartney, *The Public Life of the Earl of Macartney*, Volume 1 (1807), p. 49.
25 Stuart and Portarlington, *Gleanings from an Old Portfolio,* Volume 3 (1898), p. 162.

Chapter 3

1 Spence, *The Search for Modern China* (1991), p. 95.
2 Crossley, 'The Rulerships of China' in *The American Historical Review* 97.5 (1992), pp. 1468-1483.
3 Spence, 'Portrait of an Emperor, Qianlong: Ruler, Connoisseur, Scholar', *ICON Magazine/World Monuments Fund* (Winter 2003–2004), p. 24.
4 Spence, *The Search for Modern China* (1991), p. 101.
5 Robbins and Macartney, *Our First Ambassador to China* (1908), p. 286.
6 Spence, 'Portrait of an Emperor, Qianlong: Ruler, Connoisseur, Scholar', *ICON Magazine/World Monuments Fund* (Winter 2003–2004), p. 27.
7 Barrow, *Some Account of the Public Life, and a Selection from the Unpublished Writings of the Earl of Macartney*, Volume 1 (1807), p. 227.
8 Spence, *The Search for Modern China* (1991), p. 115.
9 Barrow, *Some Account of the Public Life, and a Selection from the Unpublished Writings of the Earl of Macartney*, Volume 1 (1807), p. 381.
10 Spence, *The Search for Modern China* (1991), p. 99.
11 Robbins and Macartney, *Our First Ambassador to China* (1908), pp. 374-5.
12 Torbert, *The Ch'ing Imperial Household Department: A Study of Its Organization and Principal Functions, 1662–1796* (1977), pp. 99-100.
13 Hevia, *Cherishing Men from Afar: Qing Guest Ritual and the Macartney Embassy of 1793* (1995), p. 48, Waley-Cohen, 'China and Western technology in the late eighteenth century' in *The American Historical Review* 98.5 (1993), p. 1,534.
14 Quoted in Hevia, *Cherishing Men from Afar: Qing Guest Ritual and the Macartney Embassy of 1793* (1995), p. 52.
15 Chun, 'The Meaning of Crisis and the Crisis of Meaning in History: An Interpretation of the Anglo-Chinese Opium War.' *Bulletin of the Institute of Ethnology Academic Sinica* 55 (1984), pp. 190-1.
16 Wills, *Pepper, Guns, and Parleys: the Dutch East India Company and China, 1622–1681* (1974), pp. 136-142.
17 Barrow, Macartney, *The Public Life of the Earl of Macartney*, Volume 1 (1807), p. 351.
18 *Ibid.*, p. 352.

Chapter 4

1 Barrow, Macartney, *The Public Life of the Earl of Macartney*, Volume 1 (1807), p. 342.
2 Staunton, *An Authentic Account of an Embassy from the King of Great Britain to the Emperor of China*, Volume 1 (1798), p. 337.

3 Robbins and Macartney, *Our First Ambassador to China* (1908), pp. 185-195.
4 Müller, *East of Bali: From Lombok to Timor Tuttle* (1997), p. 217.
5 Robbins and Macartney, *Our First Ambassador to China* (1908), p. 228.
6 *Ibid.*, p. 239.
7 Anderson, *Narrative of Embassy to China* (1795), p. 83.

Chapter 5

1 Robbins and Macartney, *Our First Ambassador to China* (1908), p. 240.
2 *Ibid.*, p. 345.
3 Foster and Morse, *The Chronicles of the East India Company Trading to China, 1635–1834* (1926), p. 215.
4 Staunton, *An Authentic Account of an Embassy from the King of Great Britain to the Emperor of China*, Volume II (1798), p. 83.
5 *Ibid.*, p. 119.
6 *Ibid.*, p. 120.
7 Hevia, *Cherishing Men from Afar: Qing Guest Ritual and the Macartney Embassy of 1793* (1995), p. 147.
8 Peyrefitte, *The Immobile Empire* (1992), p. 81.
9 Staunton, *An Authentic Account of an Embassy from the King of Great Britain to the Emperor of China*, Volume II (1798), p. 162.
10 Robbins and Macartney, *Our First Ambassador to China* (1908), p. 264.
11 Staunton, *An Authentic Account of an Embassy from the King of Great Britain to the Emperor of China*, Volume II (1798), p. 184.
12 Robbins and Macartney, *Our First Ambassador to China* (1908), p. 295.
13 *Ibid.*, p. 400.
14 *Ibid.*, p. 258.
15 *Ibid.*, p. 260.
16 *Ibid.*, p. 257.
17 *Ibid.*, p. 261.
18 Hevia, *Cherishing Men from Afar: Qing Guest Ritual and the Macartney Embassy of 1793* (1995), p. 149.
19 Barrow, Macartney, *The Public Life of the Earl of Macartney*, Volume 1 (1807), pp. 84-85.
20 Anderson, *Narrative of Embassy to China* (1795), p. 73.
21 Peyrefitte, *The Immobile Empire* (1992), pp. 111-112.
22 Robbins and Macartney, *Our First Ambassador to China* (1908), p. 270.
23 *Ibid.*, p. 275.
24 Barrow, Macartney, *The Public Life of the Earl of Macartney*, Volume 1 (1807), p. 61.
25 *Ibid.*, p. 60.
26 Han, *History of the Population and Geography of Beijing* (1996), p. 137.
27 *Greater London, Inner London Population & Density History* on demographia.com, retrieved 2 November 2016.
28 Staunton, *An Authentic Account of an Embassy from the King of Great Britain to the Emperor of China*, Volume II (1798), p. 299.
29 Robbins and Macartney, *Our First Ambassador to China* (1908), p. 277.
30 *Ibid.*, p. 277.
31 *Ibid.*, p. 289.
32 *Ibid.*, p. 289.

33 Staunton, *An Authentic Account of an Embassy from the King of Great Britain to the Emperor of China*, Volume II (1798), pp. 299-300.

Chapter 6

1 'UK media hype over visit unprofessional', *Global Times*, 18 June 2014.
2 Hevia, *Cherishing Men from Afar: Qing Guest Ritual and the Macartney Embassy of 1793* (1995), p. 157.
3 Rockhill, 'Diplomatic missions to the court of China: the kotow question I' in *The American Historical Review*, Volume 2, no. 3 (1897), p. 428.
4 Fairbank, 'Tributary trade and China's relations with the West', *The Journal of Asian Studies*, 1.02 (1942), p. 135.
5 Fairbank, *Trade and Diplomacy on the China Coast*, Volume 1 (1953), p. 32.
6 Hevia, *Cherishing Men from Afar: Qing Guest Ritual and the Macartney Embassy of 1793* (1995), p. 50.
7 Kuhn, *Soulstealers: the Chinese Sorcery Scare of 1768* (2009), pp. 122-24.
8 Rockhill, 'Diplomatic Missions to the Court of China: the Kotow Question I', *The American Historical Review*, Volume 2, no. 3 (1897), p. 438.
9 Peyrefitte, *The Immobile Empire* (1992) p. 32.
10 Rockhill, 'Diplomatic Missions to the Court of China: The Kotow Question II', *The American Historical Review*, Volume 2, No. 4 (July 1897), p. 627.
11 Robbins and Macartney, *Our First Ambassador to China* (1908), p. 269.
12 Peyrefitte, *The Immobile Empire* (1992) p. 119.
13 Robbins and Macartney, *Our First Ambassador to China* (1908), p. 266.
14 *Ibid.*, p. 266.
15 *Ibid.*, p. 272.
16 *Ibid.*, p. 284.

Chapter 7

1 Robbins and Macartney, *Our First Ambassador to China* (1908), p. 280.
2 Staunton, *An Authentic Account of an Embassy from the King of Great Britain to the Emperor of China*, Volume II (1798), p. 341.
3 Robbins and Macartney, *Our First Ambassador to China* (1908), p. 271.
4 *Ibid.*, p. 290.
5 Staunton, *An Authentic Account of an Embassy from the King of Great Britain to the Emperor of China*, Volume II (1798), p. 341.
6 Campbell, *The Asiatic Annual Register Or a View of the History of Hindustan and of the Politics, Commerce and Literature of Asia*, Volume 8 (1809) p. 38.
7 Staunton, *An Authentic Account of an Embassy from the King of Great Britain to the Emperor of China*, Volume II (1798), p. 348
8 Robbins and Macartney, *Our First Ambassador to China* (1908), p. 295
9 *Ibid.*, p. 267.
10 *Ibid.*, p. 294.
11 Staunton, *An Authentic Account of an Embassy from the King of Great Britain to the Emperor of China*, Volume II (1798), p. 365.
12 See Chayet, 'Architectural wonderland: An empire of fictions' in Dunnell, Elliott, Forêt, Philippe, *et al. New Qing Imperial History: The Making of Inner Asian Empire at Qing Chengde* (2004).
13 Peyrefitte, *The Immobile Empire* (1992), p. 85.

14 *Ibid.*, p. 85.
15 Robbins and Macartney, *Our First Ambassador to China* (1908), p. 301.

Chapter 8

1 MacMillan, *Nixon and Mao* (2007), p. 4.
2 Anderson, *A Narrative of the British Embassy to China* (1795), p. 146.
3 Staunton, *An Authentic Account of an Embassy from the King of Great Britain to the Emperor of China*, Volume II (1798), p. 229.
4 Robbins and Macartney, *Our First Ambassador to China* (1908), p. 305.
5 *Ibid.*, p. 307.
6 Staunton, *An Authentic Account of an Embassy from the King of Great Britain to the Emperor of China*, Volume II (1798), p. 237.
7 Murray J., *The Quarterly Review*, Volume XVI (1817), p. 400.
8 Staunton, *An Authentic Account of an Embassy from the King of Great Britain to the Emperor of China*, Volume II (1798), p. 232.
9 Hevia, *Cherishing Men from Afar: Qing Guest Ritual and the Macartney Embassy of 1793* (1995), p. 179.
10 Staunton, *An Authentic Account of an Embassy from the King of Great Britain to the Emperor of China*, Volume II (1798), p. 238.
11 Robbins and Macartney, *Our First Ambassador to China* (1908), p. 308.
12 *Ibid.*, p. 310.
13 Staunton, *An Authentic Account of an Embassy from the King of Great Britain to the Emperor of China*, Volume II (1798), p. 249.
14 Robbins and Macartney, *Our First Ambassador to China* (1908), pp. 312-13.
15 *Ibid.*, pp. 314-6.
16 Barrow, *Travels in China* (1804), p. 201.
17 *Ibid.*, p. 117.
18 Anderson, *Narrative of Embassy to China* (1795), p. 230.
19 Robbins and Macartney, *Our First Ambassador to China* (1908), p. 321.

Chapter 9

1 *South China Morning Post*, 'Thatcher reveals Deng's threat to seize Hong Kong in a day', 17 October 1993.
2 Proudfoot, *Biographical Memoir of James Dinwiddie LLD Astronomer in the British Embassy to China, 1792–1793* (1866), p. 58.
3 Robbins and Macartney, *Our First Ambassador to China* (1908), p. 330.
4 *Ibid.*, pp. 331-333.
5 *Ibid.*, p. 332.
6 Barrow, *Some Account of the Public Life, and a Selection from the Unpublished Writings of the Earl of Macartney*, Volume II (1807), p. 302.
7 Qianlong, *Letter to George III* (1793), USC Annenberg, USC US-China Institute.
8 *Ibid.*
9 *Ibid.*
10 *Ibid.*
11 *Ibid.*
12 *Ibid.*
13 *Ibid.*

14 *Ibid.*
15 Qianlong, *Qianlong's Rejection of Macartney's Demands: Second Edict* (1793), Asia for Educators, Columbia University.
16 *Ibid.*
17 *Ibid.*
18 *Ibid.*
19 *Ibid.*
20 *Ibid.*
21 *Ibid.*

Chapter 10

1 Robbins and Macartney, *Our First Ambassador to China* (1908), p. 336.
2 *Ibid.*, p. 346.
3 *Ibid.*, p. 357.
4 *Ibid.*, p. 357.
5 *The Evangelical Magazine Volume* XIV (1808) p. 486.
6 Robbins and Macartney, *Our First Ambassador to China* (1908), p. 347.
7 Barrow and Macartney, *The Public Life of the Earl of Macartney*, Volume II (1807), p. 341.
8 Robbins and Macartney, *Our First Ambassador to China* (1908), p. 346.
9 *Ibid.*, p. 360.
10 *Ibid.*, p. 363.
11 *Ibid.*, p. 364.
12 Hevia, *Cherishing Men from Afar: Qing Guest Ritual and the Macartney Embassy of 1793* (1995), pp 202-3.
13 Robbins and Macartney, *Our First Ambassador to China* (1908), p. 365.
14 *Ibid.*, p. 367.
15 *Ibid.*, p. 368.
16 *Ibid.*, p. 371.
17 *Ibid.*, p. 371.
18 *Ibid.*, p. 372.
19 *Ibid.*, p. 372.
20 *Ibid.*, p. 375.
21 *Ibid.*, pp. 380-1.
22 *Ibid.*, p. 376.
23 *Ibid.*, pp. 376-77.
24 *Ibid.*
25 *Ibid.*, pp. 380-1.
26 Barrow, *Travels in China* (1804), p. 130.
27 Robbins and Macartney, *Our First Ambassador to China* (1908), pp. 381-2.
28 *Ibid.*, p. 383.
29 *Ibid.*, p. 383.
30 *Ibid.*, pp. 383., 384, and 388.
31 Barrow and Macartney, *The Public Life of the Earl of Macartney*, Volume II (1807), p. 396.
32 Robbins and Macartney, *Our First Ambassador to China* (1908), p. 385
33 *Ibid.*, p. 386.
34 Barrow and Macartney, *The Public Life of the Earl of Macartney*, Volume II (1807), p. 397.

35 *Ibid.*, p. 399.
36 Robbins and Macartney, *Our First Ambassador to China* (1908), p. 390.

Chapter 11

1 Robbins and Macartney, *Our First Ambassador to China* (1908), p. 386.
2 Barrow and Macartney, *The Public Life of the Earl of Macartney*, Volume II (1807), p. 322.
3 Robbins and Macartney, *Our First Ambassador to China* (1908), p. 347.
4 Gelber, *The Dragon and the Foreign Devils* (2007), p. 164.
5 Peyrefitte, *The Immobile Empire* (1992), pp. 490-1.
6 *Ibid.*, p. 492.
7 Barrow and Macartney, *The Public Life of the Earl of Macartney*, Volume II (1807), p. 341.
8 *Ibid.*, p. 350.
9 *Ibid.*, p. 352.
10 *Ibid.*, p. 352.
11 Robbins and Macartney, *Our First Ambassador to China* (1908), p. 310.
12 Barrow and Macartney, *The Public Life of the Earl of Macartney*, Volume II (1807), p. 338.
13 Robbins and Macartney, *Our First Ambassador to China* (1908), p. 317.
14 *Ibid.*, p. 263.
15 Winterbotham, *An Historical, Geographical and Philisophical View of the Chinese Empire* (1795), p. 2.
16 Robbins and Macartney, *Our First Ambassador to China* (1908), p. 387.
17 Hevia, *Cherishing Men from Afar: Qing Guest Ritual and the Macartney Embassy of 1793* (1995), p. 10.
18 *Ibid.*, p. 103.
19 Robbins and Macartney, *Our First Ambassador to China* (1908), p. 367.
20 Hevia, *Cherishing Men from Afar: Qing Guest Ritual and the Macartney Embassy of 1793* (1995), p. 196.
21 Robbins and Macartney, *Our First Ambassador to China* (1908), p. 335.
22 *Ibid.*, p. 405.
23 Quoted in 'Break Free from Shadow of Historical Humiliation', *The Global Times*, 15 January 2010.

Bibliography

Anderson, A., *Narrative of Embassy to China* (London, Debrett, 1795).

Barrow, J., *Travels in China* (London, Cadell and Davies, 1804); *A Voyage to Cochinchina* (London, Cadell and Davies, 1806).

Barrow, J. and Macartney, G., *Some Account of the Public Life, and a Selection from the Unpublished Writings of the Earl of Macartney*, Volumes I and II (London, Cadell and Davies, 1807).

Berg, M., 'Macartney's Things. Were They Useful? Knowledge and the Trade to China in the Eighteenth Century' from *Global Economic History Network Conference*, Vol. 4 (London, LSE Lecture, 2002), pp 1–35.

Bernstein, R., 'China's Tibetan Theme Park', *The New York Review of Books*, 12 September, 2011 chinafile.com/library/nyrb-china-archive/chinas-tibetan-theme-park, accessed 25 November 2020.

Black, J., *British Foreign Policy in an Age of Revolutions, 1783–1793* (Cambridge University Press, Cambridge, 1994).

Boxer, C. R., *Four Centuries of Portuguese Expansion, 1415–1825: A Succinct Survey*, Vol. 3. (Los Angeles, University of California Press, 1961).

'Break free from shadow of historical humiliation', *The Global Times*, 15 January, 2010.

Campbell, L. D., *The Asiatic Annual Register Or a View of the History of Hindustan and of the Politics, Commerce and Literature of Asia*, Volume 8 (London, Debrett, 1809).

Chang, H., *Commissioner Lin and the Opium War* (New York, Norton Library, 1964).

Chatterjee, P., *The Black Hole of Empire: History of a Global Practice of Power* (Princeton, Princeton University Press, 2012).

Chayet, A., 'Architectural wonderland: An empire of fictions', in. *New Qing Imperial History: The Making of Inner Asian Empire at Qing Chengde* (Abingdon, Routledge, 2004), pp. 33–52.

Chun, A. J., 'The Meaning of Crisis and the Crisis of Meaning in History: An Interpretation of the Anglo-Chinese Opium War' in *Bulletin of the Institute of Ethnology Academic Sinica,* No. 55 (1984), pp. 169–228.

Cobbett, W., *Cobbett's Parliamentary History of England*, Vol XXIII, 1782–1783 (Hansard, London, 1820).

Crossley, P. K., 'The Rulerships of China' in *The American Historical Review* 97.5 (1992), pp. 1468–8.

Cruise O'Brien, C., *The Great Melody: A Thematic Biography of Edmund Burke* (University of Chicago Press, Chicago, 1992).

de Beer, G. and Rousseau, A. M. (eds), *Voltaire's British Visitors, Studies on Voltaire and the Eighteenth Century* (Oxford, Voltaire Foundation, 1967).

Ding, G., 'Stability of Gulf countries comes from within', *The Global Times*, 17 July 2019.

Dixon, S., *Catherine the Great* (London, Profile Books, 2010).

The Evangelical Magazine, Volume XIV (London, Benjamin Bensley, 1808).

Fairbank, J. K. 'Tributary trade and China's relations with the West' in *The Journal of Asian Studies 1.02* (Cambridge, Cambridge University Press, 1942).

Fairbank, J. K., *Trade and Diplomacy on the China coast: The opening of the Treaty Ports, 1842–1854*, Vol. 1 (Cambridge, Cambridge University Press, 1953), pp. 129–149.

Foster, W. and Morse, H. B., *The Chronicles of the East India Company Trading to China, 1635–1834* (Oxford, The Clarendon Press, 1926).

Gelber, H. G., *The Dragon and the Foreign Devils* (London, Walker Books, 2007).

Gittings, D., 'Thatcher reveals Deng's threat to seize Hong Kong in a day', *South China Morning Post* (17 October 1993).

Greater London, Inner London Population & Density History on demographia.com/dm-lon31.htm retrieved 2nd November 2016.

Grove, A., 'HP again reject Xerox billion dollar acquisition offer', *E-News Telecast*, 25 November 2019.

Han, G., *History of the Population and Geography of Beijing* (Beijing, Peking University Press, 1996).

Hansard's Parliamentary Debates, Vol. 6 (London, Hansard, 1806).

Hansard's Parliamentary History, March 30, 1790 (London, Hansard, 1790).

Hasan, M., *History of Tipu Sultan* (New Delhi, Aakar Books, 2005).

Hevia, J. L., *Cherishing Men from Afar: Qing Guest Ritual and the Macartney Embassy of 1793* (Duke University Press, Durham, North Carolina, 1995).

Hill, G., 'Gleanings in Family History from the Antrim Coast: The Earl of Macartney' in *Ulster Journal of Archaeology, First Series, Vol. 9* (1861/1862), pp. 1–16.

Kenny, K., *Ireland and the British Empire* (Oxford, Oxford University Press, 2006).

Kessler, L. D., 'Ethnic Composition of Provincial Leadership During the Ch'ing Dynasty' in *The Journal of Asian Studies* 28.03 (Cambridge, CUP, 1969), pp. 489–511.

Kuhn P., *Soulstealers: the Chinese Sorcery Scare of 1768* (Cambridge M.A., Harvard University Press 2009).

London, M., 'Tomi Lahren blasts "The Kaepernick Circus": Stop the "poor me" charade', *Fox Nation*, 20 November 2019.

Macartney, G., *An Account of Ireland in 1773 by a Late Chief Secretary of that Kingdom* (Michigan, Gale ECCO, Print Editions, 2010).

MacMillan, M., *Nixon and Mao* (New York, Random House, 2007).

Marshall, P. J., 'Britain and China in the late 18th Century', in Bickers, R. (ed.), *Ritual and Diplomacy. The Macartney Mission to China 1792–1794* (London, British Association for Chinese Studies and Wellsweep Press, 1993), pp. 11–21.

Mercier, L. S., *L'An deux mille quatre cent quarante* (Dublin, W. Wilson, 1772).
Meyer, C., *Getting Our Way: 500 Years of Adventure and Intrigue: the Inside Story of British Diplomacy* (London, W&N, 2013).
Morse, H. B., *The International Relations of the Chinese Empire, Vol. 1* (Oxford, The Clarendon Press, 1910); *The International Relations of the Chinese Empire, Vol. 2* (Oxford, The Clarendon Press, 1929).
Moses, L. W., 'T'ang tribute relations with the Inner Asian barbarian' in *Essays on T'ang Society: the Interplay of Social, Political and Economic Forces* (Leiden, Brill, 1976), pp 61–89.
Müller, K., *East of Bali: From Lombok to Timor* (Berkeley, Periplus Editions, 1997).
Murray J., *The Quarterly Review*, Volume XVI (London, John Murray, 1817).
Parker, G.,'Red carpet for China leader falls short', *The Financial Times*, 20 June 2014; 'Five days on the road with George Osborne in China', *The Financial Times*, 25 September 2015.
Peyrefitte, A., *The Immobile Empire* (Vintage Books, New York, 1992).
Platt, S. R. *Imperial Twilight: The Opium War and the End of China's Last Golden Age* (New York, Knopf Doubleday, 2018).
Pritchard, E. H., *The Crucial Years of Early Anglo-Chinese Relations, 1750–1800* (Washington: Pullman, 1936).
Proudfoot, W. J., *Biographical Memoir of James Dinwiddie LLD Astronomer in the British Embassy to China, 1792–1793* (Liverpool, Edward Howell, 1866).
Qianlong, *Letter to George III* (1793), USC Annenberg, USC US-China Institute; *Qianlong's Rejection of Macartney's Demands: Second Edict* (1793), Asia for Educators, Columbia University.
Robbins, H. H. M. and Macartney, G., *Our First Ambassador to China: An Account of the Life of George, Earl of Macartney, with Extracts from His Letters, and the Narrative of His Experiences in China, as Told by Himself, 1737–1806* (London, John Murray, 1908).
Rockhill, W. W., 'Diplomatic missions to the court of China: the kotow question I.' *The American Historical Review*, No. 3 (Oxford, OUP, 1897), pp. 427–442.
Rossabi, M., 'The tea and horse trade with inner Asia during the Ming,' *Journal of Asian History*, 4.2 (Wiesbaden, Harrassowitz Verlag, 1970), pp. 59–88.
Smith, A., *Wealth of Nations* (W. Strahan and T. Cadell, London, 1776).
'Sotheby's in London to auction Emperor Qianlong's musket', *China Daily*, 7 November 2016.
Spence, J. D., *The Search for Modern China* (New York, W. W. Norton & Company, 1991); 'Portrait of an Emperor, Qianlong: Ruler, Connoisseur, Scholar' in *ICON Magazine* (World Monuments Fund, New York, Winter 2003–2004), pp. 24–30.
Couchman, N., 'Athletes in the ascendant', *Sport Business*, 25 November 2019.
Staunton, D., 'David Cameron all but kowtows to visiting Chinese leader', *The Irish Times*, 21 October 2015.
Staunton, G., *An Authentic Account of an Embassy from the King of Great Britain to the Emperor of China*, Vols. 1–2 (George Nichol, London, 1798).
Staunton, G. 'Staunton's Account of the Chinese Embassy' in *The Critical Review, Or, Annals of Literature* (London, 1797), pp. 371–381.
Stuart, L., and Portarlington, C. S. D., *Gleanings from an old portfolio: containing some correspondence between Lady Louisa Stuart and her sister Caroline, Countess of Portarlington, and other friends and relations* Vol. 3. (London, D. Douglas, 1898).
Sui, C., 'Why China insists foreign organisations kowtow to its nationalistic red lines', *South China Morning Post*, 29 October 2019.

Torbert, P. M., *The Ch'ing Imperial Household Department: A Study of Its Organization and Principal Functions, 1662–1796* (Cambridge M.A., Harvard University Asia Center, 1977).

'UK media hype over visit unprofessional', *The Global Times,* 18 June 2014.

Waley-Cohen, J., 'China and Western technology in the late eighteenth century' in *The American Historical Review* 98.5 (1993).

Wills, J. E., *Pepper, Guns, and Parleys: the Dutch East India Company and China, 1622–1681* (Cambridge M.A., Harvard University Press, 1974).

Winterbotham, W., *An Historical, Geographical and Philisophical View of the Chinese Empire* (London, J. Ridgway, 1795).

Wood, F., 'Closely observed China: from William Alexander's sketches to his published work' in *The British Library Journal* 24.1(British Library, London, 1998), pp 98–121.